To Die Game

Laurence M. Hauptman, *Series Editor*

"My band is big enough. . . .
They are all true men. . . .
We mean to live as long as we can
—and at last, if we must die,
to die game."

HENRY BERRY LOWRY

TO DIE GAME

The Story of the Lowry Band,

Indian Guerrillas of Reconstruction

William McKee Evans

With a New Foreword by
James M. McPherson

Syracuse University Press

Copyright © 1995 by Syracuse University Press, Syracuse, NY 13244-5160

All Rights Reserved

First Edition 1995

95 96 97 98 99 00   6 5 4 3 2 1

First published in 1971 by Louisiana State University Press.

Designed by Jules B. McKee

The paper used in this publication meets the minimum requirements of American National Standard for Information Sciences—Permanence of Paper for Printed Library Materials, ANSI Z39.48-1984. ∞™

Library of Congress Cataloging-in-Publication Data

Evans, William McKee.
    To die game : the story of the Lowry band, Indian guerrillas of Reconstruction / William McKee Evans ; with a new foreword by James M. McPherson.
        p.   cm.—(Iroquois and their neighbors)
    Includes bibliographical references and index.
ISBN 0-8156-0359-2 (paper : alk. paper)
    1. Lowry family.   2. Reconstruction—North Carolina.   3. Lumbee Indians—Social conditions.   I. Title.   II. Series.
    F259.E9   1995
    975.6'332041—dc20   95-20527

Manufactured in the United States of America

To the memory of
Sally McNeill Evans (1852–1947)
whose recollections of Lowry band days
inspired this book

William McKee Evans, emeritus professor of history at California State Polytechnic University, Pomona, first became familiar with the oral tradition of the Lowrys during his youth in Robeson County, North Carolina. He is also author of *Ballots and Fence Rails: Reconstruction on the Lower Cape Fear*, which won an award from the American Association for State and Local History. He is presently working on a book about the transformation from a religious justification of slavery in the Old World to a racial justification in the New. An early part of this study appeared in the *American Historical Review*.

Contents

List of Illustrations

Foreword

James M. McPherson

In Robeson County, North Carolina, about one hundred miles west of Wilmington, live today more than thirty thousand people who call themselves Lumbee Indians. Of mixed white and Indian ancestry, their forebears were speaking English at least as early as the eighteenth century, an oddity which gave rise to the hypothesis that they were descendants of Sir Walter Raleigh's lost colony on Roanoke Island. In 1835 the legislature designated the Lumbees "free persons of color" and deprived them of the rights to vote and to bear arms. Squeezed out of much of their land and robbed of their rights, they had little love for Southern whites.

During the Civil War many young Lumbee men hid in the swamps to avoid conscription into Confederate labor battalions and carried on a running guerrilla war with Home Guard troops. In December 1865 Henry Berry Lowry, a Lumbee, was arrested for the wartime killing of a Confederate official—an act committed in retaliation for the murder of three of Henry's cousins by the Home Guard. While awaiting trial, Henry escaped from jail and took to the swamps with two of his brothers and a number of friends and relatives (including at least two blacks and one white) to form the nucleus of the Lowry band, an outlaw gang nearly as notorious as their contemporaries Jesse and Frank James.

For more than five years the Lowry band terrorized the county, bushwhacked leaders of posses and of militia companies, and eluded all efforts at capture (or in several cases escaped from jail after capture). The Lowrys carried out most of their raids against large planters and Conservative Party political leaders. They evaded capture for so long because, like all successful guerrilla groups, they were supported by a sizable element of the local "peasant" population, in this case Lumbees and freed slaves who disliked the white establishment. Legends grew up about Henry Berry Lowry's Robin-Hood-like tendency to share with the poor his plunder from the rich. The Lowry band dissolved in 1872 when Henry suddenly disappeared, never to be heard of again. Four of his followers were subsequently hunted down and killed by whites seeking the state bounties of several thousand dollars on the heads of every prominent gang member.

William McKee Evans has written an absorbing narrative of the Lowry band, rescuing them from undeserved obscurity. Unlike many of those who have written about the James brothers, he does not romanticize his subjects or downplay the cold-blooded nature of some of their crimes. He has also avoided the pitfall of antiquarianism by linking the Lowry story with broader Civil War and Reconstruction themes: internal resistance to Confederate authority; class and racial alliances during Reconstruction; the violence of Reconstruction politics. The Lowrys had a significance beyond local outlawry and blood feuds. Like blacks, they supported the Republicans. In 1867 they temporarily ceased their gang activities in the hope that the new Republican regime would provide dark-skinned peoples with the equal justice the Lowry band professed to be fighting for. But when the Republicans failed to carry out the root-and-branch destruction of Conservative influence or to prosecute white murderers of Indians vigorously enough, the Lowrys returned to the warpath. Evans argues that the Republicans' irresolute efforts to suppress the band alienated many Indian voters while failing to satisfy white demands and aided the Conservative return to power in 1870.

Historians' debates about the effectiveness of Republican Reconstruction policies have echoed partisan positions taken by contemporaries. Some believe that the Republicans went too far in their effort to overturn the old order of white supremacy and force radical racial change in the South. Other insist that they did not go far enough. Evans belongs to the latter school. In his judgment, Henry Berry Lowry had a clearer vision of the means necessary to combat white racism and Conservative power than did the law-and-order Republicans. Indeed, Evans comes close to endorsing the Lowrys' method of an eye for an eye as the only way to deal with Ku Klux Klan violence and white counterrevolution. The radical Republicans could have successfully brought off their social revolution, he thinks, if they had borrowed a leaf from the Lowry band.

Reconstruction failed in the end, and so did the Lowrys. But the legacy of Henry Berry Lowry has served the important purpose of giving the Lumbees a sense of identity and pride in their heritage. The engrossing story told by *To Die Game* is therefore a story of triumph as well as of tragedy.

Foreword to the Original Edition

Today, more than ever before, we Lumbee Indians of Robeson and adjoining counties in North Carolina must recognize the necessity for a true book about the Lowry band. Because of the pride we take in the brave acts of the Lowrys, Lumbees have taken a new interest in our own social customs. For some time we have hoped that a competent and unprejudiced historian would uncover this story in its entirety. We were delighted when we learned that this job was being undertaken by Dr. William McKee Evans.

I have known Bill for quite a while. Because he grew up in Robeson County he naturally knew much about the Lowry band even before his research began. He is a native of Saint Pauls and for a time attended Lumberton High School. He also studied at Davidson College and the University of North Carolina, where he received his Ph.D. He is now a history professor at California State Polytechnic College in Pomona and is author of *Ballots and Fence Rails,* a history of Reconstruction on the lower Cape Fear. This book was the winner of an award by the American Association for State and Local History in the year 1966.

I was pleased when I learned that someone with these qualifications was working on the life of my uncle Henry Berry Lowry and on the wonderful record of the Lowry band during the time when we Lumbee Indians were going through our worst oppression. Dr. Evans has searched archives throughout the nation for his facts and has written a most engrossing history of the Lowry band. I feel sure every Lumbee Indian will be delighted to read this book. It will likewise be of interest to whites and to blacks.

D. F. Lowry

Acknowledgments

Acknowledgments pose a special problem for a book of this kind. I wrote most of it while living in the area where stories about the Lowry band are part of an ongoing tradition. As a result, once it became known that I was writing a book about the Lowrys, I found that I might become indebted to one or two more people for additional facts or ideas about the Lowrys each time I went shopping or attended church. Thus as a practical matter I cannot specifically mention most of the persons who have made suggestions, many of them extremely valuable ones.

Especially helpful, however, have been my discussions with persons who combine a thorough knowledge of local tradition with scholarly training: Professors Adolph Dial and Clifton Oxendine, both of North Carolina State University at Pembroke; Lewis Randolph Barton of Pembroke; Professor A. Warren Williams of Lethbridge University, Lethbridge, Alberta; P. Dean Chavers of Berkeley, California; and Ada Austin Johnson, a native of Maxton. I also received encouragement or critical suggestions from a group of scholars each of whom is an authority on some aspect of southern or Reconstruction history, including Professors George B. Tindall, Hugh T. Lefler, and Joel Williamson, of the University of North Carolina at Chapel Hill; Professor Richard B. Current of the University of North Carolina at Greensboro; and Professor Sheldon Hackney of Princeton University. On a particular point of interpretation, furthermore, Professors Kenneth M. Stampp and Leon F. Litwack of the University of California at Berkeley offered their suggestions. Also the chief authority on Indian-black relations, Professor Kenneth W. Porter of the University of Oregon, gave some extremely valuable advice.

Others who read all or portions of the manuscript and offered encouragement and ideas are Helen Maynor Scheirbeck, Director of Education for American Indians, United States Department of Health, Education, and Welfare; Brantley Blue, United States Commissioner of Indian Claims; Maud Thomas Smith of Lumberton; and Hardy Bell of Saint Pauls. The Reverend John Blount McLeod of Philadelphus Church permitted me to examine some old McLeod family letters and allowed me to reproduce a rare photograph. Dr. Earl Lowry of Des Moines, Iowa, a historian of the Lowry family, discussed with me certain problems of the book and offered suggestions. John Godwin of Pembroke shared his impressive knowledge of such prominent Indian families as the Sampsons, his own family, and the now-extinct Strongs. Thomas J. Hall of Saint Pauls helped me with the genealogies of a number of white families.

Jack Sharp, editor of the *Robesonian*, a paper which is the original source of a large part of the most reliable information about the Lowry band, and Helen Seawell Sharp called my attention to the fact that, despite a destructive fire at the beginning of this century, the *Robesonian* collection of materials remains an extremely valuable one. They provided me a place to work in their busy shop and allowed me to continue using it during the evenings, long after the shop had closed for the night. The Reverend James McKenzie of Barbecue Church steered me to the collection of the Presbyterian Synod of North Carolina in Raleigh. Mr. and Mrs. Frank Wishart and their son William Clifton Wishart, of White

Plains, New York, allowed me to examine and liberally photocopy their family papers.

Of the many ways that the Reverend D. F. Lowry has been helpful, a number of which are indicated in the text and footnotes, not the least important has been in the capacity of guide. On one occasion, when he offered to locate for me the site where the militia excavated a Lowry escape tunnel, I hesitated, reminding myself that the Reverend Mr. Lowry was a man in his eighties and that the area around the tunnel was highly inaccessible and would cause difficulties enough for a far younger man. But finally I agreed, realizing that no person was better qualified either to locate the spot or to interpret what we found there. However, following an afternoon of trying to keep up with him in the unbelievably dense thickets of Back Swamp, I concluded that the nephew of Henry Berry and the son of Calvin had inherited a tolerable bit of the physical stamina that has characterized their family for two centuries.

Another helpful guide was E. M. McLaurin, the talented *Robesonian* photographer. Without his aid I do not know how I would ever have found, for example, the spot where the Wisharts had ambushed Tom Lowry because today the old rice fields are completely overgrown with swamp thicket, the home of many beavers.

Admiral A. M. Patterson, Dr. H. G. Jones, and Ruby Arnold, of the North Carolina State Department of Archives and History, and Charles Holloman generously helped me to use and interpret colonial and other early North Carolina records. Mrs. Sara Jackson of the National Archives in Washington gave me comparable assistance with army and Freedmen's Bureau documents. At Duke University, Virginia Gray and Mattie Russell found for me an extremely valuable diary as well as collections of letters that shed light on the Lumber River region.

It is hard to see how I could have finished this project without considerable assistance from my family. My father, J. Browne Evans, has been especially helpful; my mother, Alfreda Pittard Evans, and my wife, Ruth Van Camp Evans, have read the whole manuscript and offered critical suggestions. My Van Camp in-laws also have aided in many ways: George and Jerome, painstakingly working over my English; Paul and Stephen, preparing copy for the publisher; and Betsy, drawing maps and providing artwork. I greatly appreciate, furthermore, a detailed critical reading which my cousin Sarah Hook Rembert gave the manuscript, in which she shared with me some of her professional experience as an editor. Any mistakes that have survived these multiple readings, however, I recognize as my own responsibility.

In the midst of the racial strife of Reconstruction, the Lowry band started a movement which for a brief time drew support from all three races. Perhaps therefore it is no accident that, while I was writing a book about that movement, the assistance that I got was openhanded and generous. Nor is it an accident that the helping hands were black, white, and brown.

Shoe
Heel
(Maxton)

Argyle
(Alma)

Plumers

Applewhite's
place

Guerrilla farm

Red Banks

Eureka
(Pates)

Buie's
Store
(Pembroke)

OXENDINE'S

Harper's Ferry

Lumber River

McLauchlin's
place

N

Lowry Road

Henry Berry
Lowry's
place

Alfordsville

Aaron Swamp

Arrest at the elder Lowrys'

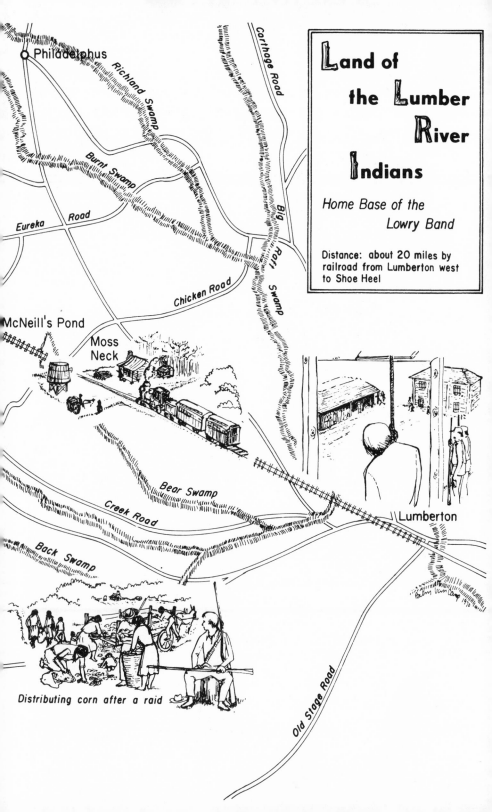

Land of the Lumber River Indians

Home Base of the Lowry Band

Distance: about 20 miles by railroad from Lumberton west to Shoe Heel

Philadelphus

Richland Swamp

Carthage Road

Burnt Swamp

Big Raft Swamp

Eureka Road

Chicken Road

McNeill's Pond

Moss Neck

Bear Swamp

Creek Road

Back Swamp

Lumberton

Old Stage Road

Distributing corn after a raid

To Die Game

1 · No Ordinary Thunder

CALVIN LOWRY SHOULD not have gone to work in the field on Friday morning. Had he been as cautious as several of his brothers on that morning of March 3, 1865, he would have kept himself prudently out of sight, perhaps hidden in the dense and tangled swamps that wind through the lowlands along the Lumber River in North Carolina. He would have kept a sharp eye out for any suspicious moves by the whites. For a long time it had not been safe for an able-bodied young Lumbee Indian such as Calvin Lowry to show himself.[1]

Many young Indians, including two of Calvin's first cousins, had been surprised by patrolling bands of the Confederate Home Guard, who had seized them, bound their hands, loaded them on trains at Moss Neck, and shipped them away to fever-devastated Wilmington, where at times free labor was scarcely to be found at any price.[2] There they

[1] During the nineteenth century there was no firmly established spelling for many family names. The same individual, for example, might be referred to as "Lowry," "Lowrey," "Lowery," or "Lowrie." Where such variations existed I use the most common present-day spelling, except for direct quotations, in which the original spelling is retained. The Lumber River Indians have been also known at various times as Scuffletonians, Croatans, Cherokees, Indians of Robeson County, and Lumbees.

[2] George Alfred Townsend (comp.), *The Swamp Outlaws: Or, the North Carolina Bandits, Being a Complete History of the Modern Rob Roys and Robin Hoods* (New York: M. De Witt, 1872), 49. Townsend compiled the reports which he and his *Herald* colleagues, A. Boyd Henderson and E. Cuthbert, made on the Lowry conflict. The bulk of the material was from the reports of Henderson. Wilmington *Daily Journal*, April 4, 1872. Mary C. Norment, *The Lowrie History, as Acted in Part by Henry Berry Lowrie, the Great North Carolina Bandit, with Biographical Sketches of His Associ-*

were condemned to wither and die in the pest holes of the lower Cape Fear, where brown-skinned Indians worked beside black-skinned Negro slaves, building an elaborate system of forts. The greatest work of engineering that the Confederacy ever undertook, the system was designed to protect Wilmington, the most important Confederate port in the upper South.[3]

But now times were changing. Each time the train stopped it brought exhilarating news of new triumphs of the Union. There were signs all about that the days of the Confederacy and of the Home Guard were nearing an end, as the soldiers in gray hurried northward before the vast Union host of Sherman, which was headed straight toward the bottom land of the Lumber River. If Calvin Lowry had gone to work in the field against his better judgment, perhaps it was because the winter of deprivation and fear was so very near an end. The sky would soon be rent by the first thunderclap of the season, and the warm rains and the balmy days would perform their annual miracle. The time had come for the brown-skinned people to return to their fields and prepare the soil for corn and tobacco, as they had done each returning spring for a thousand years.

Calvin Lowry was more fortunate than most Indians. He still had 350 acres left from his great-grandfather's estate. Few of them had fared so well. For generations, since the time of the French and Indian War, it had been a rare

---

ates, Being a Complete History of the Modern Robber Band in the County of Robeson and the State of North Carolina (Wilmington, N.C.: Daily Journal Printer, 1875), 41. All citations from Norment are from the 1875 edition of her book except where otherwise indicated.

[3] [North Carolina State Archives], *Colonel William Lamb Day: Souvenir Booklet* (Wilmington, N.C.: Carolina Printing Co., 1962), *passim*; John G. Barrett, *The Civil War in North Carolina* (Chapel Hill: University of North Carolina Press, 1963), 245–47, 266; New York *Herald*, February 23, 1865.

change in land boundaries that did not make Indian fields grow smaller and those of the white slaveholders grow larger. Near where Calvin Lowry was working stood his rifle. When questioned closely about this weapon by the whites, he would say that he brought it to the field with him to shoot crows. But he possessed it in violation of the law.

In 1835 the North Carolina legislature had designated the Indians along the Lumber River as "free persons of color," and had taken away their right to bear arms, as well as their right to vote. From time to time the substantial planters who sat on the Robeson County Court would grant a permit to some Negro or Indian to own a firearm for such a legitimate purpose as shooting crows. But no permit had ever been issued to Calvin Lowry. Furthermore the whites would not have been pleased to learn that on his father's place, buried beneath the peas in the corncrib, was the stock of another unregistered gun, and hidden at various other places about the farm were the remaining parts, not to mention a gourd of powder.[4]

It was already too late to try to get away when he saw the danger. Calvin spotted a band of about twenty-five armed whites approaching his house, and they had already seen him. It was a detachment of the Home Guard under Captain Archibald McCrimmon. He noticed that some of the men had already begun searching his house and the outbuildings. Instead of running and being ridden down and shot like an animal, why not simply ask them politely what they wanted?

[4] U.S., War Department, Records of the Army Commands (Record Group 393, National Archives), Hearings, 7–8. This document is a part of a collection of unpublished materials that a local agent of the Freedmen's Bureau, William Birnie, assembled in 1867 as a result of his investigation of some executions carried out by the Home Guard at the end of the Civil War. Besides the hearings just cited, it also includes letters and sworn depositions. Hereinafter the entire collection is cited as Investigation.

Certainly they could not send him away to the forts. The lower Cape Fear and Wilmington were already in the hands of the Union. Calvin Lowry walked calmly toward the whites.[5]

They wanted to know who he was. "I said I was a Lowry," Calvin later reported. One of them growled that he was of "bad stock." They "wanted to know if I knew anything about the robbing that was going on through the country." They also asked about the escaped "Union prisoners and if I was harboring them." [6] The young Indian did not own up to any special knowledge of either subject.

Calvin knew more than he wished to tell. He might even have been able to explain to them how the escaped prisoners and the robberies were connected. Throughout the war Indians had "lain out," hidden in the swamps to avoid conscription in the labor battalions. There they had been joined by other Indians who had escaped from the forced labor camps. At first these men could hardly be called "guerrillas." It was hard for Indians to get firearms. They were more hiding from the Confederacy than resisting it.

But as fever ravaged the lower Cape Fear, as planters protested the harsh use of their slaves whom the government had requisitioned for building the forts, as the Yankee fleet drew closer, the Confederacy's appetite for healthy Indian bodies increased. More and more Indians were hiding in the swamps and fewer and fewer growing corn. The young and the strong, who were "lying out," were becoming an intolerable burden on the old and the weak, who were tilling the soil. To make matters worse, Yankee soldiers began to escape from the Confederate prison camp at Florence, South Carolina, and to make their way to North Carolina, to the swamplands along the Lumber, where bands of poorly armed In-

[5] *Ibid.,* 6–7.
[6] *Ibid.,* 6.

dians gave them protection and shared with them their meager supplies of corn and cured meat.[7]

When further resistance based on purely defensive tactics had become virtually impossible by the winter of 1864–65, the guerrillas switched from a policy of living upon the poverty of their Indian kin to one of living upon the affluence of the white slaveholders. In a series of bold raids on plantations they had seized arms, ammunition, food, and blankets, which they broad-mindedly shared with the free Negroes and the white poor, as well as with their own kin. Public welfare measures are often viewed with some disfavor by persons from whose prosperity the necessary means are extracted. But perhaps none are regarded quite so dimly as those employed against poverty by guerrillas, their methods being more costly than charity with none of the compensating social rewards. Certainly, if the activities of the Union bands eased the pangs of hunger in Robeson County, they did nothing to soften the view of the local squirearchy toward persons who made a career of armed robbery.

The Home Guard men were looking suspiciously into Calvin Lowry's smokehouse. Had he fattened all that meat? one of them wanted to know. The Indian replied that he had. In actuality they had found little to connect Calvin with the guerrillas. They had found a rifle, but a diligent search of any number of Indian farms might yield unregistered firearms. They had found a little more food than befitted a poor man during these lean and hungry times, but what could they prove? Nevertheless they placed Calvin under arrest.

The Home Guard detachment led Calvin to a neighboring farm, the old Lowry homestead, where he, his nine brothers, and two sisters had grown up. There they surprised his aging father, who was at work in his field. Captain McCrim-

[7] Wilmington *Review*, February 15, 1889; Don Carlos Seitz, *Braxton Bragg: General of the Confederacy* (Columbia, S.C.: State Co., 1924), 506–507.

mon began by arresting every Indian in sight: Calvin's parents, Allen and Mary Cumba Lowry; his sisters, Purline and Sally Jane; one of his brothers, William; and Anne Locklear, a girl who was visiting.[8] Then he ordered a complete search of the house and farm. One of the men, finding a demijohn of brandy, offered to buy it from Allen Lowry. The old Indian said that it was not for sale. Without further belaboring the point the man took a drink of the brandy and then passed it around among his friends.[9]

But the whites found what they were looking for: hidden arms, ammunition, blankets, clothing, and, perhaps most significant of all, the golden head of a cane bearing the name of a prominent gentleman from whom it had been taken by some guerrillas. A Lowry horse and cart were impressed and the "plunder" loaded. William and Calvin Lowry were bound together with a rope and loaded onto the cart with the other prisoners. The whole group was thus transported a mile away to the plantation of Robert McKenzie, a leader of the Home Guard.

The McKenzie plantation was swarming with life when the Home Guard detachment arrived with the prisoners from the old Lowry place. Other small detachments were bringing in other Indians. Among the captives Calvin spotted another one of his brothers, Sinclair. When all had arrived, the Home Guard numbered about one hundred officers and men. It was now apparent how they had been able to bag so many Indians. By breaking up into relatively small units, they had carried out a number of individual raids at the same time. This strategy had hampered the operation of Robeson County's "grapevine telegraph," which would have normally warned threatened families of approaching danger. The prisoners were crowded into Robert McKenzie's new

[8] Deposition of Mary Lowry, May 28, 1867, in Investigation.
[9] Hearings, 7, in Investigation.

smokehouse, from which the guerrillas had recently seized fifteen hundred pounds of cured meat. The building was locked and an armed guard was placed on it.[10]

The important question that Captain Hugh McGreggor, the company commander, and the officers of his staff had to decide was what to do with the prisoners. Since they were civilians, should they not be turned over to the regular civil authorities for trial? Turn them over to Sheriff Reuben King, long intimidated by the guerrillas,[11] to be placed in the ramshackle county jail at Lumberton? While there might be doubts whether all the prisoners were guerrillas, it was at least certain that all the guerrillas were not prisoners; one captive reportedly had spoken confidently of "a large number of men hid in the swamps . . . who would come to their rescue." [12] Within the past two weeks these desperadoes had raided the county courthouse itself, seizing a sizable portion of the arms and ammunition of the official military establishment.[13]

But, assuming that these prisoners could be held long

[10] Deposition of Robert McKenzie, May 29, 1867, in Investigation.

[11] Hearings, 5, in Investigation. There is a tradition in my family that may serve to illustrate the extreme weakness of Confederate authority in Robeson County. My granduncle, Neill McNeill, a Republican legislator during Reconstruction, had emerged as a leader of the local Unionist faction during the war. According to a story that has been told many times, one day late in the war McNeill returned home to his small farm near the Big Marsh Swamp to find his daughters crying. They told him that while he had been away, the Home Guard had come and had seized their brother Dan'l, and had taken him away. McNeill laid his rifle on the floor of his buggy and drove to Lumberton, where High Sheriff Reuben King (later assassinated by the Lowry band) was holding Dan'l and other conscripts in jail. McNeill is supposed to have told King simply, "I have come for my boy." King, already at war with the major Indian families of the county, hesitated for several tense moments, undoubtedly contemplating whether he wanted to extend the conflict to the large, if not very affluent, McNeill clan. Finally the sheriff walked over and unlocked the jail door. Neill McNeill and Dan'l rode home in the buggy together. A short time later guerrillas or Union troops freed all the prisoners and burned the jail to the ground.

[12] Deposition of McKenzie, May 29, 1867, in Investigation.

[13] Wilmington *Daily North Carolinian*, February 15, 1865.

enough to be put on trial, what charges could be brought against them? Most could be charged with little more than having been suspiciously well fed during the course of a winter in which every honest Indian should have been starving. Against old Allen Lowry, perhaps they had a case. But considering the reputation of Allen Lowry and his forebears, it is not so certain that they could have obtained a conviction. While there is one dubious report that he was sentenced by the county court to a public flogging for theft,[14] this does not appear to have tarnished his good name of long standing in the community. Even an enemy of his family conceded that he had been faithful in church attendance and was respected by his neighbors, both Indian and white.[15] A friendlier source calls him a "great hunter," a man of such generosity that he was "willing to share his last cent" with his neighbors, including those who were white.[16] Was any jury impaneled under normal circumstances going to convict this "tall, fine looking"[17] old patriarch for theft because stolen property had been found on his farm?

If there were any doubts whether one could obtain a conviction in a court of the antebellum type, what prospect did the future hold for protecting white-skinned property rights against dark-skinned misery? How long would justice continue to be administered by conservative, slaveholding squires, with their strong sense of property? During the past month Sherman's army, like a hurricane, had roared northward from Savannah, toppling as it came the towering authority of family names in communities where they had been rooted for generations. Across a broad belt of South Carolina it had swept the institution of slavery from its path; and the

[14] John H. Coble and Luther McKinnon to William Birnie, June 8, 1867, in Investigation.
[15] Norment, *The Lowrie History*, 33.
[16] Townsend (comp.), *The Swamp Outlaws*, 46–47.
[17] Norment, *The Lowrie History*, 33.

dark multitude who owned nothing had looked on while Union soldiers, in rifling the big houses of plantations, had demonstrated how property might be more equitably distributed. It could only be a matter of days before Robeson County would be shaken by the fury of Sherman.

If robbery was to be severely punished, if insubordination was to be sharply rebuked, the planters along the Lumber River could hardly look forward to a more favorable opportunity than that which presented itself on Friday at the McKenzie plantation. Bolstered by gentlemen from neighboring Richmond County and a few Confederate regulars,[18] the Home Guard had not been able to offer such a show of strength for a long time. Perhaps it did not present such a splendid military spectacle as had the antebellum county militia. The clarion cry of Confederate patriotism had taken its toll of youth; the Conscription Act had taken even more. The Home Guard was what was left of the military establishment.

Yet, if the rank and file included men whose hearts were dead to the sentiments of country or men whose bodies failed to recommend themselves even to a desperate Confederate recruiting officer, the Home Guard was fortunate to have a high proportion of officers, gentlemen who were much more representative of the old county militia, since the Conscription Act exempted large slaveholders and men wealthy enough to hire substitutes.[19] Among the officers who gathered at the McKenzie place were a number of magistrates, most of them planters who administered justice in their local communities and convened as the county court to decide important questions. There were also other prominent planters there as well as two clergymen and a lawyer.[20]

[18] Wilmington *Daily Journal*, April 4, 1872.
[19] Confederate States of America, *Statutes at Large*, 1862, Chap. 45.
[20] Calvin Lowry and Sinclair Lowry to Birnie, October 24, 1867, in Investigation.

Considering the disturbed state of the country and the nearness of the Yankee army, what better opportunity would there be to convene a court and to administer justice?

The dignitaries who had gathered at the McKenzie plantation hurriedly convened a court. In their methods of carrying out justice, the Home Guard leaders were as informal and unconcerned with legal niceties as the guerrillas had been in their methods of carrying out famine relief. The accused were not only denied a chance to present their case, but they were not even present at the trial. The prisoners remained locked in the smokehouse while the court deliberated.

But the right of the accused to be heard was not completely ignored. From time to time someone from the court would go out to the smokehouse, ask some prisoner a question, and then return to relate what he had heard. One of these visitors was reported to have reminded Allen Lowry that none of his ten sons had ever served in the labor camps, though the youngest was about sixteen. Indeed the old Indian had once been warned that "if he did not get up his boys [out of the swamps] to go to the government fortifications, they would have to suffer for it." To this he replied that, since his sons were now men, they "were free from him and he could not rule them." [21]

A proposition that one planter made to a prisoner would seem to show more concern for the practical problem of producing a crop during the coming year than for any abstract concept of justice. Robert McKenzie was said to have told Sinclair Lowry, his Indian neighbor, "that he would get him clear of being shot if he would work six months for him." [22] McKenzie also reportedly accused Allen Lowry of having threatened his life. Lowry denied it, whereupon the planter answered that it "was a lie for John Purcell had told

[21] Deposition of Calvin Lowry, October 14, 1867, in Investigation.
[22] Deposition of Sinclair Lowry, June 1, 1867, in Investigation.

him" of the threat. This line of questioning was apparently pursued no further when the older man replied, "Send for John Purcell." [23] But it would not be so easy to turn aside questions about the golden head of a gentleman's cane.

Of all the prisoners, the prospects of William Lowry appeared darkest. He had been living at the old Lowry place, where clearly identified "plunder" had been found, and he lacked the long-standing prestige of his father. Furthermore a witness identified him as having been one of a band of "about thirteen men, five of whom were white," who had rifled his plantation.[24]

As a result he and his brother Calvin, to whom he was bound, decided to attempt a desperate ruse that might allow William to escape. The two prisoners complained to the guards of thirst. Still tied together, they were taken out of the smokehouse and led to the well by three or four guards. William still had in his pocket a "little dirk" which the whites had overlooked when they had searched him and taken his pocketbook and other personal objects. "After we got our water," Calvin later reported, "William and myself stepped to a fence nearby." Taking advantage of a momentary lapse of vigilance by the guards, William "cut the rope and run. One man popped a cap at him as he turned the corner of the house [.] they then jumped over the fence and run into the field where they could see him and fired on him . . . they then cried out they had him and went on down there and got him then carried me back [to the smokehouse?] where the company was . . . and handcuffed me to my father . . . [They] brought William Lowry up where Mr. Coble questioned him very close about the Yankees and Robbers[.] William denied knowing anything about them and he told him that he had better tell the truth his time

[23] Hearings, 8, in Investigation.
[24] Deposition of William A. Sellers, May 27, 1867, in Investigation.

was short and not to go off with a lie in his mouth." [25]

The Reverend John H. Coble, who besides being a Home Guard chaplain was pastor of Center Church, recalled a very different version of this interview. He said that at this time William "confessed that he belonged to the gang and that he was concerned in robbing the Messrs Sellers and Mrs Dr McNair. He likewise gave the names of his accomplices." [26] But George Dial, an Indian prisoner who was holding the wounded man in his arms at the time he was supposedly making his confession to the Reverend Mr. Coble, denies that William admitted anything. [27]

The effort of William Lowry to escape brought the Home Guard to an abrupt decision. The company voted to execute the four adult male Lowry prisoners. But one of the whites, Hector J. McLean, voted against the motion and protested the decision after the vote had been announced. [28] He called Chaplain Coble to one side and pointed out that nothing which could be identified as plunder had been found in the houses of either Sinclair or Calvin Lowry, whereupon Coble addressed the troops, saying that "it would be better to clear 99 guilty men than to punish one innocent man." [29] Moved by the words of the preacher, the Home Guard approved a new motion to execute the two who had been living at the Lowry homestead, William Lowry and his father.

They led his father out and placed him on a cart where William lay. Outside Captain McGreggor was drafting a twelve-man firing squad. [30] George Dial, watching from the smokehouse, saw one of the Home Guard men "put a spade

[25] Hearings, 8, in Investigation.

[26] Coble and McKinnon to Birnie, June 8, 1867, in Investigation.

[27] Deposition of George Dial, October 19, 1867, in Investigation. In this investigation the witness' name is spelled "Dyal." I am using the more common present-day spelling of this name. See note 1.

[28] Deposition of Hector McLean, May 2, 1867, in Investigation.

[29] Hearings, 3–4, in Investigation.

[30] Deposition of McLean, May 27, 1867, Hearings, 4, in Investigation.

and shovel in the cart" with William and Allen Lowry.[31]

Perhaps because Robert McKenzie did not want an execution taking place on his land, the cart was driven back to the old Lowry homestead. There the wounded prisoner and his father were bound to a stake and blindfolded. Emmanuel Fullmore, a black who had been impressed by the Home Guard to drive the cart, did not want to see what was to follow; he withdrew into the woods.[32] Back in the McKenzie smokehouse, Mary Lowry, her daughters, two of her sons, and the other captives, waited and listened. They heard the crack of distant rifle fire,[33] then presently the sound of the returning cart.

Some Home Guard leaders appeared at the smokehouse door and informed the prisoners that William and Allen Lowry had been shot and then asked Calvin and Sinclair Lowry if they would not like to tell the whereabouts of the "Union soldiers and their camps." [34] But fortunately for the two brothers, a spring shower burst upon the plantation and the interrogations were suspended for the day.[35]

The next morning, Saturday, March 4, 1865, the ordeal was resumed. First it was Calvin's turn, with a Home Guard major asking the questions. The officer began by asking Calvin if "they had told him what they had done" to his father and brother. The Indian replied that he had "heard that they had killed them." "Yes, they had killed them and buried them," the major continued. Now, would he like to tell "where the camps of the Union soldiers were"? Calvin still professed that he knew nothing. Roderick McMillan, who would later be a Conservative sheriff of Robeson County, "went at him with his bayonet." But McLean, who the day

[31] Deposition of George Dial, October 19, 1867, in Investigation.
[32] Deposition of Emmanuel Fullmore, May 27, 1867, in Investigation.
[33] Deposition of Calvin Lowry, October 14, 1867, in Investigation.
[34] Ibid.
[35] Hearings, 9, in Investigation.

before had successfully protested the decision to shoot Calvin and Sinclair, "stopped him and took hold of the bayonet." [36]

Next came the turn of George Dial, with Captain McGreggor, the execution officer of the day before, asking the questions. Despite McLean's objections to the use of torture, Dial was blindfolded and, while the captain asked him questions, McMillan "stuck the point" of his bayonet in him. They threatened to "kill him . . . and put him in the hole with Allen and William Lowry." [37] Dial was induced to reveal that he knew the location of "a small cave," probably used to store arms or provisions.[38]

The heavy-handed interrogation techniques of the Home Guard were getting results. They learned, though the record does not indicate exactly who told them, that a wounded Yankee soldier was being cared for at the house of Amanda Nash, a white schoolteacher who performed small services for the guerrillas. Possibly it was from Calvin Lowry that they extracted this information; certainly he knew the Union soldier, who had once been a guest in his father's house.[39] When the Home Guard went out to check the report, they took him along.

But if it was indeed Calvin who endangered Mrs. Nash and her patient, this disclosure was likewise an admission that heretofore he had not been entirely frank with the Home Guard. In any event, Calvin Lowry and George Dial were handcuffed together, and a detail under Captain McCrimmon took them out to check the new information and to "hunt camps." [40]

Perhaps to encourage a more cooperative attitude on the

[36] Deposition of Calvin Lowry, October 14, 1867, in Investigation.
[37] Deposition of George Dial, October 19, 1867, in Investigation.
[38] Hearings, 9, in Investigation.
[39] Ibid., 10.
[40] Ibid., 9.

part of the prisoners, the detachment first stopped at the old Lowry homestead, where the Indians were shown the spot where Calvin's father and brother had been killed the day before.[41] Next they went to Calvin's farm. His wife had escaped the Home Guard dragnet of the day before. But in the meantime, she had crept back to the farm, locked the house and outbuildings and again disappeared,[42] probably to seek the protection of the guerrillas.

The Indian woman's precaution, however, did not long detain Captain McCrimmon's men, who apparently hoped that a second and more thorough search of the farm might uncover new evidence. They "broke open the back door of the dwelling house," Calvin later recalled. They "broke open my [dairy?] and also some of the gable end of the smoke house . . . [They] also broke down the crib door."[43] But apparently they found nothing further to implicate the Indian farmer.

Next they visited the cave that George Dial had promised to show them, though there is no indication what they found there. They then continued to the house of Amanda Nash, where the wounded Yankee was receiving care. Captain McCrimmon left some of his men on the road, and led the rest to the house to take the soldier. Mrs. Nash raised such a vigorous objection to their moving him that they returned to the road without their prisoner. After further deliberation, however, they changed their minds and decided either to "go and take him out or kill her." She surrendered her patient. They then got a cart and moved the Yankee to the McKenzie plantation, where they put him into the smokehouse with the Indian captives.[44]

The next morning, Sunday, March 5, 1865, the Reverend

[41] Deposition of Calvin Lowry, October 14, 1867, in Investigation.
[42] Hearings, 9, in Investigation.
[43] Ibid.
[44] Ibid.; deposition of Calvin Lowry, October 14, 1867, in Investigation.

Mr. Coble and Captain McGreggor appeared at the door of the smokehouse. The minister began reading a law to the prisoners, which one remembered as having stated that "if they fed or harbored any more Union Soldiers or gave a deserter a meal [or] victuals, or if there was any more mischief through that neighborhood, they would have to Suffer for it." [45] Then, to their surprise, the captives were informed that they were all free to leave except Calvin Lowry and the wounded Yankee. As they filed out of the smokehouse they became aware of a possible reason for their release: their ears picked up the sound of distant battle. George Dial recalled that "when he was let go . . . he heard the firing distinctly." [46]

Captain McGreggor merely wanted Calvin to drive a cart to Lumberton carrying a guard and the Yankee, who was to be turned over to Neatham Thompson, a Confederate official. Thompson grumbled to the Home Guard soldier about the sick prisoner. He said he "did not know why they had brought him here. They ought to have left him along the road somewhere." [47] Calvin was then allowed to return home.

The next day, Monday, March 6, 1865, a group of Indians gathered at the spot where, on Friday, Allen and William Lowry had crumpled before the firing squad. They opened the shallow grave in which both men had been unceremoniously stuffed. [48] The time had come for the warm, wet south wind to blow in the spring, to bring the first storms of the season. But it was no ordinary thunder that rumbled on the southern horizon, as the dark-skinned people washed and dressed the bodies of their fallen kin and prepared them for a decent burial. [49]

[45] Deposition of Calvin Lowry, October 14, 1867, in Investigation.
[46] Deposition of George Dial, October 19, 1867, in Investigation.
[47] Deposition of Calvin Lowry, October 14, 1867, in Investigation.
[48] Deposition of Sinclair Lowry, June 1, 1867, in Investigation.
[49] Ibid.

2 · "A Mixt Crew, a Lawless People"

THE RECONSTRUCTION PERIOD was a time of unprecedented social upheaval throughout the South. But in this entire region, from the Potomac to the Rio Grande, there was probably not a single locality torn by more bitter or sustained strife than that which took place in Robeson County, North Carolina, and in the immediately neighboring counties of North and South Carolina. Was there some special inclination toward violence in the character of the people who lived along the Lumber River?

Perhaps the answer is to be found not so much in the character of the people as in the character of their history. The emancipation of the slaves confronted the people of this section, as well as those in the rest of the South, with a bitter conflict over a redefinition of the status of the blacks. But along the Lumber River people were still engaged in a bitter conflict over the status of the Indians. Indeed a peculiar feature of this area has been the special extent to which the people of each generation must face not simply the troubles of their own making, but also the unfinished business of their ancestors, the survival of ancient wrongs. This was a place in which to a special extent no tide of history had ever swept quite clean, where relics of the past persisted to confront the present with curious contrasts. For example, prehistoric men along the Lumber River constructed a certain dugout canoe. In the twentieth century these canoes were still being built, their basic design only slightly influenced by the coming of iron and steel cutting tools.

Old ideas, furthermore, have proved almost as enduring as prehistoric canoes. So have old quarrels, which elsewhere might long have been forgotten. As an example, for most Americans the revolutionary war ended with the Treaty of Paris of 1783. But it has never been so simple to settle anything in Robeson County, where the savage blood feuds set in motion by that conflict reverberated well into the nineteenth century. Writing in 1875, Mary Bridgers Norment still remembered the name and address of a Tory who had inflicted a saber wound on the hand of a certain patriot during the Revolution. Along the Lumber River local history might be read in the habits and beliefs of one's neighbor.

In no respect is this tendency of the past to survive into the present more manifest than in the important role that Indians continue to play in the life of the region. Elsewhere in eastern America the great wave of white conquest swept all before it, obliterating almost all traces of earlier peoples, reducing the Indians to little more than a shadowy legend. But the Indians of Robeson County are no legend. They are brown-skinned men and women planting their corn and tobacco on the lands where Indians have grown corn and tobacco many centuries. About one quarter of all American Indians east of the Mississippi River live in North Carolina along the Lumber River,[1] and the census report of 1960 showed that about 30 percent of the people living in Robeson County were still Indians. Perhaps one can detect a hint that the Reconstruction period was not the first time in the history of this region that hunted and hounded men could defy their pursuers and endure.

Perhaps geography is a key to the peculiar development of the valley of the Lumber River. There is much excellent farm land in the area, and in the twentieth century Robeson

[1] Brewton Berry, *Almost White* (New York: Macmillan Co., 1963), 14, 152.

County has sustained a rich agriculture and a relatively dense farming population. But this has not always been the case and appears to have come as a direct consequence of the construction of the railroads and all-weather roads. With the growth of transportation, the agricultural population of Robeson began to overtake and surpass that of most neighboring counties.

Before the development of transportation, however, the valley of the Lumber was relatively backward and sparsely populated. This was because the productive land is cut up and crisscrossed by pocosins, or "bays," the curiously oval-shaped swamps characteristic of the eastern Carolinas. These have no particular significance now that good roads have been constructed, but in early historic and prehistoric times they may well have acted as a sort of filter determining the kind of people who settled the region. This was because in primitive days the chief mode of transportation was the dugout canoe; and in the Lumber River region the navigable watercourses were separated from the farm lands by tangled, almost impenetrable swamps. This difficulty was enough to discourage men from settling in the region. But not all men. What kind of people chose to make their homes in these fertile but swamp-encompassed fields?

Though very little work has been done yet in the archaeology of this region, perhaps it can already supply us with some hints as to the answer. Relics of tools and weapons, tiny bits of pottery give clues to the settlement of the area by individuals from a wide variety of cultural groups, suggesting that this region, isolated by encircling swamps, may have long been a refuge for the remnants of defeated, half-annihilated peoples.[2]

[2] Chapman J. Milling, *Red Carolinians* (Chapel Hill: University of North Carolina Press, 1940), 219; John Reed Swanton, *Probable Identity of the "Croatans"* (Washington: U.S. Office of Indian Affairs, 1933), 2.

What people have found refuge along the Lumber River? Although this is a question that arouses considerable interest among Robeson County Indians today, it cannot be answered precisely. Present-day cultural patterns do not point to particular Indian tribes. So far as anyone has been able to determine, moreover, the Lumber River Indians spoke English and had the same habits as back-country whites in the mid-eighteenth century, when they were "discovered" by European immigrants. Indeed a curious feature of the Lumber River valley in the eighteenth century is that the Indians spoke English, while the largest group of white settlers, the Highland Scots, did not.

What brought about a virtual eclipse of native culture and the adoption of European ways, apparently before the area was generally settled by Europeans? In the 1880's Hamilton McMillan, a local historian, made a bold leap toward an answer. He suggested that these Indians were "Croatans," descendants of the tribe which may have given refuge to and finally absorbed the English colony Sir Walter Raleigh helped to found on Roanoke Island, off the north coast, in the 1580's.[3]

Three centuries separated Sir Walter Raleigh and Hamilton McMillan, during the first two of which very little was known about the Lumber River valley. Yet these Indians show a considerable admixture of white ancestry, and McMillan was able to demonstrate a certain correspondence between their family names and those of the Roanoke Island settlers. This theory has intrigued local historians ever since, and has been explored at some length by Lewis Randolph Barton, himself a Lumber River Indian.[4] While our present knowl-

---

[3] Hamilton McMillan, *Sir Walter Raleigh's Lost Colony* (Wilson, N.C.: Advance Press, 1888), *passim*.

[4] Lew[is Randolph] Barton, *The Most Ironic Story in American History: An Authoritative, Documented History of the Lumbee Indians of North Carolina* (Charlotte: Associated Printing Corp., 1967), 53–58 and *passim*.

edge of the seventeenth and eighteenth centuries hardly seems sufficient to test fairly the "Lost Colony" theory, at the same time, at least one thing appears certain: if any of the half-Indianized descendants of the Roanoke settlers found refuge in the valley of the Lumber, so did the survivors of other defeated peoples. The movements of Indian tribes in early historic times and the histories of particular families both suggest a complex origin for the Lumber River Indians.

At the time of the earliest explorations various tribes apparently lived in or near the valley of the Lumber. About 1700, for example, the region itself and the territory immediately to the south and west appear to have been occupied by Siouan-speaking peoples. But just to the north and east were Iroquoian tribes, including the mighty Tuscarora. Also to the east were relatively weak Algonquin-speaking peoples, including at one time the tribe which may have absorbed the English settlers from Roanoke Island.[5]

Furthermore the coming of the whites to the area brought about a considerable shifting and mixing of Indian tribes. The Siouan peoples of the Carolinas, for example, pressed by the Cherokees to the west and possibly frightened by the Spaniards to the south, were moving northward until they encountered other Siouan tribes pressing southward from Virginia, where the English had landed. As a result, by the beginning of the eighteenth century, some half-dozen small Siouan peoples had converged around the upper Pee Dee, into which the Lumber empties.[6]

Meanwhile Europeans had once again landed in eastern North Carolina. The Tuscarora nation attempted to expel them and for twenty-two months during 1711-12 made

[5] Hugh Talmadge Lefler and Albert Ray Newsome, *North Carolina: The History of a Southern State* (Chapel Hill: University of North Carolina Press, 1963), 24–25.

[6] These would include the Cheraws, Catawba, Eno, and Keyauwee of the Carolina Sioux, as well as Occaneechi, Saponi, and Tutelo of the Virginia Sioux. Swanton, *Probable Identity of the "Croatans,"* 3.

a series of attacks on New Bern, where a group of Germans and Swiss had gained a foothold. But, when faced with the prospect of annihilation by the Europeans, many Indian peoples reacted in a manner that seems discouragingly modern: they recognized the destructive power of the whites. Yet, in their diplomacy, tribal leaders attempted to use the new threat to promote some old quarrels. Thus the whites were able to create a coalition of peoples antagonistic to the Tuscarora, and to turn the tide of the war.[7]

The attacks on New Bern were turned back and the Tuscaroras forced on the defensive. Finally on June 23, 1713, the great Tuscarora fortress of Nohoroco fell to the whites and their Indian allies; during the savage four-day battle more than five hundred defenders lost their lives. Nohoroco was the key to a system of forts that the Tuscarora had constructed to defend their towns on the Neuse River.[8] As a result, resistance ceased, not only by the Tuscarora, but by the other nations as well. The Europeans, who hitherto had arrived only in small bands, now came in swarms and within a short while had occupied the country as far west as the Appalachians.

The main body of the Tuscarora withdrew to the north, where they joined their Iroquoian-speaking kinsmen around the Great Lakes; and their descendants reside now around Niagara Falls in New York and Ontario.[9] A few Tuscaroras withdrew southward, finding their way to the Lumber River valley. The Lowry clan of Robeson County trace their descent in part from the Tuscaroras.[10]

[7] Charles R. Holloman, "Palatines and Tuscaroras," *We the People*, January, 1966, pp. 21–22.

[8] Charles R. Holloman, "Fort Nohoroco: Last Stand of the Tuscaroras," *We the People*, December, 1965, p. 18.

[9] *Ibid.*, 32.

[10] Norment, *The Lowrie History*, 5, 7, 27; John C. Gorman, "Henry Berry Lowry Paper" (MS in North Carolina Department of Archives and History, Raleigh), 1.

It may seem curious that the largest concentration of Indians in the eastern United States should be found only one hundred miles from the Atlantic and not much farther from the locations of the first English colonies in America. An important reason, as we have seen, was that in primitive times the Lumber River region, compared to the surrounding territory, was a less accessible and therefore a less desirable place to settle. Thus, like many other powerful peoples before them, the whites for a time spurned this region and hurried on past to occupy the fertile, well-drained, and easily accessible Piedmont land to the west. Therefore the Indians concentrated in the upper Pee Dee and Lumber River area were completely surrounded by a Caucasian frontier, which closed about them in an ever-tightening ring. If, during the past two hundred years, the brown-skinned people in this region have acquired a reputation for reacting fiercely to any affront to their dignity, for challenging a slight that others might allow to pass, perhaps it is because they have come to realize that long ago retreat ceased to be a practical possibility.

Though some Indians survived along the Lumber, many others did not. During the eighteenth century a half-dozen tribes and as many languages disappeared. We have only sketchy information as to what brought about the decimation of these people and the destruction of their cultures, but it appears to have been largely the result of disease, the white man's germs proving even more deadly than his gunpowder. Since the Indians had no hereditary resistance to European diseases, the epidemics of the eighteenth century by no means struck down the two races impartially. "It is pretty certain," wrote the Charlestown *Gazette* in 1759, "that the smallpox has lately raged with great violence among the Catawba Indians, and that it has carried off near one half of that nation, by throwing themselves into the river as soon as they found themselves ill. This distemper has since appeared among the inhabitants at the Charraws and Waterees, where many families are down." [11]

The Catawbas, who in 1700 had been able to count 1,500 fighting men, by the middle of the century could muster only 450. Yet their decline continued unchecked although they received into their ranks the surviving members of a kindred tribe, the Cheraws, a people for whom the disease had brought an even greater disaster.[12] A short time later a white official reported that the Catawbas "consisted within these few years about 300 fighting men but last year small pox ravaged their towns which made them desert them and leaving their sick behind to perish; by an account from their King Haglar to me they are reduced to 60 fighting and as many old men and boys and a suitable number of women." [13]

The germs of the Europeans did not strike down Indian and white impartially. Neither did their alcohol. Perhaps drinking alcohol is not good for any people. Yet in certain cultures whatever ultimate evils may result from its use are not dramatically evident. In other cultures, including those of a number of Indian peoples, the introduction of distilled liquor brought an element of chaos into their society. King Haglar of the Catawbas, whose territory in the mid-eighteenth century apparently included the Lumber River region, made

[11] The Right Rev. Alexander Gregg, History of the Old Cheraws; Containing an Account of the Aborigines of the Pedee, the First White Settlements, Their Subsequent Progress, Civil Changes, the Struggle of the Revolution, and the Growth of the Country Afterwards, Extending from about A.D. 1730 to 1810, with Notices of Families and Sketches of Individuals (New York: Richardson and Co., 1867), 16, quoting Charleston Gazette, December 8, 15, 1759.

[12] Ibid., 17.

[13] William L. Saunders (ed.), The Colonial Records of North Carolina (Raleigh: State of North Carolina, 1886–90), VI, 616, hereinafter cited as Saunders (ed.), Colonial Records.

these observations to a royal commission which was trying to find out why some white settlers were having trouble with Indians:

Brothers here is One thing You Yourselves are to Blame very much in, That is You Rot Your grain in Tubs, out of which you . . . make Strong Spirits. You sell it to our young men and give it them many times; they get very Drunk. . . . this is the Very Cause that they oftentimes Commit those Crimes that is offencive to You and us. . . . it is also very bad for our people, for it Rots their guts and Causes our men to get very sick and many of our people has Lately Died from the Effects of that strong Drink . . . .
 . . . I desire a stop may be put to the selling strong Liquor by the White people to my people. . . . If the White people make strong drink let them sell it to one another to drink in their own families. This will avoid a great deal of mischief which otherwise will happen from my people getting drunk and quarrelling with the White people. . . . I have no strong prisons like you to confine them for it, Our only way is to put them underground.[14]

But unfortunately for King Haglar, if his followers had a thirst for alcohol, the white traders had one for profits; and, although the white men did indeed have many "strong prisons," these would not primarily be used to confine the destructive social consequences of that particular addiction. By 1798, except for a small enclave of Catawbas on the upper Wateree and the Cherokees in the Appalachians, tribal life had disappeared from the Carolinas.[15]

Closely connected with the breakup of tribal organization was the disappearance of distinctly Indian culture. Ancient languages died as old lips fell silent. Here and there one may still encounter a river or stream with a strange-sounding name, the meaning of which is often forgotten, surviving as

[14] *Ibid.*, V, 143, 581.
[15] Gregg, *History of the Old Cheraws*, 18–19.

the pitiable relic of a language that was once heard about council fires.

Yet in the isolated and backward valley of the Lumber a hardy race of brown-skinned men and women endured despite the ravages of gunpowder, alcohol, and smallpox. In time they would be called "Scuffletonians," "Croatans," and "Lumbees," as well as other names. Were they Indians? Their bodies probably bore the genes of a half-dozen Indian nations,[16] but their ideas and habits mirrored the cultural heritage of the English settlers. Their houses, their dress were those of the white pioneers, as were their inclinations toward hard drinking and lusty violence. They spoke exclusively English; and though they spoke it in a distinctive manner, they did not retain native words that their white neighbors would not understand. The old Indian heritage was as much a closed book to them as it was to the whites. Like the whites they practiced evangelical Christianity, and by the nineteenth century most of them had become Baptists or Methodists.[17] In no significant way did they seem to be different from the backwoods whites.

Yet, however much the Scuffletonian might resemble the conqueror in language, custom, and religion, a subtle distinction still lingered. Perhaps it was because he could not adopt also a European skin color. A few shades of difference in skin pigment was all that was necessary to divulge a chapter of local history. One glance at a man's face and a person could tell whether he belonged to the seed of the conqueror or of the vanquished.

Though at first the Europeans bypassed the Lumber River region for the more desirable Piedmont, nevertheless toward the middle of the eighteenth century came an increasing

[16] A leading authority on southeastern Indians believes that the tribes leaving the largest contingents in the Lumber River area were the Keyauwee and Cheraws. Swanton, *Probable Identity of the "Croatans,"* 5.

[17] Barton, *The Most Ironic Story in American History,* 93–96.

trickle of settlers from the new races, both whites and blacks. They made their homes in the Indian farming communities along the Lumber River, known collectively to the whites as "Scuffletown" and to the Indians as "the Settlement." [18]

Some of the new immigrants may have come to "Scuffletown" for reasons similar to those that had brought the older settlers, for among them were escaped slaves looking for a community that would give them shelter and protection.[19] Others may have come because they did not have legal land titles within the frontier of white settlement. A certain royal official reported during the French and Indian War that the area was inhabited by "a mixt Crew, a lawless people," who "possess the land without patent or paying quit rents"; and who had "shot a Surveyor for coming to view the vacant lands being encircled in great swamps." [20] Thus the proud Scuffletonians made their debut on the pages of recorded history.

[18] The exact location of "Scuffletown," as well as the origin of the term, is uncertain. Indeed a stranger who came looking for a town by that name was likely to be thoroughly confused by the directions that he got from local Indians, at least until they learned something about the purpose of his visit. Scuffletown "was similar to the end of a rainbow," the Reverend D. F. Lowry explains. "You never could find the place. If you were headed south and inquired about it, it was 15 miles down the road and when you had driven . . . 15 miles down the road and asked . . . , it was 10 miles up the road." He thinks that the name originated with an inn located at Harper's Ferry on the Lumber River. During the American Revolution both the inn and the ferry were operated by James Lowry (*ca.* 1710–1810), considered the common ancestor of thousands of present-day Lowrys in the region. There was music and dancing at the inn. "The people would also scuffle and wrestle, hence it became known as Scuffle Town." (Letter to author from D. F. Lowry, n.d.) Barton and other historians of the Lumber River region have suggested another possible origin for the term. They believe that it is a corruption of the name "Scovilletown." (Telephone conversation with Lewis Randolph Barton, August 1, 1970.) Many Robeson County communities have in fact derived their names from such a prominent family as the Scovilles.

[19] In early-eighteenth-century North Carolina, however, not all slaves were Negroes. After their defeat in 1713 many of the Tuscaroras were sold into slavery. Holloman, "Palatines and Tuscaroras," 29.

[20] Saunders (ed.), *Colonial Records*, V, 161.

The large-scale settlement of the area by whites did not begin until about a decade before the American Revolution. The first large group of whites were the Scottish Highlanders, whose experience in some respects paralleled that of the Indians. Just as the defeat of the Tuscaroras in 1713 had served to set in motion the disintegration of tribal society in the Carolinas, so the defeat inflicted two years later by the royal government on some rebellious Scottish clans had started a similar process in the Highlands, a process that resulted in the complete breakup of a society governed by kinship relations. Many of these uprooted Scots found their way to the Lumber River valley, where they made their homes beside detribalized Indians.[21]

In other ways the Scots were quite different from the Indians, and unlike some of the earlier white settlers they were not absorbed into the Scuffletonian community. For one thing the Scots were divided by greater class distinctions. Among them were tweed-wearing, Highland aristocrats, men and women who were literate, who spoke English fluently. But there were also unlettered, Gaelic-speaking Scots, many of them indentured servants, called "Buckskins" because, it is said, they wore leather breeches as did the Indians; and it was with deerskins that they repaid their indentures and became free men.

A difference in language would for a long time continue to divide the Scots and the Indians. The Indian community was not only a melting pot for a number of Indian language groups, but also had absorbed some of the earlier white and black settlers as well. The Scuffletonians adopted English at such an early period that we have no written records of their using the old languages. The Buckskins, on the other hand, already having a common language, Gaelic, could be more

[21] Duane Gilbert Meyer, *The Highland Scots of North Carolina, 1732–1776* (Chapel Hill: University of North Carolina Press, 1961).

leisurely in learning English. As late as the Civil War the old Celtic tongue still sounded before the red glow of the Buckskin's hearth. Because the Indians adopted English perhaps a century before the Scots, they use a slightly older form of the language. For this reason, even in twentieth-century Robeson County, a person's speech sometimes gives a clearer indication as to which racial community he belongs than does his physical appearance.

Though a large number of Indians survived in the Lumber River valley, they did not prosper. Much of the best farm land in the area had been "granted" by the British Crown to various whites. Yet the royal government can by no means be blamed for all of the misfortunes of the Scuffletonians. Indeed the Crown "granted" some former Indian land to Indians. But, already land-poor in the eighteenth century, the brown-skinned people grew poorer, until by the time of the Civil War many were completely landless.[22]

What brought about this increasing poverty of the Indians? To some degree they were merely sharing the impoverishment that the Buckskins and other whites in the South were undergoing. All were beginning to suffer from the effects of slavery.

At first it is not obvious why a farmer who tilled his own acres should be affected if the plantation next door used slaves. But the yeoman's cotton had to be sold in competition with that produced by a slave gang working under the cowhide whip of a driver and subsisting on coarse staples at a brute level. However much importance a small farmer might attribute to his white skin and free status, these distinctions did not give any special quality to the cotton that he produced, nor did they impress Liverpool buyers in their bids

---

[22] U.S., Bureau of Census, Eighth Census of the United States (1860), Free Population, North Carolina, XIII, Robeson County (unpublished reports in National Archives).

for the product of his labor. In the South, as a result, deeper economic distinctions began to develop in the community of the free. The crude equality of the eighteenth-century backwoods began to give way to a society divided between those families that enjoyed the benefits of slave labor and those that worked in competition with it.

But the Indians fared worse than the Buckskins. Slavery brought not only new ways of organizing the production of cotton but also new ideas. The defenders of the system everywhere were cultivating an elaborate body of racist ideas which served not only to justify human inequality, but also to solidify the whites in upholding an institution that could not exist without broad community support. It was inevitable that these ideas would be directed against people who were not slaves. This indeed happened in 1835 with the ratification of a new North Carolina constitution: nonslave blacks lost most of the attributes of citizenship, including the right to vote and the right to bear arms. These new restrictions were aimed at blacks rather than Indians. But the Scuffletonians had no tribal organization or culture to prove that they were Indians. They merely had dark skin, which the whites were regarding increasingly with suspicion or contempt. Consequently, the wording of the document, "free persons of mixed blood," came to be applied to both the Lumber River Indians and the Cherokees in the Appalachian Mountains.[23] After 1835 people would continue to talk of "free Negroes" and "free people of mixed blood," but in reality the rights that all of the dark-skinned people enjoyed made them more than slaves but less than free men.

Furthermore there is reason to believe that the new half-free status of the Scuffletonians caused their already small fields to shrink even smaller. Since the Indian's legal rights

[23] N.C., *Constitution* (1835), Art. I, Sec. 3, Cl. 3; Barton, *The Most Ironic Story in American History*, 92.

were now more restricted, since he was now confronted with more pronounced white supremacy, he may have begun to fare more poorly in the white man's courts, especially when he became involved in a dispute with a white. Of great importance was the litigation that took place in the civil courts, which decided such controversies as land titles and the attachment of property for the recovery of debts. Concerning the gradual impoverishment of the Lowry family between the Revolution and the Civil War, one observer noted that "their land was levied upon to pay debts. Being Indians, with an idea that their ancestors held all this land in fee simple they could not understand [how] it would be taken from them, and for years they looked upon society as having robbed them of their patrimony." [24]

The movement for secession and southern independence evoked little enthusiasm in the Lumber River valley, with its large Indian and Buckskin population. The conscription acts evoked even less, as there were few people who could avail themselves of the escape clauses, which exempted large slaveholders and persons having enough money to hire substitutes.[25] For the Indians conscription meant not only more hardship but further humiliation as well.

To be sure, the unhappy experience that the Lumbee Indians had with Confederate North Carolina did not reflect a universal policy of Confederates against Indians. On the contrary, in dealing with the Cherokees, Creeks, Chickasaws, and other large acculturated tribes in what later became Oklahoma, the Jefferson Davis government offered more generous treaties than those that the United States had been in the habit of breaking.[26]

---

[24] Townsend (comp.), *The Swamp Outlaws*, 48, quoting "Mr. Leech" [Giles Leitch?].

[25] Confederate States of America, *Statutes at Large*, 1862, Chap. 45.

[26] Annie Heloise Abel, *The Slaveholding Indians* (3 vols.; Cleveland: Arthur H. Clark Co., 1915–25), I, 158–80.

But in explaining why the Confederacy courted the friendship of the Indians on the frontier it is significant to note that in this region the assaults on Indian power were just beginning. Much of the traditional social organization of these tribes, much of their motivating ideology, much of their military power was still intact. Furthermore, since they were located in the region between Confederate Texas and Arkansas on one hand and Unionist Kansas on the other, they had military strength that they could offer to either side. The Confederacy made the highest bids. The slaveholding elite of these tribes accepted these offers, raised regiments; and they and thousands of their humbler kinsmen were disastrously defeated by a Union army at Pea Ridge, Arkansas, March 6–8, 1862.[27]

As far as Confederate North Carolina was concerned, on the other hand, the Indians of that state had been legislated out of existence by the Constitution of 1835. Since then there had been only "free persons of color." With the outbreak of the war, persons not having the right to bear arms were conscripted into labor battalions and assigned to work beside black slaves constructing a system of forts around the mouth of the Cape Fear estuary, which protected Wilmington.[28]

It would have been difficult for the government to build these forts with free labor, particularly during the yellow-fever epidemic of 1862–63, which sent a large part of the free population scurrying to the higher and healthier ground in Piedmont North Carolina. The epidemic was particularly severe at Wilmington, the center of both military and economic activity in the area. In an effort to fumigate the air,

[27] *Ibid.*, II, 29–36.
[28] U.S., War Department, Captured Confederate Records, Payrolls (Record Group 109, National Archives); anonymous manuscript on the origins of the Lowry band, in the possession of Clifton Wishart, White Plains, N.Y., 6, hereinafter cited as Origins of Lowry Band.

tar barrels were burned on the street corners of the stricken city. The heavy, pungent smoke blackened the entire landscape, covering everything with a shroud of gloom. A resident noted that as of October 18, 1862, "there had been five hundred new cases in the past week and 150 interments . . . . The streets were empty, business was entirely suspended, nothing broke the sickly silence save the rolling sound of a hearse or the physicians' vehicles or here and there, a solitary footfall." [29] With a grim singleness of purpose the Confederate command continued work on the forts, though the epidemic wiped out perhaps 10 percent of the people who remained on the lower Cape Fear.[30]

Yellow fever subsided considerably after 1863, but human misery persisted around the forts. The planters whose slaves were being used on the project were indignant about the ill usage that their property was receiving. As a result of their protest, the North Carolina legislature passed a resolution complaining to the Confederate command about conditions in the labor camps. In his reply to the resolution, General Braxton Bragg made no effort to minimize the problem except to point out that the bad conditions were by no means confined to slaves, and "to a great extent have been shared" by Confederate soldiers. He admitted that the rations were too light for men engaged in heavy work, that the men were inadequately clad for winter, that they were forced to work in water when gathering sod and rafting timber, that there was a shortage of hospital facilities, living quarters, and fuel.[31]

All suffered hardship, but the experience of the Indians converted their hardship into a sense of outrage. To the Scuffletonian conscript it must have appeared that he had very nearly reached the destination toward which his people

[29] Wilmington *Review*, February 15, 1889.
[30] Barrett, *The Civil War in North Carolina*, 259.
[31] Seitz, *Braxton Bragg*, 506–507.

had been pressed during a century of degradation. Piecemeal they had lost their lands, their civil rights, and their social status. Now at last the line that separated the brown-skinned Indian labor conscript from the black-skinned Negro slave must have seemed a subtle legal distinction indeed!

Some Indians managed to escape from the forts and to return home to the Settlement. In order to avoid recapture, however, they had to take up a practice that the Heroes of America[32] and other North Carolina Unionists called "lying out"—camping in the woods as a means of staying beyond the reach of the Confederate Home Guard. The most important group of these refugees that the conscription officers sought in the junglelike swamps of Robeson County was the Lowry band, the nucleus of which appears to have been originally four sons of Allen Lowry and certain of their kinsmen, as well as male members of families with which they were connected by marriage.

The Lowrys soon discovered, however, that their native swamps had become hiding places for men who were not Indians. They found that Yankee soldiers, who had escaped from the Confederate camp near Florence, South Carolina, had also found refuge there. This discovery confronted them with some of the larger implications of the war. Initially at least, had they been accepted on a basis of equality, the Indians would have been willing to serve the Confederacy.[33] But having been brought into conflict with the local representatives of Confederate authority, by about 1863 they had

[32] This was a pro-Union secret society. It appears to have been based largely in North Carolina, though it may have had some influence in South Carolina and in parts of Virginia. It may have been the substance to the reports of a "treasonable society" said to have been active among North Carolina soldiers in the Army of Northern Virginia. Joseph Grégoire de Roulhac Hamilton, "The Heroes of America," *Publications of the Southern Historical Association*, XI (1907), 10–11 and *passim*.

[33] Townsend (comp.), *The Swamp Outlaws*, 47; Norment, *The Lowrie History*, 150.

Henry Berry Lowry and His Gang in the Swamp

come to sympathize with the Union cause. They soon began accepting Yankee soldiers into their band, which had been previously based on kinship and marriage.

In the meanwhile, passive resistance was becoming increasingly difficult. Too many Indians were "lying out"; not enough were growing corn. Although the Scuffletonians were no strangers to hunger, they had never known such misery as that which now came upon them with war, since more and more people had to share less and less food. A contemporary writer has related how, under these conditions, the Lowry band moved from a policy of subsisting on the poverty of their Indian kin to one of living on the affluence of their more prosperous neighbors:

It is a notorious fact that the inhabitants of Scuffletown often live for days without any thing to eat except Huckle Berry's [sic]; and in the winter season they have been known to live for days without anything whatever to eat. These Scuffletonians for reasons herinafter mentioned regarded the Genl Govt [sic] and its soldiers as their best friends, consequently they were more than proud when these escaped prisoners came amongst them to show them every attention they could and to entertain them as highly as possible. . . . The refusal of our state and Genl Govt [the Confederacy] at the same time to accept them as soldiers produced feelings of bitterness toward our Govt and aroused their Indian feelings of enmity against their white neighbors, who were their best friends.[34]

Moreover the escaped prisoners, "by reading and talking to" the Scuffletonians, "presented such pictures to their minds as were best calculated to strengthen their feeling of friendship" toward the Lincoln government. The big problem was food. The Scuffletonian wishing "to entertain them a little better than they were themselves accustomed to live . . . determined to have some meat to eat. Old Allen Lowry whose Guest these escaped prisoners were . . . sent his sons Henry Berry, Steve, & Bill to Mr. Barnes' fields where his fattening hogs were . . . . They killed two of the finest . . . and carried them home." [35]

But James P. Barnes, a wealthy slaveholder and minor local official of the Confederacy, missed his hogs, became suspicious of his Indian neighbors, obtained a search warrant, searched the Lowry place, and found the ears of two recently slaughtered hogs bearing his earmarks. The sons of Lowry, whom he suspected, were nowhere to be found; and he did not wish to prefer charges against their father, with whom he used to hunt and fish. Nevertheless he warned Allen Lowry that neither he nor his kin was ever again to set foot on Barnes's land; and, in the months that followed,

when an officer came along to get hands to work on the Breast Works about Wilmington Mr. Barnes would invariably pilot

[34] Origins of Lowry Band, 2–3.
[35] *Ibid.*, 3.

them through his neighborhood. These boys of Allen Lowry were frequently taken to labor on these fortifications. . . . on the 21st day of December 1864 they ambushed him between his house and the Post office . . . . After first shooting him down Henry Berry walked up to him and with an old shot Gun while Mr. Barnes was begging him not to shoot him any more for "I am dying. You have killed me" shot him through the hand (which was imploringly held up) into the face and head. His screams brought Mr. Willis Moore and Archd McNair and some negroes. He barely had time to tell them who had shot him before he died.[36]

Having killed Barnes, the Lowry band next turned their attention to a Confederate official whom they disliked far more, James Brantley Harris. Harris was a white merchant and liquor dealer who had settled among the Scuffletonians some years before. With the outbreak of war he had been made the local Confederate conscription officer and had been provided with a Home Guard detail to help him beat the bushes in search of Indians who might prove useful in the fever-ridden pest holes of the lower Cape Fear.

It is doubtful that the Scuffletonians would have liked any Confederate conscription officer. But it is significant that Harris was disliked by people who were white and staunch supporters of the Confederacy. One remembered him as being "a rough man," [37] another as "not sustaining a fair character . . . being feared by all who knew him." [38] In his capacity as recruiting officer he was "the roughest of his class, overbearing and abusive" to the Indians, and he was "charged with being too familiar with the wives and daughters of his customers and from this first sprang enmities between himself and the Lowreys." [39]

[36] *Ibid.*, 5–6.
[37] *Report of the Joint Select Committee to Inquire into the Condition of Affairs in the Late Insurrectionary States (Ku Klux Conspiracy)* (Washington: Government Printing Office, 1872), II, 286, hereinafter cited as *Ku Klux Conspiracy.*
[38] Norment, *The Lowrie History*, 42.
[39] Wilmington *Daily Journal*, April 4, 1872.

The exact cause of the quarrel may have been simply "the discharge of Mr. Harris' duty as Militia officer," as one source indicates,[40] or it may have been that "being a libidinous wretch he took possession of some of the lightest damsels in the settlement, and one of these was courted honorably by a cousin of young Henry Berry Lowry." [41] In any event, whether in pursuit of duty or of amorous adventure, the conscription officer aroused the bitter enmity of a young Lowry, who was reported to have exploded that "the Country was not large enough to hold him and Harris." [42]

Fearing for his life, the 230-pound conscription officer on a Sunday night prepared an ambush near a house where his adversary was expected to make a visit. He patiently waited. Presently in the half-light a youthful silhouette appeared before him. "Who's there?" he called. "Lowry," the answer came back. Harris fired. Later he found that he had indeed killed a boy, a member of the Lowry clan, but the wrong one. He had slain Jarman Lowry, with whom he had no special quarrel.[43]

Although the Robeson County grand jury apparently overlooked this particular murder, Harris a short time later again had occasion to fear for his life. Wesley and Allen Lowry,[44] two of the slain boy's brothers, whom the conscription officer had previously sent to work in a labor battalion at the forts, had now been granted a short furlough and were returning home to the Settlement to visit their parents.

[40] Origins of Lowry Band, 7.
[41] Townsend (comp.), *The Swamp Outlaws*, 49.
[42] Origins of Lowry Band, 7.
[43] *Ibid.*, 6–7.
[44] This youth was a son of George Lowry and a nephew of the Allen Lowry (*ca.* 1800–65) mentioned in Chapter 1. The names Wesley and Allen are the names remembered by the Reverend D. F. Lowry and others of their kinsmen. A white, who may have been more prone to confuse the names of Indians, called them "Bill" and "George." *Ibid.*, 8.

To forestall an attempt on his life, Harris led his Home Guard detachment to their place, arrested Wesley and Allen on the pretext that they were absent without leave, and informed their parents that he was taking them to Moss Neck, where they would be put on a train for Wilmington. The two young Indians were handcuffed and led away. However, before reaching the station, Harris told his Home Guard squad that "they might go back, as he could manage his prisoners the rest of the way himself." [45] A short time later the dead bodies of Wesley and Allen Lowry were found near the Moss Neck station. According to one report, probably originating with Harris himself, "they made an attack upon him, but . . . he killed them both right there with a lightwood knot." [46]

On January 15, 1865, the elephantine conscription officer was riding in his buggy, accompanied by an Indian woman. He reined his horse to a halt, and the woman got out. Harris drove on. Suddenly there was a deafening barrage of gunfire. Harris vanished from view, apparently disappearing into the floor of his buggy. The horse, wild with panic, ran away, racing madly for home. Just before the frightened animal dashed into Harris' yard, the lifeless body of his master fell from the buggy.[47]

Having now killed both a civil and a military officer, the Lowry band could hardly expect that the government would allow such a challenge to pass unnoticed. And they were not ready for a major onslaught. Not having enjoyed the legal right to possess firearms, Indians were naturally poorly prepared, as were the escaped Union prisoners. The vulnerability of the Lowrys no doubt prompted their next move,

[45] Wilmington *Daily Journal*, April 4, 1872.
[46] Origins of Lowry Band, 8.
[47] *Ibid.*, 9.

Moss Neck

a bold raid on the Robeson County courthouse at Lumberton, where they seized arms and ammunition intended for the local militia.[48] For provisions they began a series of raids on the more prosperous planters, but carefully avoiding the property of the Buckskins and Indians.[49] It was probably as a result of these Robin Hood tactics that they were able, as one Conservative put it, to find "some few degenerate white natives who were ready and willing to take up cudgel with them, to inflict injury on their former neighbors and friends."[50] One such raid, however, which they made on February 27, 1865, on Argyle Plantation near present-day Maxton, probably did more to arouse their enemies against them than anything else they had done.

The Confederate party was small in Robeson County, but it included many of the wealthy and well-educated citizens. One of the warmest friends of the cause was the widow Elizabeth Ann McNair of Argyle, who after surviving another Scottish husband would be remembered as the widow Neil McNair MacRae. Like some Highland chieftainess, she reigned over Argyle, which was tilled by about thirty slaves

[48] Wilmington *North Carolinian*, February 15, 1865.
[49] *Ku Klux Conspiracy*, II, 294.
[50] Wilmington *Daily Journal*, April 4, 1872.

and stood like a rock of Confederate defiance in a swamp of Buckskin indifference and Indian subversion.

As a knowledgeable person, the widow in the winter of 1864–65 probably no longer had any real hope of victory in the war. It seems more likely that her Confederate pugnacity stemmed from her sense of loss. Her only child, Harlee, a seventeen-year-old artilleryman, had just died in the Confederate service at one of the Cape Fear forts.[51] Harlee had not gone down to the forts out of compulsion. When people with wealth and slaves gave their sons, it was from a sense of commitment; and it was not easy to abandon a cause for which so much had been committed.[52]

Against the guerrillas the widow was by no means defenseless. Not only was she playing host to two families of her kinsmen; but Argyle, with its private railroad stop, was also a favorite port of call for fashionable young men of the Confederate army. If forty returning summers had stolen away some particle of her youthful charm, time had dealt more kindly with Argyle Plantation and Elizabeth's fortune. Two of her young army friends were house guests at Argyle the night the Lowrys made their raid.

Following a gun battle, some of the guerrillas succeeded in getting inside the plantation big house. There they were greeted by a most unladylike barrage of gunfire apparently coming from the lady's own bedroom. Later, after they had had time to reflect on the matter, the widow's many friends, while perplexed by this curious circumstance, were not without explanations for it: one thought that the lady herself had probably developed some skill with a Colt repeater.[53]

[51] Robert C. Lawrence, *The State of Robeson* (Lumberton, N.C.: Robert C. Lawrence, 1939), 189.

[52] U.S., Bureau of Census, Eighth Census of the United States (1860), Free Population, North Carolina, XIII, 999, Slaves, North Carolina, IV, 62–63.

[53] Origins of Lowry Band, 10.

Another suggested that although the lady fired the shots herself, the pistol belonged to a young lieutenant from Fayetteville, who "being ill had been given the use of Mr. McNair's own room that night, for the time being." [54]

After another brief exchange of fire, the widow and her friends and kinsmen were forced to give up. But Elizabeth McNair remained defiant. One of the guerrillas, Owen T. Wright, a Yankee regular, had been wounded in the attack. She now claimed to have fired the shot that brought him down. One of the Indians wanted to shoot her on the spot, but another Yankee, an officer, intervened on the lady's behalf. The raiders took possession of the widow's wagons and teams and even impressed a few of her slaves to drive them. They moved Wright, the wounded soldier, several miles away and left him in the care of another widow, Amanda Nash, a white schoolteacher said to have been a secret Lowry sympathizer, who for years performed small favors for the band. [55] The next morning at dawn the teams and slaves returned to Argyle, the wagons empty. [56] The Scuffletonians would share a little of Argyle's bounty, but Elizabeth McNair might also have to endure some of Scuffletown's misery.

Perhaps the most important result of the raid on Argyle was that it goaded the Home Guard into more resolute

[54] John C. MacRae to Donald MacRae, March 3, 1865, in Hugh MacRae Papers, Duke University Library; William Clifton Wishart (ed.), Commentary on Francis Marion Wishart Diary (Wishart Papers, in possession of Clifton Wishart, White Plains, N.Y.), 29. This document is an incomplete typescript which William Clifton Wishart (1871–1965) made of his father's diary. All citations of this document refer to the editor's valuable notes and commentary rather than to the diary itself, which is cited in this book always from his father's original. Hereinafter cited as W. C. Wishart, Commentary on Diary.

[55] This is a tradition that has come down through Mrs. Nash's daughter, whose name was also Amanda Nash and who was also a teacher.

[56] Norment, The Lowrie History, 60–61; Wilmington Daily Journal, April 4, 1872; Townsend (comp.), The Swamp Outlaws, 50; John C. MacRae to Donald MacRae, March 3, 1865, in MacRae Papers; Origins of Lowry Band, 9–10.

action. Relatively impotent throughout the war,[57] and further demoralized by the assassination of James Brantley Harris, the Home Guard now found its ranks strengthened by the friends and the kinsmen of the widow McNair, a number of whom were Confederate regulars. Perhaps also their spirits were stiffened by the strong-willed Calvinist lady who adopted as her life motto the device "I will find a way or make one." [58]

Thus reinforced, the company was reorganized, electing Captain McGreggor of Richmond County as commander, and began a series of actions against the Lowrys. On March 3, 1865, the Home Guard men raided a series of farms where they suspected that guerrilla loot might be found. The search of houses and the interrogation of suspects culminated in the execution of William Lowry, who was probably an active guerrilla, as well as his aged father, who probably was not. But just at the point where the campaign appeared to be meeting with dramatic success, the Home Guard called a halt: search and interrogation were discontinued, suspects set free. To the south one could already hear the sound of the cannons that brought famine and freedom.

On Thursday morning, three days after the executions of William and Allen Lowry, the Reverend Washington Sandford Chaffin arose before dawn, as was his custom. He rarely failed to watch the approach of the new day. It seemed a fitting time to contemplate the use that he had made of all of his other days, and to savor visions of days still to come. But this particular morning was scarcely one conducive to quiet meditation. A smell of smoke hovered in the air. Outside was a confused din of voices. The Reverend Mr. Chaffin walked to the window and looked out on Lumberton's main

[57] *Ku Klux Conspiracy*, II, 294.
[58] Lawrence, *The State of Robeson*, 190. The Latin motto, *Inveniam viam ut faciam*, is more precisely translated as "I will find the way in order that I may act."

street. There were piles of burning cotton here and there, which yesterday the local Confederate authorities had ordered destroyed. People were hurrying about in "great excitement." More rumors, he thought. This had been going on for days.

He opened his diary to March 9, 1865, and started to make his entry for the day. But a great cry rose in the street, and again he went to the window. He saw two riders "straining their steeds down the street toward Major Blount's—hollering 'The Yankees are coming, the Yankees are coming.' Almost instantly the street was swarming with Yankees . . . cavalry, charging in every direction. A neighbor started to run, and was twice fired upon before my door. There were some 300 to 500 of them, I suppose. They robbed me of Mrs. Chaffin's watch—also stole Kate [Chaffin's horse]. They burned the county bridge, railroad bridge and depot, entered many houses & committed many depredations." [59]

But at this moment General William T. Sherman's forces were having troubles of their own, occasioned not so much by Confederate resistance as by Robeson County swamps. "The trials that this and other divisions endured . . . between Lumber River and Little Rockfish Creek beggar description," wrote Major General John A. Logan.

To be fully appreciated the scene of their operations should have been visited; the whole corps worked night and day as pioneers until the treacherous country was passed. No sooner had the second division fairly commenced crossing the Lumber River than rain set in with great violence completely washing the bottom out of the roads. . . . the roads were so bad that in places no ground could be found solid enough for the animals to stand upon, and wagons had to be pulled out of the mire by

---

[59] Washington Sandford Chaffin Journal (MS in Duke University Library), March 9, 1865, and *passim*.

relays of men. . . . General Corse moved on until 9 p.m. [March 9], corduroying almost every foot of the road and making four miles . . . . One of the swamp bridges had sunk and his command bivouacked with Juniper Swamp and Creek, swollen into quite a stream, flowing between his brigades.[60]

The difficulties that Sherman was encountering influenced his policies, and his policies would influence events in the Lumber River valley for some time to come. His army had been living off the country. This ancient practice, which had tarnished the historical reputations of Attila the Hun and Genghis Khan, had likewise not improved Sherman's public image in Georgia and South Carolina. Upon reaching North Carolina, Sherman had intended to modify his policy, since in that state the Lincoln government was supposed to have many friends; and the Union cause could hardly be expected to thrive on a famine created by a Union army. He planned to try to curb the exuberance of his foragers, who sometimes behaved as if every night were Halloween.[61]

In the Lumber River valley the hope of finding Union sympathizers was not unfounded. Local persons, especially Indians, volunteered to act as scouts, to guide the army through their native swamps. But Sherman did not change his policy. Were his soldiers, with their fixed habit of looting, likely to wait patiently for the supplies that might never arrive over the bottomless roads that lay behind them? Was the general, used to making decisions based narrowly on military considerations, likely to leave his troops in the mud for a time in order not to sacrifice the native Unionists to the vengeance of their neighbors? Sherman chose to get his sol-

[60] *The War of the Rebellion: A Compilation of the Official Records of the Union and Confederate Armies* (Washington: Government Printing Office, 1880–1901), Ser. I, Vol. XLVII, Pt. 1, pp. 231–32.
[61] Barrett, *The Civil War in North Carolina*, 298.

diers out of the mud; and if this decision left the local Unionists in even deeper difficulties, this was not a military problem.[62]

Like many Indians, Solomon Oxendine had been conscripted for a time into a labor battalion at Fort Fisher, and had come to sympathize with the cause of the Union. One of his kinsmen, in fact, had volunteered as a guide for the Sherman forces. Yet the foragers came also to his own yard and seized his only draft animal. "I and my wife begged for the mule," he later reported, but the Yankees "said they were in this low country . . . and they were obliged to have good teams to get out. They took my mule and . . . I have not seen him since." [63] Nearly a decade later the government would pay Oxendine and other Unionists for their losses. But in 1865 they had the problem of how to grow a crop without draft animals.

Rich people could sometimes produce much more impressive figures of their losses than those that Oxendine suffered with the seizure of his mule. Dr. Hector McLean, for example, discovered that if there was any honor in having General Logan and his brigade at his Edinboro Plantation, the privilege was decidedly an expensive one. He claimed that following their three-day visit he was poorer by 4 mules, 6 horses, 5 cattle, 124 hogs, 2,000 bushels of corn, 600 bushels of potatoes, 300 bushels of peas, 100 bushels of wheat, 20 bushels of rice, 6,500 pounds of fodder, 7,000 pounds of bacon, 60 gallons of syrup, 100 chickens, and some 25,000 fat lightwood fence rails which were used for campfires and for corduroying muddy roads.[64]

[62] *Ibid.*, 297–98.

[63] U.S., Treasury Department, Records of the Accounting Office, Southern Claims (Record Group 217, National Archives).

[64] U.S., Treasury Department, Records of the Accounting Office, Southern Claims (Record Group 233, National Archives), File 17, p. 179.

Many people suffered hardships as a result of Sherman's visit. Yet it seems ironical that in this victorious campaign of a Union army, some of the people who lost most heavily were the local supporters of the Union. They suffered material losses like the rest. But more seriously, some were now abandoned to the desperate wrath of their neighbors for having lent a hand to this hunger-creating army.

The Home Guard, momentarily thrown off balance by the coming of Sherman, was quick to regain the initiative. The Lowrys, on the other hand, did not recover so easily. Their ranks had been depleted by the departure of the Union regulars who left with Sherman. Furthermore, just before the arrival of Sherman, the Home Guard had obtained some important information about the Lowry band.

Under their heavy-handed interrogation, a suspect had revealed that Amanda Nash was caring for a wounded Union soldier, Owen Wright. The Home Guard descended upon her. On this occasion they appear to have accepted Mrs. Nash's explanation that she had acted under duress and had cared for Wright because she feared reprisals, but they were nevertheless able to extract further information from the wounded man himself, between the time he was captured and the time he was finally set free by Sherman's forces. Wright may have found the days he spent in Lumberton in custody of Neatham Thompson, the local Confederate enrolling officer, less agreeable than the time he was in the care of Mrs. Nash. In any event he was by some means induced to reveal the names of persons who had helped him following his escape from the prison camp at Florence, families with whom he had taken meals, and is supposed to have informed the authorities that at Sinclair Lowry's place there were "25 or 30 concealed guns." [65]

[65] Deposition of Sinclair Lowry, June 1, 1867, in Investigation.

Wright may not have realized how much trouble his revelation would bring down on the heads of the people who had befriended him.

About April 1, 1865, Thompson and some twenty men from the Home Guard descended in a fury on Sinclair Lowry's place. The Indian carpenter denied any knowledge of hidden arms. The Home Guard began their search. Lowry, for his part, merely stayed in the house and waited. Widely recognized for his craftsmanship, he enjoyed the respect of many whites as well as Indians; and he was not generally considered to be a part of the guerrilla band led by his brothers—first William, then Henry Berry. There was some security in having a good name among the whites and it was probably for this reason that their mother, Mary Cumba Lowry, had come to live with him, since the Home Guard had made her a widow about three weeks earlier.[66]

Suddenly there was a burst of gunfire. Lowry checked quickly to see if his family was safe. Somebody was missing. He found that his mother, whom he thought was safely in the kitchen, had vanished. At the risk of getting shot himself, the Indian dashed from the house. In the yard he met a Home Guard man who, strangely enough, asked him "for a pitcher to get some water," which he was going to "carry to a sick person." Lowry gave him a pitcher but "followed after the man about two hundred yards, and in the woods off the road he saw his mother—Mary Lowry—trying to walk." When he reached her "she threw her arms around his neck . . . . He sat down with her, and after resting, tried to get her to walk again but she was so frightened that she fainted away . . . . He sent to the house for a blanket to carry her home." [67]

A Home Guard firing squad had taken her into the woods. They had tied her to a stake and blindfolded her, just as

[66] *Ibid.* Mrs. Lowry was sometimes called "Polly" as well as "Mary."
[67] *Ibid.*

they had done her son and husband. A voice then inquired if she would not like to tell where the guns were hidden and where her other sons were. But the old lady declined. Then the voice of Neatham Thompson gave the order, "Fire!" But the gunfire was deliberately misaimed, since the purpose of the action was to make her more cooperative. When the smoke cleared, however, Mary Lowry was in no condition for questioning; she was completely unconscious. Thompson then ordered her cut down and sent for water to revive her.[68]

The tactics of the Home Guard had been generally effective: by terrorizing one suspect they could induce him to betray others, who in turn would be seized and likewise induced to yield information implicating still others. Thus the interrogations tended to spread and become more devastating. They had certainly succeeded in terrorizing Mary Lowry. But they left without finding out the whereabouts of her guerrilla sons, or where their arms were hidden. The vicious cycle of terror-betrayal-terror was interrupted when it reached Mary Lowry.

But unfortunately the bitterness of many whites against local Union people was far from spent—a bitterness deepened by the misery that Sherman had left in his path and rendered more desperate by each new Confederate defeat. On May 1, 1865, two Indians, William Locklear and Hector Oxendine, were on their way to the house of a white neighbor, who they thought might help them recover some horses "the Rebels took from us." But before reaching their destination they were arrested by William Humphreys and some other hostile whites. Locklear was allowed to go free, but before he left he heard Humphreys tell his companion, "I am going to keep you under guard tonight . . . . I am going to carry you to Andrew Carlisle's where you did the damage, and then we are going to put you through . . . . You . . . had no

[68] *Ibid.*; deposition of Mary Lowry, May 29, 1867, in Investigation.

business to go off with the Yankees and they . . . could not have made you done anything if you were not a mind to have done it." [69]

The next morning Andrew Carlisle received an oral message delivered by a Negro servant, asking him to take his gun over to his father's plantation, near by, "and help to shoot a buck." Carlisle understood. Like Locklear and Oxendine, he too had lost his horses. But, unlike them, it had been Sherman's men, rather than the retreating Confederates, who had done the damage; and Hector Oxendine had been the very Indian guide who had led Sherman's men to his plantation. Indeed he would come and "help to shoot a buck"! [70]

At the plantation of the elder Carlisle, a Negro servant watched as a band of armed whites led away their Indian prisoner. Some time later one of the whites returned and ordered him "to take a spade and hoe and go over to the swamp . . . ." And upon reaching the designated spot: "There was Hector Oxendine killed." A group of whites "were sitting off a little way talking . . . . I was ordered to dig Hector Oxendine's grave." [71] The next day the Oxendine kin located the spot, exhumed the body and returned home with it. [72]

Exactly one week later, at Appomattox, Virginia, two generals shook hands and their followers returned home, the savage cruelties that they had inflicted upon each other for four years now becoming as last week's nightmare, half-remembered. Why remember injuries inflicted by hands that served not an individual but rather a machine of war? Every

---

[69] Deposition of William Locklear, August 23, 1867, in Investigation.

[70] Deposition of Jack Carlisle, August 23, 1867, deposition of Davy Crawford, August 23, 1867, in Investigation.

[71] Deposition of Jack Carlisle, August 23, 1867, in Investigation.

[72] Deposition of Elias Carlisle, August 23, 1867, in Investigation.

person connected with a heinous act of war has his orders and can thus point a finger to somebody else. Responsibility is in this way spread ever more thinly over an ever larger circle of people until all concept of wrong evaporates and patriotic men can be held blameless for the crimes that their hands commit. With all guilt absolved, forgiveness becomes easy. But this was not so in the Lumber River valley. There it would take more than a cordial handshake by two generals to erase what war had written.

3 · "Only Payin' 'Em Back!"

On October 16, 1865, as midnight drew near, the silence of Willis Moore's plantation was ripped by a gunshot. Presently Patrick Barnes, a black servant on the plantation, heard the voice of his patron: "Patrick I have shot someone. Go and see who it is." Barnes obeyed. Going out to the corncrib, he caught sight of a human figure "standing leaning on a basket containing some corn." He recognized the man. It was Wesley Moore, who had once been a slave on the Moore plantation. "Wesley what are you doing here[?] How come you to take this corn?" But the wounded man gave no clear reply, only "kept murmuring on [,] calling on the Lord."

Barnes returned to the big house and asked the planter, "What are you going to do with Wesley? Are you going to let him lie there and die[?]" "I am not going to have anything to do with [him]," the white man replied. "I have sent after Lieutenant McNair of the Local police who can do with him as he pleases."

A short time later, A. J. McNair, the officer of a rural police company, arrived. He also wanted to know why the wounded man had stolen corn. "Mr. McNair," Moore replied, "I had no earthly use for the corn except to get me some bread—potatoes hurt me." The officer and the planter conferred for a moment. Then they decided to send for a doctor. But Wesley Moore died from his wound.[1]

[1] *State v. Willis P. Moore*, October 21, 1865, U.S., War Department, Bureau of Refugees, Freedmen, and Abandoned Lands (Record Group 105, National Archives), hereinafter cited as Freedmen's Bureau Records.

Eight months earlier, before Sherman had come, would Willis Moore have fired that fatal shot in the dark? Would he have risked killing a slave worth perhaps $1,500 in order to save a bushel of corn? Or, more basically, had it been necessary for slaves to steal their cornbread? Planters would have thought that they were wasting money and corrupting blacks had they fed their slaves the same food that white people ate, but at the same time, they had considered it poor business practice to feed their slaves short rations when it came to such coarse plantation staples as cornmeal.

Many of the early results of emancipation did not appear promising. On May 15, 1865, somebody had stood in the door of the courthouse at Lumberton and declared that the slaves were henceforth and forever free. To Wesley Moore and countless others these words had meant that a slave could leave his master, and he and a great many others did so. Emancipation had indeed set free one's feet, but the stomach remained a slave to the habit of eating. Most of the food along the Lumber was securely locked in stoutly built corncribs and smokehouses, protected by vicious dogs, by the firearms of the planter, and never far away were the sabers and pistols of the police company.

Thus in 1865 a black's free feet often had to transport his captive stomach back to the fleshpots of Egypt. There he had to stand, hat in hand, before his former master, or somebody else who possessed salt pork and cornmeal, and make all the obeisances considered appropriate for a well-mannered slave. He was thus forced to recognize that in the new free society, as in any other, men who control food are the taskmasters of those who do not, no matter what words to the contrary might be intoned from the courthouse door.

What did the abolition of slavery in America in fact mean? Did it simply mean the continuation of more servitude carried out by a different arrangement—a hungry black being shot to death for stealing corn? Even after a century of debate Americans would still not be able to agree on what black freedom means, but their basic positions on this question had already emerged by 1865. Then people were called Radicals or Conservatives, depending upon which of two approaches they preferred, though much more was involved in their differences than racial ideology.[2]

The Radical thought that the Negro was to take his place as an equal member of a society that had already been enriched by the contributions of many nationalities. The Radical was hostile to any idea that there could be different classes of citizenship or that there could be partial citizenship for any group; specifically he was opposed to any special legal disabilities covering the blacks. Some Radicals thought that to give the black legal rights, however, without also allowing him some measure of economic power was to engage in pious hypocrisy, while leaving the freedman to appear as a helpless supplicant before the smokehouse of his former master. To avoid such bogus equality they favored granting each black family a homestead, which would be carved from the public lands or from the large estates of leading Confederates.

[2] Although the motivation of the Radicals is a complex problem which is not within the scope of this book, the term *Radical* is here construed to mean that faction of the Republican Party which frequently advocated the cause of the blacks. Although Radicals indeed advocated the cause of the blacks, some historians have raised doubts as to the depth of that commitment, suggesting that the Radicals used emancipation and civil rights as a smoke screen for a takeover of the federal government by a new power elite.

To some historians, the Radicals' duplicity is demonstrated in their abandonment of the blacks at the end of Reconstruction. Unfortunately in politics it is not common to find a group continuing to make "idealistic" commitments to allies that it no longer needs. By 1877 it had become apparent that the devastation of the South, the vast growth of northern industry and population, the weakening of political agrarianism, the rise of a business community with enough millions to domesticate the Democratic as well as the Republican Party—all combined to reinforce, to consolidate the new regime. The Republican Party could now afford to be independent of the blacks, and even racist. It needed to raise few issues that went beyond the primary interests of its rich patrons. Its Radicalism was dead.

The Conservative, on the other hand, was disturbed by the prospect of the blacks' sudden leap from slavery to full citizenship. He felt rather that they should be required to undergo some type of apprenticeship before taking an equal place in American life, during which the various civil rights enjoyed by citizens would be extended to them, one at a time, as they proved themselves worthy of greater responsibilities. The Conservative also stressed that although slavery had been abolished, menial occupations still existed; and he reasoned that the blacks, with their generations of experience in performing such jobs, were better qualified to do them than anyone else.

As in the case of Radicalism, Conservatism represented a considerable range of opinion, extending all the way from the unreconstructed Rebel, seeking a legal subterfuge for continuing slavery under a different name, to those who were willing to concede important rights to the freedmen. But essentially American opinion concerning the question was divided in those days, as it has been sometimes since, between those who believed that slavery had its good points which should be conserved and those who believed that slavery had been inherently evil and that its relics should be torn root and branch from American life.

The nationwide conflict between the Conservatives and the Radicals, concerning the nature of the society to be reconstructed in the South, essentially shaped events in the valley of the Lumber River as elsewhere. Unfortunately for the black and the brown, however, the Conservatives held the upper hand in the government during presidential Reconstruction, which began during the war and continued until 1868. Thus with the acquiescence of the President, the local governing bodies of the Old South—institutions that had been shaped by slavery—could begin to function again.

The Robeson County Court, for example, continued to

meet at Lumberton, its function hardly interrupted by the Union victory. This body not only dispensed justice but was also the chief institution of local government. It was composed of the justices of the peace, or "squires," of the county, who had been appointed for life by the governor upon the recommendation of the county representatives in the General Assembly. A squire tried minor cases in his own neighborhood and was the local representative of state authority. The squires assembled as a court in Lumberton to try important cases as well as to carry out such administrative functions as regulating the militia, the roads, and the schools, and handling other county business.[3]

In Robeson County not all of the squires were well-to-do patricians. Particularly in the more primitive and isolated areas there were Buckskin squires. Some of these had been Whigs and during the war, like many of the Indians, had sympathized with the Union. But although they had a certain influence, these men did not control the county court. On the contrary, the court tended to be dominated by a comparatively few rich families. During presidential Reconstruction, for example, Thomas A. Norment was chairman of the court; his son, William Stokes Norment, was county solicitor; his brother-in-law, John Alfred Rowland, was clerk of the court; and his grandson, Owen Clinton Norment, was a captain in the county militia, which enforced the decisions of the court.[4]

Reuben King, who at this time may have been the wealthiest person in the county, also occupied an influential position. He was sheriff; and, although he had no sons, a son-in-law, William Ive Brown, was constable, and another, Albert Moody, held various county posts.[5] The Wishart family held

[3] Lefler and Newsome, *North Carolina*, 307–308.
[4] Freedmen's Bureau Records, report, April 3, 1867; Lawrence, *The State of Robeson*, 223; Norment, *The Lowrie History*, 83.
[5] William Birnie to Allen Rutherford, October 24, 1867, in Freedmen's Bureau Records.

a similar position in regard to the military establishment.[6] These posts do not appear to have been particularly lucrative and may not have been attractive to persons for whom salary was an important consideration. But they were positions of power and influence.

Essential for reconstructing the South along Conservative lines was the revival of the old society's military establishment. This was a touchy business for the Conservatives, one that could easily stir up the wrath of the victorious North. Indeed one of the most important advantages that the South had enjoyed during the Civil War was having begun the conflict with that high degree of military readiness that is so essential for maintaining the stability of a slave society. The war was more than half over before the North had found the quality of military leadership that the South had possessed from the firing of the first shot.

Nevertheless on the question of a military revival the Conservatives were willing to risk exciting the northern Radicals, because they knew that the planters, through their property, through their control of food, possessed the means for putting the blacks in what they called "their place," the necessary means for making the blacks the "mudsills" of the New South even as they had been of the Old. But if the blacks were to be put in their place, the white man's chickens, his salt pork, his cornmeal, and his firewood would have to be defended from the black man's misery. While most Conservatives were reconciled to some sort of labor contract system in place of slavery, at the same time, they did not want the contracts to be drawn between parties having approximately equal bargaining power. From their point of view, a favorable contract might result from the negotiations between a planter with a well-filled smokehouse,

[6] Lawrence, *The State of Robeson*, 11–12.

on one hand, and a shivering beggar with an empty stomach, on the other.

The Home Guard had been the strong arm of Confederate authority on the local scene. Thus, in theory at least, the organization evaporated following the defeat of the Confederate armies. But the old way of life, requiring the subordination of dark skin, had never been able to exist long without a Home Guard or something very much like it. Indeed Sherman's troops were hardly out of sight before a group of Robeson County squires had gathered in Lumberton to discuss what to do about the disturbed state of the country. Their first idea was to create "a strong secret, military association," which is about what the Ku Klux Klan would later become. But at this time more sophisticated counsels prevailed and they finally decided to organize simply a "police guard," to function openly and protect property.[7]

At this time the creation of a secret military organization indeed seemed a bad idea even from the point of view of the Conservatives themselves. Their social order could be established in the South simply through the defense of all the traditional American property rights except the right to own slaves. Johnson, who became President a short time later, was himself a southerner and knew perfectly well that the local military efforts of the Conservatives were aimed against freedmen, toward preserving a few relics of slave society, and not toward organizing a new rebellion against the federal government, as some Radicals suspected.

As a result, Union military officers in the South were not alarmed by this virtual reincarnation of the Confederate Home Guard. On the contrary they gave the Conservative bands official recognition, issued arms to them, and charged

[7] Chaffin Journal, April 15, 1865.

them with the duty of maintaining law and order in their communities. These bands were known variously as "police guards," "county militia," "regulators," and sometimes even "Home Guards." The members were required by the occupation authorities only to take the presidential loyalty oath, and were asked no embarrassing questions about past loyalty.[8]

Yet a certain amount of conflict was inevitable between the southern military establishment and the northern army of occupation. The Union army was honeycombed with Radicals. A local commanding officer of the Union army, who happened to be a Radical, might view with alarm this marching and drilling by the "Rebels," many of whom were Confederate veterans, under the command of their former officers, and even wearing parts of their old uniforms. He would almost certainly not agree with his southern counterpart, the commander of the neighborhood Police Guard,[9] as to exactly what is to be included in maintaining law and order, as to precisely how to reconcile the right of a property owner to the enjoyment of his possessions with the right of a black to eat and to use firewood.

President Johnson's solution to this conflict was to remove Radical officers from their commands wherever feasible and to move the army of occupation out as quickly as possible, allowing the Conservative courts and militia to reconstruct the South as they saw fit. On June 21, 1865, he removed General Joseph Roswell Hawley, the Radical commander of the military district of Wilmington, and replaced him with a Conservative.[10] But mainly he concentrated on getting the army out. Thus by the end of presidential Reconstruction in

[8] A copy of the oath used in Robeson County is included in the Catherine McGeachy Buie Papers, Duke University Library.

[9] James E. Sefton, *The United States Army and Reconstruction, 1865–1877* (Baton Rouge: Louisiana State University Press, 1967), 26 and *passim*.

[10] U.S., War Department, Special Order No. 98, in Joseph Roswell Hawley Papers, Library of Congress.

1868 the army of occupation was only a token force.[11] In the meanwhile the Conservative state government revived the antebellum Black Codes, which defined the status of free blacks and Scuffletonians as that of a submerged caste suspended somewhere between slavery and full citizenship.

Although the Negroes, the Indians, and the Unionists along the Lumber River were undoubtedly disappointed by the earlier result of Reconstruction, most of them had little time to concern themselves with political disappointment. Like most other people in the area, they were chiefly concerned to find food. Even the Reverend Mr. Chaffin confided to his diary in the spring of 1865 that he had been to the army "Commissary's department seeking something to eat. There is a vast amount of suffering here, I learn." And the next day he noted meeting "several *freed* negroes going to Fayetteville. They were in very destitute condition." [12] Even as late as 1868 a northern Radical noted "great suffering among many of the freed people and poor white people, for want of corn and meat. Those that have small means, are unable to purchase corn for the reason that it is the *fixed determination* of the Rebels to starve out the loyal people of the county both white and black." [13]

Considering the faminelike conditions that prevailed along the Lumber River after the war, it is surprising that there were not more outbreaks of black violence, as the freedmen had fewer resources than either the Buckskins or the Indians. Occasionally a black would make a desperate effort to grab something to eat, but mostly they persevered and hoped. They persevered because the rigorous school of slavery had taught them that to endure is to survive. They hoped be-

[11] Joseph Grégoire de Roulhac Hamilton, *Reconstruction in North Carolina* (New York: Columbia University Press, 1914), 239.
[12] Chaffin Journal, March 16, 17, 1865.
[13] Alfred Thomas to Jacob F. Chur, April 3, 1868, in Freedmen's Bureau Records.

cause their strange new existence, with all its hardships, and which as yet they only dimly understood, nevertheless seemed rife with new possibilities.

They were becoming aware, for example, that their cause was being championed by white Radicals. The activities of the Freedmen's Bureau were being extended, as measure after measure was passed over President Andrew Johnson's vetoes. The relief program of the bureau, though far from lavish, was giving a little bargaining power to the black when he negotiated a work agreement with the man who stood in front of the corncrib. Though he still needed the planter's food, the planter could grow little food or cotton without his labor, and his free feet could take him elsewhere. He could try the railroad construction projects or perhaps he could find work in the turpentine forests.

But life seemed to offer the freedman even more intoxicating possibilities. If Lincoln could set free a man's feet, perhaps another President could liberate also his stomach. Some Negroes along the Lumber River were getting "extravagant ideas in relation to confiscated lands," an agent of the Freedmen's Bureau noted.[14] They were beginning to suspect that freedom had something to do with the possession of fields where the corn ripens and of woodlands where the pork fattens, that the substance of freedom has something to do with property.

In a material sense, the plight of the Scuffletonians was not so critical as that of the freedmen. Nevertheless there is some reason to believe that they looked at their life less optimistically than did the blacks. The half-freedom that the black and the brown peoples were accorded under the Black Codes was a new experience to the Negro and one that he could well believe was an important milestone on the road

[14] James Sinclair to Charles J. Wickersham, October 23, 1865, in Freedmen's Bureau Records.

to full citizenship. But such a status was not new to the Scuffletonians. This was the condition they had lived under for thirty years, and by no means did they regard it as a step toward full citizenship. To them it was a step toward slavery.

Scuffletonian memories were long, but of all the history that they could recall, there was little that brought them joy. They could remember the lands and the dignities that they had enjoyed in the eighteenth century. A number of them, particularly the Lowrys, had favored the patriot cause in the American Revolution, while most of the Scots had sided with the Tories. But, though it was widely reported that the patriots had won that conflict, such did not appear to be the case in Scuffletown. The Scots remained in possession of most of the land, and the wasting away of Indian status continued. The outcome of the Civil War was hardly less ironical: many Indians had supported the Union. The Union had won. But hardly had the smoke cleared before the federal government turned over local military and political power to former Confederates, who were thus assisted in their reprisals against friends of the Union.

Even the prospect of acquiring a little land was perhaps a less intoxicating dream to the Indian than it was to the Negro. The Scuffletonian did not have to learn the relationship between freedom and property. He had long known that such freedom as existed was likely to be found in some unpromising briar patch squeezed in between the white man's plantation and the swamp. But, though many Indians were still clinging to such tracts of land, at the same time, in order to make a living, they had had to hire themselves out to work for white men.

For generations they had thus been able to survive. However they had not forgotten the difficulties encountered along the way. People who were poor, who had dark skin, who were deprived of education, who were not recognized as citizens, might indeed retain or acquire a little land of some sort. But the experience of the Scuffletonians had also taught that such a prospect did not necessarily throw open to them a shining future.

Thus, while in a purely objective sense the plight of the Indian may have been less critical than that of the black, at the same time the miseries of the Scuffletonians were not mitigated by a joyous sense of emancipation, by the vision of a radiant new life. The end of the war had brought rather what seemed to be a betrayal by pretended friends. The "damned Yankees have fooled him twice, but could not do it again," Thomas Lowry is reported to have remarked when a northern journalist attempted to win his confidence.[15] Bitter and frustrated, the Indians once again took up the primitive, impoverished, and half-free life that they had known for generations.

A visitor to the Indian communities along the Lumber River noted that the "people have few or no horses, but often keep a kind of stunted ox to haul their short, ricketty carts, and a man with such a bovine hubin [sic] and pair of old wheels is esteemed rich." He added,

To visit a Scuffletown shanty, representative of the whole, is to pass by a cow lane or foot track, up through a thicket and suddenly come upon a half-cleared field of old pine and post oak, enclosed by a worm fence without a gate. . . .

The yellow woman commonly has a baby at the breast, and from half a dozen to a dozen playing outside on the edges of the swamp.

The bed is made on the floor; there are only two or three stools; only one apartment comprises the whole establishment.

The Scuffletowners go out to work as ditchers for the neighboring farmers, who pay them the magnanimous wages of $6 a month.[16]

---

[15] Wilmington *Daily Journal*, March 19, 1872.
[16] Townsend (comp.), *The Swamp Outlaws*, 43–44.

A white resident of the area described a typical cabin as

constructed of pine poles about five or six inches in diameter,
notched one above the other until it reaches the height of eight
feet and then covered with pine boards; the chimney built
against one end of the house on the outside of poles and clay
as far up as the body of the house goes, and the balance of the
chimney with sticks and clay, where it narrows to the funnel or
smoke hole; a door is cut on the front side and the chinks
stopped with clay; no windows generally; sometimes a cut hole
is left on the door with numerous peep holes in the body of
the cabin. A little distance from the cabin will be found in the
yard a well of water, or rather a hole dug in the ground, surrounded with a cypress gum or curb to keep the children from
falling in and getting drowned. In the corner of the chimney on
the outside will be found a half barrel sawed off and set up on
boards one foot above the ground for running off lye, from
wood ashes, for the purpose of making soap, the other half of the
barrel being used as a washtub. A poor, half-starved *fice dog*,
used for hunting "possums" and "wild varmints," will generally
be found inside of the enclosure. The two or three acres cleared
are ploughed and planted in corn, potatoes, and rice, which
come up *puny*, grow *puny* and mature *puny* . . . .
The above picture is true of the great majority of the Scuffletonians, but there are a few honorable exceptions. The Oxendines lived in better style and in much more comfortable dwellings, in fact, were well-to-do citizens, whilst the old set of the
Lowrie family lived in good, comfortable houses, several of them
being good mechanics, or house carpenters.[17]

A militia officer described a visit to a Scuffletonian home
in 1871: "Took down Swamp path to Elias Jones', where we
got water and had some meat cooked. Jones gave us some
fresh pork, but my God it was bad! A house ten by fourteen
made of pine boards; and no floor, only the dirt. A wife,
seven children, a gun and four dogs constitute his inhabitants. One broken chair, two plates, one broken fork, no cups

[17] Norment, *The Lowrie History*, 43–44. Emphasis in the original.

or anything of the kind. Had no meal and no meat only the pork." [18]

The Union army had come and gone from the bottom lands of the Lumber River, but the life of the Indian remained unchanged. The faces of authority remained unchanged. If the Union triumph in the spring of 1865 fired Scuffletonians with hope for a better future, those expectations were thoroughly chilled by the onset of winter.

But there was at least one Indian who was little preoccupied with the disappointing results of the Union victory as the winter approached. Henry Berry Lowry, still in his teens despite his service in the wartime band of his kinsmen, was contemplating marriage to his pretty sixteen-year-old cousin, Rhoda Strong. Henry Berry was not the only person who found Rhoda attractive. Even a writer for the pro–Ku Klux Klan Wilmington *Journal* remembered her as having a "really pretty face which is by the way almost white." [19] Another male visitor found her "remarkably pretty," having "large dark, mournful looking eyes, with long lashes, and a very well developed figure"; but at the same time he felt "compelled to add" that she smoked a pipe and used snuff.[20]

But during these troubled times, Henry Berry and Rhoda were not going to be able to spend many years together. Yet the impression that Rhoda had formed of him would remain with her to the end of her life. Even in her old age,

[18] Francis Marion Wishart Diary (MS in possession of Clifton Wishart, White Plains, N.Y.), September 17, 1871. The Wishart diary and notebooks are transcribed by the following rules: (1) Capitals and punctuation, which are rarely found in the original, are added without brackets; (2) words added to clarify the meaning are placed in brackets; (3) Wishart's symbols and abbreviations are written out as full words; therefore (4) no word will be transcribed as a misspelling unless Wishart spells it out to the proper number of letters or more and does so incorrectly. Hereinafter references to this document will be cited as Wishart Diary.

[19] Wilmington Daily *Journal*, December 25, 1873.

[20] New York *Herald*, March 26, 1872.

when in the year before her death she talked of Henry Berry, whom she had not seen in more than thirty years, she still remembered him as "the handsomest man she ever saw." [21]

The wedding was set for December 7 at the old Allen Lowry homestead—an arrangement that created some dissension within the Lowry family. An older kinsman was afraid that a full-scale Indian wedding held at this spot, twice raided during the past year, would surely attract the attention of their enemies. The Conservatives, as the Confederate faction in the county were now called, were growing bolder as they became aware that President Johnson, commander in chief of the occupation forces, shared many of their ideas about Reconstruction. But Henry Berry, the youngest of Mary Lowry's ten sons, insisted on being married in his mother's house. [22]

Also the ceremony could easily have been performed by the young groom's brother, Patrick, who was a Methodist minister. But instead an arrangement was made for the marriage to be formalized by a white friend, Hector J. McLean, a Buckskin squire. The Lowrys had a warm feeling for the squire. Though he had been required to serve with the Home Guard, McLean had used his influence in May to prevent the firing squad execution of Calvin and Sinclair Lowry. Indians also remembered that he had tried to prevent the use of torture when the Home Guard had been questioning suspects.

On the appointed day the Strongs and the Lowrys arrived by the score along with their other kin and friends. The ceremony was followed by an "enfare," or wedding feast. An Indian guest would probably have had to think far back, beyond the lean years that war had brought, in order to recall such a display of good food; and when enemies of the

[21] Lumberton *Robesonian*, June 25, 1908.
[22] New York *Herald*, March 26, 1872.

Henry Berry Lowry

Lowrys heard of it, they shook their heads and muttered. But there had been no guerrilla raids or recorded armed robberies since the war had ended in the spring.[23]

A possible explanation for this display of plenty during a time of want is the position that Henry Berry and his mother held in the eyes of their kin. The youth was generally credited with having killed the tyrant James Brantley Harris the past February, thus having avenged the murders of his cousins, Jarman, Wesley, and Allen. In a similar position was Mary Lowry, the mother of ten sons and two daughters and the oldest, or nearly the oldest, member of a large and moderately prosperous clan which included skilled craftsmen, yeoman farmers, and several clergymen. In the spring she had undergone a rigorous interrogation by the Home Guard but had not given information that would injure others. The Lowrys would find the means whereby

[23] Origins of Lowry Band, 20.

such a mother and such a son would be able to give an enfare that would do their family honor!

"The supper was set in the yard in front of his mother's house. The table was about 75 feet long and was literally groaning under the many good things it supported." [24] But while these festivities were taking place,

Leut. A. J. McNair . . . of the Home Guard [sic] who had heard of the Heros wedding in prospectus repaired to the groom's residence at about the hour the ceremony was expected to take place with a few of the Guard. They did not arrive in time to witness the ceremony after the supper was over they made their appearance and very politely asked Henry Berry to consider himself their prisoner remarking at the same time he might trouble himself to cross his hand behind his back. . . . his first impulse, which is natural with characters of his nature, was to rebel—refuse to submit. Some very threatening conversation here ensued on both sides. He finally saw however that his case was a hopeless one unless he could incite the multitude there assembled (some 200 persons in all and including 2 white men—the squire and a neighbor of his) to oppose his arrest. Realizing what would be his fate he first refused to submit when the officer in charge told one of the Guard to "shoot him." As soon as a gun was leveled upon him he jumped behind the squire[,] crossed his hands behind him and said "men are you going to see one man tie me here tonight?["] This appeal to the crowd created a great deal of excitement, and aroused a general spirit of resistance in his favor among them; though it was not long before his more timid friends were stampeded. It is thought that about one half of the crowd dispersed. McNair now started off with his prisoner, when the squire overcome with sympathy for his newly married couple attempted to interfere for the release of the prisoner—demanding the authority for the arrest and trying to awe them by speaking of the greatness of his office—that he was a justice of the peace himself, and that if the party did not desist he would have them arrested. The squire finally became leader of the crowd and followed McNair with about 75 Scuffletonians for

[24] Ibid.

some three hundred yards, when McNair and his detachment of the Guard took a stand. There happen to be a bridge over a large ditch just at this point, and as the first man of the pursuers attempted to cross it he was met somewhat forcibly by the but end of a musket. The second attempt to cross the bridge recd a similar check when the charge was stopped. At this juncture the squire told the crowd to hold on and let him try a personal effort in Henry Berry's behalf. He crossed the bridge, and after haranguing the Guard for a while with his threats &c he himself was taken under arrest. The Guard now had two prisoners instead of one and were now masters of the situation.[25]

Squire McLean was later released "on parole and under promise to behave better in the future," but Henry Berry was held under guard for several days in Lumberton, where the county jail had been burned by Sherman's forces after they had freed a Union prisoner being held there. Later the young Indian was incarcerated in the Columbus County jail at Whiteville.[26]

The squire's demand that the Police Guard show legal cause for seizing Henry Berry may have had some effect. In any event a proper warrant was issued for his arrest. The Robeson County Court had generally shown a certain promptness in serving legal papers on Indians, but the alacrity with which this particular order was executed set something of a record, the arrest having been carried out the day before the warrant was issued.[27]

He was charged with the wartime killing of James P. Barnes, who had been applying his skill as a turkey hunter to helping the Home Guard hunt Indians. Henry Berry was not charged, however, with killing James Brantley Harris. Per-

---

[25] *Ibid.*, 17–19.
[26] *Ibid.*, 19–20.
[27] *Ibid.*, 17. This arrest took place December 7, 1865; the warrant authorizing the arrest, however, bears the date December 8, 1865. Warrant in Henry Berry Lowry Papers, North Carolina Department of Archives and History, Raleigh.

haps the Conservatives thought that it would be impolitic to link the killing of such a bloodthirsty ruffian with that of the respected Barnes.

When *State v. Henry Berry Lowry* came up for a preliminary hearing, the youth treated the whole proceeding with proud contempt. He declined to answer questions or even to cross-examine witnesses who appeared against him.[28] But he never had to stand trial for murder before the court of his enemies. He somehow managed to escape from the Columbus County jail. He reportedly cut or "filed his way through the iron bars of his cell and broke down the wall of the jail while the jailer and family occupied rooms beneath." [29] Thus, as a local white reported, he was able to "escape to the woods with handcuffs on, and make his way back to his wife in Scuffletown . . . . This was the first escape ever effected by a criminal confined in jail at Whiteville. How he came in possession of a file, no one in the confidence of the whites can tell." [30] However there is a tradition in Robeson County that Rhoda, his young bride, brought a cake to him in jail in which she had concealed the file.

But the friends of the Confederacy now had control of the entire state power mechanism, from the governor's mansion down to the county courthouse, and they had a few old scores to settle before the war would be over for them. Thus, without showing the slightest interest in bringing to trial the killers of such Indians and Unionists as Jesse Jones and Hector Oxendine, as well as Allen and William Lowry, they were still searching for a poor white named Breton Brigman as late as March, 1866, with a capias charging him with harboring a Confederate deserter. And for the capture of Henry

[28] *State v. Henry Berry Lowry*, Henry Berry Lowry Papers, North Carolina Department of Archives and History, Raleigh.
[29] Origins of Lowry Band, 20–21.
[30] Norment, *The Lowrie History*, 13.

Berry the county court issued at least thirty-five capiases, which were distributed liberally among the county sheriffs of North and South Carolina. Furthermore, to make the hunt profitable, the newly elected Conservative governor, Jonathan Worth, offered a reward of three hundred dollars —more than a Scuffletonian day laborer could earn in four years.[31]

Yet Sheriff King and the other authorities found it simpler to issue thirty-five capiases for the arrest of Henry Berry than

Calvin Oxendine   Henderson Oxendine

to execute one of them. The youth had fled to the swamps, where he had eluded the Home Guard during the war. There he was joined by kinsmen and friends. Among these were Rhoda's brothers, Andrew and Boss Strong. Though Boss in 1866 was only about fourteen years old,[32] he nevertheless became Henry Berry's closest friend and most trusted

[31] *State v. Brigman*, March 22, 1866, Robeson County, Unclassified Criminal Action Papers, North Carolina Department of Archives and History, Raleigh; Fayetteville *Eagle*, December 31, 1868. Among the Henry Berry Lowry Papers in the North Carolina Department of Archives and History there are 35 capiases issued to county sheriffs in various parts of the Carolinas, each of them returned with a notation by the sheriff that he could not find or could not take Lowry.

[32] Many people at this time did not keep a record of birthdays. One often, therefore, had only an approximate idea of his own age.

Thomas Lowry   George Applewhite

lieutenant. He was also joined by his own brothers Stephen and Thomas; by his first cousins Calvin and Henderson Oxendine, whose murdered kinsman Hector was still unavenged; and by John Dial, an Indian apprentice blacksmith. Like Boss Strong, Dial was only about fourteen years old, but he already had a substantial reason for disliking the authorities: his father had been prodded with a bayonet point during the course of an interrogation by the Home Guard.[33]

But it was not only Indians who were drawn toward Henry Berry Lowry. Two Negroes, both former slaves, joined his band: George Applewhite, a highly skilled mason and plasterer from Wayne County; and Eli Ewin, a shoemaker usually known as "Shoemaker John." He was also joined by Zachariah T. McLauchlin, a Buckskin boy about the same age as Dial and Boss Strong. Why would a white youth identify himself with a harassed band consisting of a half-dozen Indians and two Negroes? Though there is no definite evidence that McLauchlin was a member of the Lowry band before 1870, he had been suspected for a number of years,

[33] Deposition of George Dial, October 19, 1867, in U.S., War Department, Records of the Army Commands (Record Group 98, National Archives), File R–10.

largely because of his close association with Scuffletonians. To have Indian friends was natural in the community where he and his widowed mother lived. Their closest neighbors were the Oxendines and Dials, Indian families having boys his age.

Had McLauchlin been a well-brought-up young Buckskin, perhaps he would not have cared to have attended Indian corn-shuckings. Such a riot of turkey-roasting, singing, lovemaking, drinking, sometimes ending in outrageous brawls, would have been much too extravagant for his austere Presbyterian taste. He would scarcely have noticed how pretty were the honey-colored girls who danced the throbbing jubas. But Zachariah's education had been neglected. A "sensual, heathenish type," "a low-bred youth," "probably the meanest specimen of the Scotch that could be found in the county," McLauchlin helped his mother on their small farm during the day, but "at night-fall sallied forth to join his chosen comrades" for some highly un-Calvinist amusements. He "entered the band in good earnest" in 1870 after being denounced to the authorities by a white girl.[34]

The Lowry band was thus reconstituted; and although he was not quite twenty, Henry Berry was now its unquestioned leader. It would seem that such a group could not escape the Police Guard, strengthened by the return of Confederate veterans. But six years later some members of the band would still be free and even offering rewards for the capture of their pursuers.[35] Yet, except for when the militia was around, these men did not vanish into the swamps. On the contrary Henry Berry "as well as his followers were often on the public highways or at work for the citizens. They ventured to attend church occasionally at New Hope [Chapel]

[34] Townsend (comp.), *The Swamp Outlaws*, 31; Norment, *The Lowrie History*, 18, 98.
[35] Wilmington *Star*, September 19, 1872.

. . . in Scuffletown, but it was observed that they always went armed." [36]

It seems clear that the arms of less than a dozen men were no match for the militia. They survived because of a one-way flow of information in Robeson County. The Lowrys were usually well informed as to the whereabouts of the militia: the authorities were usually misinformed as to the whereabouts of the Lowrys.

Sheriff King, the county court, and the militia officers would have had an easier time had they been generally regarded as guardians of impartial justice. But many people, particularly blacks and Indians, regarded them primarily as a source of oppression. Like many another local Black Code regime during presidential Reconstruction, their military power was much more compelling than their moral authority; and they would soon discover that there are definite limits to purely military power.

The Lowry band employed tactics which, under conditions like those prevailing in Robeson County, have sometimes made discriminating bandits more popular than law enforcement officers. They directed their raids against prosperous Conservatives, especially those who had harmed their own families or other Indians; Indians, blacks, and Buckskins could expect little trouble from them. This policy of robbing the big houses of the planters but respecting the cabins of the poor did not actually deprive them of much valuable loot. At the same time it insured that a large number of the people would never regard them as common thieves, would not cooperate with the efforts of the militia to capture them. Far from it. It was not to the courts or militia that many people turned for justice, but to the Lowry band.

A black woman at Shoe Heel (later Maxton) showed a northern newspaper correspondent her mouth. She had only

[36] Origins of Lowry Band, 15–16.

two teeth left. She told him that, while she was a slave, her master had knocked out her other teeth with "an oak stick," and added, "Oh, dis was a hard country, and Henry Berry Lowery's jess a paying 'em back. He's only payin' 'em back! It's better days for the black people now." [37] The young man who broke down the wall of Whiteville jail was finding some friendly latchstrings hanging from the log cabin doors of all three races.

[37] Townsend (comp.), *The Swamp Outlaws*, 27.

4 · "Ought to Be Some Stop Put to These Speeches"

IN THE FALL OF 1865 a document was laid on the desk of Major Charles J. Wickersham which must have puzzled him. It was a petition from some "citizens of the county of Robeson" calling upon him as chief agent of the Wilmington district of the Freedmen's Bureau to remove Colonel James Sinclair from the local bureau office at Lumberton "for the reason that he has been obnoxious to the people." [1] The word *citizens* always meant *whites* and usually meant *Conservative whites*. Yet Sinclair was a former Confederate officer, had been appointed by a Conservative general—and even then only "provisionally until the arrival of the superintendent of the Sub District." Why were these people in such a rush to get a man with Sinclair's qualifications out of the Lumberton bureau office?

Indeed the signers were with few exceptions Conservatives. Yet they probably hated this former Confederate colonel more than they did Henry Berry Lowry. Sinclair, a Presbyterian clergyman, was a native of Scotland who had begun his ministry in Robeson County just before the war and immediately following the completion of his studies at Western Theological Seminary in Pittsburgh. Shortly after Sinclair arrived in the Lumber River region his father, also a minister, followed him into the area and began preaching to a

[1] Petition of Giles Leitch *et al.*, September 16, 1865, in Freedmen's Bureau Records.

Gaelic-speaking congregation at Barbecue Church. The younger Sinclair's marriage to Mary E. McQueen may have marked the beginning of his undoing.

The young Sinclair had Radical inclinations. The Mc-Queens were prominent slaveholders and gunpowder secessionists. He was never able to tear his frail and ailing wife away from her devoted family. As a result he spent the war years and much of Reconstruction frantically trying to solve a problem for which there was no answer: how was he to act out the dictates of a Radical conscience without at the same time bringing dishonor to his wife and her kin?

When the secession movement got under way, he had preached a sermon against it from the pulpit of Ashpole Church. This produced such an explosion of rage in polite plantation society in general and among the McQueens in particular that ruffian elements in the community began to mutter about a possible lynching. Intimidated, ostracized, isolated, and remorseful about the injury that he had caused his wife, the young minister allowed the McQueens to arrange a colonel's commission for him in the Confederate army.

But even by this concession he did not succeed in wiping clean the stain with which he had besmirched their family honor. At a battle near New Bern, North Carolina, he had commanded his men to "bring their guns to order and await orders" at a time when more enthusiastic Confederates thought that the command should have been to have fired on a certain Union detachment.[2] Some newspapers criticized Sinclair bitterly, the Richmond *Examiner* using the word "traitor." In a storm of controversy he resigned his commission and returned to his home in Lumberton. However in the course of the debate the Scot made statements that

[2] *Report of the Joint Committee on Reconstruction, Part II: Virginia, North Carolina, South Carolina* (Washington: Government Printing Office, 1866), II, 167.

laid him open to sedition charges. At dawn one morning
Confederate judicial officers descended upon his residence
and took him away to Wilmington as a prisoner.

But suddenly he was set free. The sedition charges against
him evaporated, and he was made an editor of the *North
Carolinian*, an extreme Confederate newspaper in Wilmington. All of this was probably arranged by the McQueen
family to give him a second chance to redeem himself. Certainly the material that he wrote for that paper must have
brought more pleasure to the clan McQueen than it did to
the tortured conscience of the author. But once again his
rehabilitation was short-lived. The war was hardly over before the erring son-in-law began to fall back into the same
infidelities from which he had already been twice rescued.

The younger Sinclair had begun to preach to the blacks.
This would have been fine had he bent his efforts toward
teaching them to respect property. But he seemed to be
catering to their unrest. They were growing dissatisfied with
the position that they had always occupied in the antebellum churches. They were no longer content to sit in a
special balcony for blacks and listen to a white preacher
deliver a message pleasing to the substantial planters who
paid his salary. Sinclair helped some blacks organize a church
of their own at Lumberton. He served as their preacher and
sometimes said things that were not pleasing to substantial
planters. He said that he was opposed to President Johnson,
that Negroes were being persecuted, and that his own life
had been threatened.[3]

But if in his religious activities Sinclair seemed to be
showing ingratitude toward the McQueens, a family that had
tried earnestly to help him, this was nothing compared to his
other interests. In August, 1865, he agreed to serve temporarily as the Lumberton agent of the Freedmen's Bureau.

[3] Wilmington *Herald*, August 21, 1865.

There was no other institution so detested by the planters. It was not the army of occupation but the bureau that stood in the way as the Conservatives attempted to put back together a few of the broken pieces of the old way of life. As long as the bureau passed out free cornmeal and salt pork, in however miserly quantities, how was the black ever going to be persuaded to put his X mark on what the Conservatives regarded as a realistic contract and thus take what they saw as his proper place in the New South?

Not all people would judge with equal harshness the kind of job—even with the bureau—that a man might accept in order to tide over his family during a time of famine. But Sinclair went beyond the bare requirements of his job. He did not confine himself simply to administering relief to the hungry. Blacks brought him samples of the rations that planters were issuing to them, and the preacher carefully measured the meal and weighed the salt pork. And a planter whom Sinclair thought was feeding too lightly was likely to have to listen to an indignant lecture delivered with a sputtering Gaelic accent. So far as polite plantation society was concerned, the minister had reached the end of the road.

It was at this time that unpleasant reports concerning Sinclair's moral character began to reach the ministers and ruling elders of the Fayetteville Presbytery, to which the Scot was affiliated. Judging these reports, if true, to be "seriously detrimental to the cause of Religion and morality generally," this governing body of the denomination, meeting at Barbecue Church, where the accused pastor's father preached, appointed a committee to investigate the allegations.[4]

At least one member of the committee, the Reverend John H. Coble, had some previous experience with investigations.

[4] Minutes of the Fayetteville Presbytery, October 6, 1865 (MS in Archives of the Synod of North Carolina, Raleigh).

Called "the Devil's Priest" by Radical enemies, the Reverend Mr. Coble had served as a Home Guard chaplain; and one of the ways which he had made himself useful to that organization was by warning captured Indian suspects of the wrath of Heaven if they tried to protect their relatives by lying. Upon investigation, the committee was satisfied that the allegations against Sinclair had substance. They therefore prepared a list of charges against him with specifications of each. These included public drunkenness, the sale of intoxicating liquor, "adultery—with negress," and falsehood.[5]

In what may have been an effort to prejudice Sinclair's case, one of the ruling elders on the committee, William McL. McKay, published the charges in a newspaper on the eve of the minister's trial before the presbytery. Denouncing the charges as "infamous libel and slander," Sinclair confronted McKay and demanded an explanation. But "in reply to my remonstrance," the preacher later wrote, McKay "did strike at me, and whereas I endeavored to defend myself . . . [I] was arrested and tried" before a Conservative squire. He was speedily convicted of assault and jailed.[6]

Though he probably had already been released, the minister did not appear for trial before the presbytery the following week. The proceeding, however, was undertaken without the benefit of his presence. None of the misdeeds of which he was accused, some of them extending back over a number of years, appear to have come to the attention of the presbytery prior to Sinclair's brief connection with the bureau the previous fall. This action, though not mentioned in the list of charges, was one that could be more easily verified than a number of those enumerated, and in the eyes of some

[5] *Ibid.*, October 27, 1865.

[6] Statement of James Sinclair, February 27, 1866, in Robeson County, Unclassified Criminal Action Papers, North Carolina Department of Archives and History, Raleigh.

church leaders may have been about the least pardonable deed ever attributed to the preacher. He was nevertheless convicted of every specification of every charge; and, despite the vehement opposition of his aged father, every vote was recorded as unanimous.[7]

Both Sinclairs now withdrew from the southern Presbyterian church and affiliated with the northern branch of that denomination. The father was commissioned "by a presbytery on the wrong side of the Mason-Dixon line" to preach to a congregation of freedmen in Harnett County,[8] while the son was commissioned to continue his work in the Lumberton area. If the northern Presbyterians believed the charges upon which their southern brethren had just convicted the younger Sinclair, they could be sure that they were getting a minister who could preach about sin with no small measure of authority.

So far as the Lumber River region was concerned, he had lost all of his friends among the people who counted. Yet he was winning friends among the people who never before had counted. Though his connection with the bureau had been brief, he had used it to increase his influence among the freedmen, a development disturbing to the Conservatives. It "was not because he preached abolitionism," a Wilmington paper remarked, "for abolitionism is now an accomplished doctrine and everybody accepts it; but because he seeks to get control over the blacks and direct when, where and for whom they shall work, what wages they shall demand, how many hours they shall labor, and so on through all their affairs." [9]

Following his service with the bureau, Sinclair tried his

[7] Fayetteville Presbytery Minutes, April 5, 1866.
[8] John A. Oates, *The Story of Fayetteville and the Upper Cape Fear* (Charlotte: Dowd Press, Inc., 1950), 621.
[9] Wilmington *Herald*, August 21, 1865.

hand at publishing. The experience that he had gained as an editor of the ultra-Confederate *North Carolinian* he applied less than a year later with the publication of the *Southern Freedman*. The venture failed however because most blacks were not yet capable of supporting a newspaper financially or even reading one.[10] Next he founded a black school at Lumberton. One Conservative predicted that the school "promises to be a nuisance. I trust he will control his pupils." [11]

Though ostracized by the Conservatives, Sinclair nevertheless did not ever come to enjoy the complete confidence of the local Unionists, either white or Indian. They would always have a certain mistrust for this former Confederate colonel, with his powerful McQueen connections, who could change sides so quickly. But with the freedmen it was a different matter. There was "considerable excitement in town," the Reverend Mr. Chaffin remarked, "on account of a speech Wesley McQueen (freedman) made at the courthouse last night. He said to the negroes, that they ought to stand by their friends, and that Rev. Jas. Sinclair was the chief corner stone of Robeson County—that for defending their rights he Sinclair had received blows at the courthouse door." [12] His influence with the blacks was likewise noted by a prominent Radical, who reported that the "building which I hoped to have for a school, I cannot rent until I will agree to exclude from it Reverend Mr Sinclair. Such an agreement would please the white people, but mortally offend the freedmen. Therefore I have respectfully declined the proposal." [13]

As an individual Sinclair was no great threat to the social

[10] *Ibid.*, November 13, 1865; *Southern Freedman, passim.*
[11] Chaffin Journal, May 7, 1866.
[12] *Ibid.*
[13] Samuel S. Ashley to E. P. Smith, January 11, 1867, in American Missionary Association Archives, Amistad Research Center, Fisk University.

order that the Conservatives were attempting to establish. One could always confound Sinclair, the Radical preacher, with some well-chosen text from the book of Sinclair, the Confederate editor. But because of some large events that were taking place in the nation, the Conservatives looked on him with anxiety and loathing. In the South the very success that the militia officers, the judges, and the legislators were enjoying in putting the black in his place was causing them some bad press in the North; and the indignation that was thereby being built up there was threatening the very foundations of Conservative Reconstruction. These were developments that might put the whole South under the control of men like Sinclair.

Having created the southern state regimes, the President was loyally defending them, saying that the South had repudiated secession and carried out emancipation, that reports of violence against the Negroes were exaggerated, and that the southerners themselves were best qualified to work out a solution to the Negro problem. But fewer Americans were now listening to the President and more were listening to Thaddeus Stevens, who was saying, in substance, that the black was being forced by savage repression and violence into a status which dangerously approached slavery; and that the southern whites, regretting nothing but defeat, were rebuilding their old political alliances through which before the war they had controlled the Democratic Party and thereby virtually dominated the nation. In the congressional elections of 1866 the Radicals made a clean sweep, increasing their strength so much that they could now push almost any measure over the President's veto, thus giving them an opportunity to impose their concept of what the New South was to be like. Restoring military government, they started the process of Reconstruction all over again, based this time on the black's right to vote and take part in politics.

The Radical capture of Congress made possible the organization of the Republican Party in the South. It appeared that a combination of white Unionists and voting blacks might be able to challenge the one-party, solid South that John C. Calhoun had envisioned. In North Carolina a state organization of the new party was formed March 27, 1867, and a local organization was established in Robeson County the following April 13, with James Sinclair delivering the major address. One observer, noting the preacher's Gaelic accent, remarked that "his tongue don't always throw off English words just as an Englishman would." He also thought that the speech, which lasted an hour and a quarter, was "all out of the *mental* reach of the great bulk of his auditors." [14]

The Radical leaders, however, did not completely trust the Republican Party organization as a vehicle for carrying out their program. In the South it had been formed too recently; it included a strong old-Whiggish business faction as well as many unstable political mavericks and illiterates; and above all most southern Republicans lacked political experience. Better organized and more consistently Radical was the Freedmen's Bureau. Shortly after the formation of the Republican Party, the Lumberton agent of the Freedmen's Bureau, William Birnie, received a letter marked "confidential." It was from his immediate superior, General Allen Rutherford, who asked him to draw up "a list of suitable persons, residing within your Sub District to be recommended for appointment as Registers of Election. This will include none but men of *Known Union Sentiments*." As a basis for this selection "you will name first honorably discharged officers or soldiers of the United States army; and if possible, one colored citizen for each precinct who must be able to read and write. You will state opposite each name

[14] Chaffin Journal, April 13, 1867.

sent in by you the age, color, limit of time he has resided in the county, and if he has served in the United States army together with other information (showing that he is a Union man) as you may have." [15]

But from the point of view of the Radicals even the bureau might not in the long run be the best institution for organizing the South according to their program. After all, as a government agency, the bureau could be abolished by a Conservative Congress in a matter of minutes, just as the Republican Party might someday be taken over by the Whiggish business faction within the party. They therefore organized the Union League, which was independent of the government and would give some organization to the Radical faction within the Republican Party. In Robeson County, the Republican Party, by playing down its Radicalism, could sometimes woo support from whites who disliked blacks and Indians but who disliked the Conservative squirearchy even more. But the Union League did not run candidates for election. Virtually a party within a party, its chief function was to spread Radical ideas.

Because the Conservatives owned most of the corncribs and smokehouses, the Union League sometimes tried to protect its members from reprisals by the planters through the practice of secrecy, a feature of the organization which allowed the Conservatives to imply that the Union League was engaged in the same type of activities as their secret society, the Ku Klux Klan. However, the league's fumbling efforts to be secretive did not fool one Conservative observer: "James Sinclair and some *niggers* seem to have some secret order in the courthouse—said to be the Union League. A goodly number of negroes are hanging around the courthouse as if waiting to be initiated. At night there was quite

[15] Rutherford to Birnie, April 25, 1867, in Freedmen's Bureau Records. Emphasis in the original.

a gathering in the courthouse to hear speeches. There were some 60 women & more men. The Bureau man [William Birnie] sat with and hugged a negro woman." [16]

Because of the inept attempts of the Union League to practice secrecy, some people confused it with the Unionist underground organization of the war years, the Heroes of America, popularly known as the "red strings," from a system of secret signals that the society used. Thus it was certainly the Union League that a white lady of the Scuffletown district heard on the road in front of her house, just before she retired for bed: "It is 11 o'clock," she wrote her mother, "and . . . the red stringers are going by on their way home from the Council whistling and hollering." [17]

Considering her neighborhood, one may surmise that the "red stringers" that she heard were undoubtedly Indians. At first the more active members of the league were either Indians or whites. But in the long run the freedmen were no more likely to accept a passive role in the league than they were in the white people's churches. As early as the spring of 1867 a circuit rider noted "negro political lecturers going among the negroes & I apprehend evil from it." [18]

So did many other Conservatives. They had always had to deal with the unrest of the Scuffletonian and the Buckskin, but the involvement of blacks was something new and sinister in the political equation. Thus the same observer, writing from Lumberton, reported that there was "considerable excitement" because of some "incendiary" speeches that the Reverend Mr. Sinclair and some Indian Republicans made to the Negroes in the courthouse. "There ought if possible to be some stop put to these speeches . . . . A

[16] Chaffin Journal, May 13, 1867. Emphasis in the original.
[17] Catherine McGeachy Buie to her mother, August 24, 1867, in Catherine McGeachy Buie Papers, Duke University Library.
[18] Chaffin Journal, May 25, 1867.

few gentlemen concluded that we ought to take steps to stop these . . . speeches by sending a commission to Col Frank at Wilmington." [19] But, though the commander of the military district was ultimately responsible to a Conservative chief in Washington, he may have noticed that the President's fortunes were beginning to wane. Thus he received the delegation "in a very friendly manner," but he "did not seem disposed to interfere" with Union League meetings.[20]

The league's work was of great importance in the election to decide the question of a constitutional convention. Congress might impose black suffrage on the South for these elections, but just how the freedmen would vote was by no means a foregone conclusion. No matter how appealing Radical ideas might sound to him, the black had to face the fact that it was almost always a Conservative who controlled his supply of food and firewood, who owned the very house he lived in and his garden plot, and who had ways of learning what meetings he attended and how he voted. By contrast the Radicals could offer very little material relief—but they could offer a captivating vision of a new life. The significance of the Union League consisted in transmitting this vision to the black, so that in 1867 and 1868 he was willing to stake his fragile livelihood on a venture to overthrow presidential Reconstruction.

Thus it was that in North Carolina as elsewhere the Republican cause flourished. Delegates were elected for a convention which, between January and March, 1868, wrote a state constitution that incorporated a number of new features: manhood suffrage without property or racial restrictions, no religious restrictions on officeholders except the debarment of atheists, popular election of county officials,

[19] *Ibid.*, May 14, 1867.
[20] *Ibid.*, May 15, 1867.

a broader system of public schools, a more lenient penal code specifying fewer capital crimes and a more advanced theory which included the concept of reforming the offender, and other progressive innovations.

The Republican victory and the new constitution made a considerable difference on the local scene. The squirearchy was abolished. The administrative duties of the county court were taken over by a board of county commissioners. Special justices of the peace settled neighborhood disputes much as the squires had; but, whereas the squires had been appointed for life, the justices regularly had to run for re-election.

There were some familiar faces among the men who formed the new regime. Squire Hector McLean, friend of the Lowrys and permanent minority on the old county court, had been elected a county commissioner. Roderick McMillan, an active member of the Home Guard, had been elected county surveyor, probably because the Republicans had no qualified person to run against him. But there were also some brown Indian faces that had never been seen on the county court of the old regime. James Oxendine, known as "Big Jim," a prosperous Indian merchant and farmer, had been elected one of the county commissioners. Also Charles E. Barton and the Reverend Patrick Lowry, an elder brother of Henry Berry, had been elected justices of the peace.

There was, however, in the new government of the county a noticeable absence of freedmen. The bureau had been unable to produce its "one colored citizen for each precinct, who must be able to read and write." [21] In the local Republican organization blacks were still playing a somewhat passive role, while Indians occupied only minor posts.

A Conservative source says that the local organization was controlled by a triumvirate of Radical carpetbaggers: James

[21] Rutherford to Birnie, April 25, 1867, in Freedmen's Bureau Records.

Sinclair and E. K. Proctor, both natives of Great Britain, and Olen S. Hayes, originally from Ohio, who had established a mercantile business at Shoe Heel following his discharge from the Union army.[22] Certainly these men were the most active and held the most important jobs. Sinclair and Proctor served in the North Carolina House of Representatives, and Hayes in the state Senate. Local offices were most often occupied by moderate, Whiggish Republicans, such as Benjamin A. Howell, a Lumberton merchant who had replaced Reuben King as sheriff. The white Republican Party also included a number of political mavericks who for various reasons had become alienated from the old establishment. The party thus brought together people of extremely varied backgrounds; and although at times it could muster a great number of votes, it was an organization highly vulnerable to internal antagonisms.

Perhaps the greatest source of strength of the local Republican Party was the almost universal support it enjoyed among Indians, who hoped that the Republicans were bringing about a system of justice in which brown skin would not be a liability in court. From the first, the Radicals had lent a sympathetic ear to their grievances, especially their complaint that the killers of Confederates were forced to hide in the swamps while the killers of Indians hunted for them. In 1866, shortly after a Conservative governor had outlawed Henry Berry, General Allen Rutherford, the Radical agent of the bureau for a group of southeastern North Carolina counties, heard of his case and advised the state head of the bureau that Lowry had been outlawed for killing Barnes, who was "one of a party engaged in hunting for escaped Union prisoners." [23]

[22] Wilmington *Carolina Farmer and Weekly Star*, July 29, 1870.
[23] Rutherford to Clinton A. Cilley, July 16, 1866, in Freedmen's Bureau Records.

But the prosecution of individuals for wartime killings was an activity that both sides could practice. In May, 1867, the Radical bureau agent at Lumberton began an investigation into the killing of certain Indians. He questioned a number of witnesses and prepared a group of sworn statements relating to the deaths of Allen and William Lowry and Hector Oxendine. He then prepared what appeared to be a strong indictment for murder against more than a score of Home Guard members for the murder of Allen Lowry. But to get a conviction, or even to get such cases tried before a court, proved to be quite another matter.

In pressing these cases Birnie knew that he had no chance in the kind of civil courts that existed during presidential Reconstruction. "As some of the most prominent men in this county are accused," he wrote, "I am of the opinion that the civil authorities will not do anything with them." [24] He therefore attempted to transfer the cases to a military court. But the office of the adjutant general in Charleston, headquarters of the Second Military District, took exactly the same view of the affair as the Robeson County Conservatives. The officer replying to Birnie's request speculated that the Lowry band had in view "not the aid of the Union, but simply seeking to enrich themselves." Despite elaborate documentary evidence that the accused might be guilty of murder, the officer chose to address himself to a different question, namely, that the slain might have been guilty of larceny. Unfortunately for the Scuffletonians, however, he did not carry his digression far enough to inquire whether Allen Lowry had taken part in the Lowry band, whether larceny was a capital crime, or whether the Home Guard had acted under the color of law as a properly constituted court. Instead the officer hurried on to conclude that it was "inexpedi-

[24] Birnie to Rutherford, September 26, 1867, in Freedmen's Bureau Records.

ent for the military authorities to institute any proceedings looking to a determination of the merits of the case: and cognizance of the charges will not be taken." [25]

Birnie went through the motions of bringing the cases before the civil authorities, but with no better luck. When they came before the county court at its spring term in 1868, the Conservative prosecutor wrote the words "nolle prosequi" across each of the indictments, indicating that the state did not choose to prosecute the Home Guard.[26]

The military authorities had refused to touch the killers of the Lowrys because they thought that the guerrillas had been robbers rather than Union men. But what about the case of Hector Oxendine? He had never been accused of appropriating Confederate property for private use. He had only been accused of aiding the Union forces. Would the army and the federal government regard this as sufficient grounds for executing a man without a trial?

In 1867 when an army officer found himself in the position of having to make a political decision, he sometimes had the consolation of being able to choose whether he would be flattened under the millstone of a Conservative commander in chief or that of a Radical Congress. Faced with such a political situation, the lawyers in the adjutant general's office would have been less than masters of their craft if they could not find some legal grounds for doing nothing at all.

A decision on the Oxendine case was returned to the Freedmen's Bureau, in which the facts were conceded to be as the bureau documents had alleged: Oxendine had been shot without trial for aiding the Union forces. But did the army actually have jurisdiction at the time and place of the murder? "It appears," the decision continued, "that no mili-

[25] Louis V. Caziarc to Rutherford, November 19, 1867, in Freedmen's Bureau Records.
[26] Lowry Papers.

tary occupation by the national authority was extended to the locality in which the crime was said to have been committed—otherwise; it is reasonable to suppose that the alleged outrage would have been prevented. . . . and the commanding general directs that no steps be taken to pursue further investigation or to bring the alleged murderers to punishment by the military authorities." [27]

The legal argument that the army had no jurisdiction in the area was not a good one. At the time of the crime the Union occupation of southeastern North Carolina was nearly two months old. During this period Robeson County had been made a part of the military district of Wilmington, an area including eight counties in which a provost marshal was attempting to maintain order. Furthermore, the argument that the occurrence of the crime was an indication that the military authority had not yet been extended to the scene of the murder was a doctrine that had startling implications for southeastern North Carolina. Indeed it would seem that, during the spring of 1865 when the military district was the only organized government in the area, the only murders that could be punished legally would be those committed on the steps of the provost marshal's office in Wilmington.

But if, during presidential Reconstruction, the military authorities were hampered by insurmountable difficulties in their efforts to prosecute white men for killing Indians, the same could not be said of the civil authorities in their efforts to capture members of the Lowry band. The Conservatives could appreciate a legal system sufficiently sophisticated to distinguish the deeds of violence committed by fair-skinned friends of the Confederacy from those committed by brown-skinned friends of the Union. But what would be the attitude of the Republicans? Their attitude was crucial, because

[27] Caziarc to Rutherford, December 26, 1867, in Investigation.

the military authority was only a temporary makeshift and, since the Republican election victory in 1866, it seemed only a question of time before the Conservative regimes of the South would be swept away by a Radical Congress.

It would soon become apparent that the Republican leaders would take a view of the Lowry band that was hardly different from that of their Conservative opponents. William Birnie had encountered some indication of this trend in the spring of 1867, almost a year before the party assumed control. In his attempts to prosecute the Home Guard for killing Indians, he had discovered that not all of his opponents were Conservatives. A newcomer to the region, having moved to Lumberton from New York in service of the bureau, he may have been surprised at a witness that one of the accused summoned in his behalf. Robert McKenzie summoned for the Home Guard none other than the Reverend James Sinclair, the most prominent figure of the Radical triumvirate which was supposed to control the Republican organization in the area.

Sinclair had switched his public political position from blue to gray several times during the course of the war; and during the final months had made statements in support of the Confederacy about as strong as one could reasonably expect from a man with a blue conscience and a gray wife. It was during this time that he had been approached by some prominent gentlemen whose plantations had been raided by the Lowry band. At their instigation he had drawn up a petition, which he agreed to present personally to Governor Zebulon Vance, and which requested that the governor "take some steps to suppress these robbers." [28]

Why did these men turn for help to Sinclair, an individual who from their point of view was thoroughly unreliable? Most likely his aid was enlisted precisely because of his rep-

[28] Hearings, 11, in Investigation.

utation as a Unionist. Vance, who was governor from 1862 to 1865, had a prewar Unionist background himself and to some extent still depended politically upon the defeated Unionist faction. More important, however, a petition drawn up by a reputed Unionist which represented the Lowrys as common robbers might serve to cut them off from the Union sentiment. For his part, Sinclair, intimidated by lynching threats, chastened by his sedition arrest, domesticated by his ailing wife and her rich Confederate relatives, had been willing to play the part that McKenzie and the other planters had prepared for him. Even as a postwar Radical, Sinclair, who was not often so consistent, found it expedient to stick to his wartime position on the question of the Lowrys. Any effort to press the prosecution of the Home Guard raised some embarrassing questions for the strongest Republican leader in the area.

But there were more general reasons why the Republican leaders felt constrained to overlook the wartime services of the Lowrys to the Union and assume the same attitude toward them as the Conservatives had. Political developments were making it expedient for the Republicans stridently to assert themselves as the party of law and order, of legal propriety. When the Johnsonian state regimes were overturned in 1868, the Conservatives lost control of all legal means for inflicting violence upon their enemies and for protecting property, including the courts, the militia, and the police. As a result they suddenly shifted their tactics from the use of legal to extralegal violence.

"I have received reliable reports, legally substantiated," a major general wrote to Governor William Woods Holden in 1868, "that several hundred Henry and Spencer rifles (many of them sixteen shooters) with accoutrements, &c., complete, have been received at Wilmington and thence distributed to organizations in this State, styling themselves 'Seymour and Blair' Clubs and 'K.K.K.'s . . .' The Constitutional right of all citizens to the possession of arms for proper purposes does not extend to the perfecting of organizations, armed with weapons of a purely military character, such as those reported as having been received in such unusual quantities at Wilmington and other points." [29] These weapons were not allowed to rust. During the next three years 26 murders and 213 floggings were credited to the Ku Klux Klan in North Carolina.[30]

It might appear that since the Conservatives had resorted to violence, the Republicans could find good use for men with the particular talents of the Lowry band. Precisely the opposite, however, was the case. Despite their Republican sympathies—and even the outlaw Henry Berry marched in "one or two processions of the republican party" [31]—the Lowry band's policy of conducting armed raids, in which they helped themselves to the possessions of wealthy Conservatives, in the long run brought even more harm to the political strategy of their friends than to the economic condition of their enemies.

Republicans could look back on the events that had taken place in the nation since the war with a great deal of pleasure. They had until recently been only a sectional party, their organization confined largely to a bloc of northern states, a party that had come to power only because of a national crisis, and even then without the backing of a majority of the votes. But after the war the party had grown mightily in numbers and influence. Yet it is significant that much of

[29] Quoted in Wilmington *Weekly Journal*, September 25, 1868. Holden was governor from 1868 to 1871, and also had served briefly as provisional governor in 1865, but had been defeated in an all-white election by Jonathan Worth, a Conservative.

[30] Hamilton, *Reconstruction in North Carolina*, 477 and *passim*; *Ku Klux Conspiracy*, II, *passim*.

[31] *Ku Klux Conspiracy*, II, 287.

this growth had come because the Republicans had taken utmost advantage of a wave of popular indignation sweeping the nation in reaction to the outbreaks of violence and disorder in the South, outbreaks which they had been able to associate with their Conservative or Democratic opponents.

After 1868 the Republican pose of strident political respectability seemed to offer prospects for an even more abundant harvest of votes than before. Because the Republicans had gained control of the entire mechanism of legal force in the South, the Conservative press was now ridiculing the new state constitutions and their prominent men were defying the laws passed by carpetbag legislatures. Thus hyper-pure legality was not a political game that both sides could play with equal advantage. Try as they might, the Conservatives would never be able to make a grand dragon of the Ku Klux Klan look as respectable as the most dubious carpetbagger judge. On the other hand, perhaps the strongest asset that the Republican leaders had was the consistency and vigor with which they had championed political propriety and opposed skullduggery. They therefore could easily have gotten along without the efforts of the Lowry band.

During the early months of the new regime, the Republicans seemed to be making good their claim of being a party that could rule by peaceful, constitutional processes, even though not all the violence and disorder that had characterized presidential Reconstruction could be properly blamed on the Conservatives. Some of it certainly was due to the bad economic conditions and general demoralization left by the war. "The blighting curse of the late war will not be erased . . . until the present generation has passed away," the Reverend Mr. Chaffin had predicted in 1867. "Every town & highway is infested with thieves." [32]

But there also appear to have been political causes for

[32] Chaffin Journal, April 11, 1867.

these conditions. For the people who were black, brown, or hungry, the institutions of local government had virtually no moral authority. No law was likely to be observed that could not be enforced with instant violence. Indeed, between 1865 and 1868, so far as Robeson County is concerned, it would scarcely be an exaggeration to say that the authority of the county court and Police Guard, at any particular moment, extended only so far as their pistols would fire, beyond which lay the domain of feud law and shapeless chaos.

But at least at the outset, the democratic innovations of the Radicals seemed to bring a considerable measure of peace and stability to the bottom lands of the Lumber River. The plain people of all three races had taken a dim view of the squirearchy and had misbehaved badly once they had noticed that its authority had been weakened and dislocated by war. But they looked with more optimism on the new regime with its democratically elected Buckskin county commissioners and brown-skinned justices of the peace. Their optimism possibly explains why in Robeson County no armed robberies were reported for almost six months after the Republicans took over, although there had been six, all unsolved, reported for May, 1868, just before the Conservatives ceded power.[33]

The members of the Lowry band shared this general optimism toward the new regime, which had elevated a number of their kinsmen to minor posts. Thus they discontinued their raids on the Bakers, the McNairs, the Townsends, and other families that had been active with the Home Guard or Police Guard—the armed robberies they had begun when Governor Worth had outlawed Henry Berry. But was it now safe for these men to come out of hiding and follow ordinary

[33] Monthly Reports of Crimes Committed, in Investigation.

jobs? In time John Dial found a job in a blacksmith shop; the smith knew his identity but did not betray him.[34] Unfortunately for the Lowrys, however, most of the people whom they could trust did not employ much labor. When it was considered safe for him to do so, Henry Berry helped his nephew, Billy Lowry, care for his bees.[35] But most of them had to live on the slender means of their relatives and friends.

In the meantime what were the attitudes of the Republican leaders toward the Lowrys? Now that Republicans controlled the courts, would they again prosecute the Indian-killers, or did the obligation of vengeance still rest with the kinsmen of the slain men? Months passed and no indictments materialized. Did this mean that for the Republican leaders the war was over, that there would be no further prosecution of individuals for half-political offenses against life and property committed during the confused period toward the end of the war? Was Henry Berry still an outlaw?

The reluctance of the Republican Party to become involved in the Lowry question may have resulted from a belief that if there was anything Robeson County did not need it was further agitation of old grievances. But there were also political reasons for the Republicans' reticence: to prosecute former members of the Home Guard was to call attention to the reputation of certain of their supporters in Robeson County, a reputation that would contribute little to the campaign image of the party as upholder of the majesty of the law and defender of property. On the other hand, to prosecute the Lowrys would tend to split and weaken the local organization of the party. In such a dilemma the Republican leaders, as long as they could, simply did nothing,

[34] Wilmington *Daily Journal*, August 19, 1868.
[35] Interview with D. F. Lowry, September 3, 1967.

undoubtedly hoping that somehow the feud might die of inactivity.

In October, 1868, Governor Holden received a prodding letter from J. W. Schenck, Jr., Republican sheriff of New Hanover County, asking whether Holden intended to honor the offer made by his Conservative predecessor, Governor Jonathan Worth, of paying three hundred dollars for the capture of Henry Berry.[36] Though the governor's reaction to this inquiry is not recorded, events would soon force his hand. Within ten days an interracial band of some thirty armed men raided the company store of J. N. McLaurin of McLaurin's Hill, South Carolina, and several nearby plantations. Though none of these raiders were positively identified, it appears that they were led by Henry Berry's men, who had grown restive at the ambiguous attitude of the government and the uncertainty of their own position. A few days later, crossing back into North Carolina, they raided the plantations of Elizabeth Carlisle, James H. McQueen, and Alexander McKenzie, all in Robeson County.[37]

Because of the stress that the Republicans were putting on legalistic propriety, the governor would probably have eventually denounced the Lowrys—but these events greatly hastened that eventuality. An opportunity to repudiate the Lowry band and represent his party as the unequivocal champion of political respectability came when he received a petition from Robeson County complaining that the local authorities were unable to bring the Lowrys to justice because the Scuffletonians "it is believed give them aid and comfort and we are led to this belief from the fact that when any attempt is made to arrest them or search for stolen goods

[36] J. W. Schenck to William Woods Holden, October 10, 1868, in Governors' Papers, North Carolina Department of Archives and History, Raleigh; Fayetteville *Eagle*, December 31, 1868.
[37] Fayetteville *Eagle*, October 26, December 3, 31, 1868.

they rally to their aid and defense bidding defiance to all law." [38]

Citing the postwar robberies attributed to the Lowrys, and the killing of Barnes, the petitioners stated that they did not believe members of the band "would submit to peaceable arrest but would defend themselves to the death and this has somewhat deterred our citizens from rising in their strength and slaying the last of them." The citizens were also reluctant to take such measures because "we believe that there are some that would accuse us of disloyalty and of killing loyal citizens. . . . We would therefore suggest to your Excellency . . . to declare all such as may be guilty of such crimes as outlaws and have them arrested dead or alive." [39]

Perhaps it is significant that, though the petition bore more than fifty signatures, there is not the name of a single prominent Republican included. Yet, though this was a Conservative request coming from a predominantly Republican county, Governor Holden nevertheless granted it; and on November 30, 1868, issued a proclamation of outlawry against Henry Berry and a number of his chief adherents.[40] Holden's action might have served some of the larger objectives of the Republican Party, particularly if the Conservatives had shown the same embarrassment about the Ku Klux Klan that the Republicans showed concerning the Lowry band. But the most tangible result was to split the local party and deliver Robeson County to the control of the less numerous but more united Conservatives, since the Scuffletonian backbone of the party would not support this act of the governor and the other leaders.

The local Republicans were quick to recognize the dangers inherent in the governor's move. In an attempt to ne-

---

[38] John MacRae *et al.* to Holden, November 25, 1868, in Governors' Papers.

[39] *Ibid.*

[40] Raleigh *Sentinel*, December 5, 1868.

gotiate a compromise, an arrangement was worked out for a meeting between Henry Berry Lowry and two minor leaders of the county organization, Dr. Alfred Thomas, who had replaced Birnie as local agent of the Freedmen's Bureau, and Sheriff Benjamin A. Howell, whose recent election had ended Reuben King's eighteen-year occupancy of that office. The meeting took place at a house near Asbury Church, one that had been built for Henry Berry and Rhoda following their marriage in 1866, and where the leader of the outlaws still resided with his wife and infant daughter, Sally Ann, at such times when the neighborhood was considered secure.

Rhoda Lowry served the visitors with what a contemporary account describes as a "sumptuous repast," after which Henry Berry gave a demonstration of his talents as a fiddler. The purpose of their visit was to persuade the Indian to surrender himself and to take his chances with the new system of Republican courts. He agreed to their proposal, but on the condition that, during the time he should spend in jail awaiting trial, nothing should be done to demean or humiliate him. The Republican leaders promised that he would be confined in a part of the jail reserved for debtors; that in place of the regular fare of two meals a day he would have three meals a day, prepared on the outside and brought in to him; that he would not be ironed; and that he would be protected against any mob action Conservative ruffians might attempt.[41]

Henry Berry returned with them to Lumberton and was confined to the debtors' section of the new jail that the Republican administration had just completed, a two-story, fortresslike structure of heavy, hewn timber situated on a little rise overlooking the Lumber River. He was not shackled and he received the food that he had been promised.

[41] Origins of Lowry Band, 24–25; Townsend (comp.), *The Swamp Outlaws*, 26; Fayetteville *Eagle*, December 31, 1868.

But this treatment of the outlaw leader caused an outcry in Lumberton. Why should a Scuffletonian be so favored, it was demanded, "while there is a white man confined and ironed for stealing a horse, a small crime compared with murder[?] The white man and the other prisoners get their common jail food, while Lowry had to be fed with delicacies, notwithstanding he was getting one more meal than the others." [42] "This good treatment, added to reports of his proud and unintimidated bearing, led to a public cry that he ought to be ironed and put on hard fare." Also, though there is no clear indication of the kind of tactics that Henry Berry and his friends planned to use at the coming trial, at the same time it was reported that "some of the towns-people, hearing of the line of defense to be assumed . . . resolved to drag him from jail and drown him in the river at the foot of the jail-yard hill." [43]

Yet, despite the assurances that Sheriff Howell and Dr. Thomas had given Henry Berry that he would have protection, despite the control of the Republicans over the militia, despite the predominance of Republican sentiment in the county, the authorities seemed to have taken no steps to insure the security of their prisoner, either by placing a special guard at the jail or by moving him to a safer location. Why?

It is perhaps significant that not one of the top three figures in the local party organization—Sinclair, Proctor, or Hayes, all of whom were members of the legislature—had associated himself with this effort to compromise the Lowry conflict by giving Henry Berry a fair trial. The attitude of Sinclair, the most influential of the three, appeared crucial if the Republican Party was to prove that in this case a person with brown skin would receive justice in their courts.

[42] "Robeson" to editor, December 14, 1868, appearing in Fayetteville *Eagle*, December 21, 1868.
[43] Townsend (comp.), *The Swamp Outlaws*, 28.

It would be interesting to know what mixed feelings Sinclair must have experienced in the darker recesses of his being, some weeks back, when the Lowry band had committed a magnificent robbery of certain members of the clan McQueen, his in-laws. But, at the same time, as a responsible Republican leader, a member of the railroad lobby in the lower North Carolina house, he could not deplore such an action too strongly. The larger interests of his party required that the voters be given a clear alternative to the pillowcase skullduggery associated with the Conservatives. A vigorous champion of the rights of the freedmen and Indians, whose votes had sent him to the legislature, he was also learning to appreciate the aspirations of the railroad magnates and the entrepreneurs whose greenbacks had financed his campaign.[44]

So varied were his commitments, in fact, that it would appear that Sinclair was a man who in a moral sense was capable of coming apart at the seams: a number of his good deeds, if he were to consider them in a slightly different light, must have appeared as sins to him, whereas many sins, upon some reflection, must have become good deeds. Could a man so torn apart be sufficiently devious as to reason that Henry Berry, bound and sent to the bottom of the Lumber River by Conservative ruffians, would cost the party fewer votes than if the Scuffletonian hero were convicted in a Republican court? Was the Reverend James Sinclair ready to play Pontius Pilate before a lynch mob?

Dark rumors swept from cabin to cabin along the Lumber River and reached the ears of Henry Berry in the debtor's cell in the Lumberton jail. He "grew suspicious and uneasy."[45] On Saturday night, December 12, 1868, Eb Jones, a Lumberton shoemaker who served also as jailor, came to

---

[44] N.C., *Report of the Commission to Investigate Fraud and Corruption Under Act of Assembly, Session 1871-1872* (Raleigh: James H. Moore, State Printer and Binder, 1872), 316–19 and *passim*.

[45] Townsend (comp.), *The Swamp Outlaws*, 26.

his cell to bring him his evening meal. When Jones "entered, he was confronted with a pistol and bowie knife, and [Lowry] ordered him not to speak at his peril." The outlaw then told the jailor that "he had not been treated as promised when he consented to come there." [46] " 'I'm tired of this,' he added. 'Open that door and stand aside. If you leave the place for fifteen minutes you will be shot as you come out!' He then walked out of the jail, turned down the river to avoid town, stopped at a house and helped himself to some crackers, and, crossing the bridge, was never again seen in Lumberton." [47]

Henry Berry was a bold and desperate man. Yet when he crossed over the Lumber River and entered the Settlement of the Scuffletonians he was moving among a folk in whom his rash deeds evoked a sympathetic response. The Republican victory and the coming of democratic methods of government had actually done little to mitigate the frustration of this troubled people.

Just after the war Radicals had spoken about the confiscation of great estates and about land for the landless. But now that the Republican Party was in a position to do something more than talk, the idea of "forty acres and a mule" was being dismissed as a fatuous dream. The Republicans were still talking about civil rights and the equality of all men before the law, to be sure. But the Home Guard had been forgiven and the Lowrys outlawed, and the former members of the Home Guard were now hunting the Lowrys. Indeed there was much in the experience of the Scuffletonians which would seem to bear out the proposition that the more things change, the more they remain the same.

There was no denying that much of what the Radical

[46] Fayetteville *Eagle*, December 13, 1868.
[47] Townsend (comp.), *The Swamp Outlaws*, 26; Origins of Lowry Band, 25.

politicians had to say sounded good, and Indians consistently preferred these men to the Conservatives. But at best politics provided a long and circuitous road to the smokehouse and the corncrib; and the courthouse was proving to be a poor place to avenge the murder of a kinsman. The Lowry band, on the other hand, was more representative of the various races than were the courts; the primitive judgments pronounced by their Spencer rifles seemed truer than those of Republican judges; and the path they had taken to the smokehouse door was certainly more direct than that advocated by the Radical politicians.

It was about dusk on Saturday evening, January 23, 1869, when Reuben King arrived at his plantation. Saturdays were always busy days for him; and he had just come from Lumberton, two miles distant, where he had spent the day collecting his bills. For Reuben King this could sometimes be a considerable undertaking because, unlike many planters, he had not faced the Confederate defeat with virtually all his resources tied up in slaves. Though he had lost more than a score of slaves, the foundations of his fortune, his lands, were quite intact. He could easily count himself among the two or three wealthiest men in the county.[48]

Even his most outstanding public honor, his position as high sheriff of Robeson, for a time after the war had not been challenged. This had not been because he was universally esteemed; no one is likely to hold a position requiring so many unpleasant duties and at the same time enjoy unanimous approval. For his part, King had aroused the bitter enmity of the Radicals. They had accused him of being "arbitrary and oppressive," with ignoring the legal rights of debtors when he had found it necessary to evict them and

[48] Fayetteville *Eagle*, February 4, 1869, quoting Wilmington *Journal*, n.d.; U.S., Bureau of Census, Eighth Census of the United States (1860), Slaves, North Carolina, IV, 50, Free Population, North Carolina, XIII, 896.

sell their farms at public auction.[49] They had once raised a great hue and cry against him, demanding that he release Noel Locklear, an Indian whose term of servitude imposed by the county court had expired some time earlier.[50] The Radicals had even gone to the military authorities about the sheriff, trying to get him removed from his position in order, as one of them said, to "save the loyal people from the relentless persecution of this official." [51] But nothing had ever come of these efforts.

Meanwhile, however, a Radical Congress had imposed an election on the South; and the Republicans by figuring into the total all the ballots cast by freedmen and Scuffletonians had at last succeeded in depriving King of his position. But, though there was now a Republican sheriff of sorts, the Conservatives had regarded the whole procedure as a coarse farce and refused to recognize the legitimacy of the new regime. To the most prominent and the best educated people in the county there was now, and for almost two decades had been, but one high sheriff of Robeson; and he was the old gentleman who, on this chill January evening, now entered the living room of his plantation big house.

A neighbor had dropped in for a visit. The two gentlemen relaxed before a comfortable fire and after a few moments King opened his newspaper to an account of a recent Baptist convention. But suddenly something made him look up from his paper: before him stood Henry Berry Lowry, who six weeks ago, almost to the hour, had walked out of the Lumberton jail. Lowry said that he had come for "his gold and silver." The old sheriff leaped from his chair and made a mad lunge for the armed Indian, whom he must have known

---

[49] Alfred Thomas to Joseph K. Wilson, March 4, 1868, in Freedmen's Bureau Records.

[50] Alfred Thomas to Thomas A. Norment, March 18, 1868, in Freedmen's Bureau Records.

[51] Thomas to Wilson, March 4, 1868, in Freedmen's Bureau Records.

was reputed to be the most expert gunman in the county. A bullet cut him down, mortally wounded. It was said to have been fired by George Applewhite, a black man, who, standing in the shadows, was covering his leader as he advanced toward King. The Lowrys ransacked the plantation for valuables and then vanished into the swamps.[52]

For Henry Berry there was now no road back toward a reconciliation with the Republican leaders—if indeed there ever had been. All of them, to a man, might have detested King, but they could not condone his murder. Some of them would castigate this deed quite as sharply as did the Conservatives. Yet these same men, torn between antagonistic loyalties, entrapped and paralyzed by legal hairsplitting, and above all outraged by the atrocities of the Klan, would continue to show a certain suppressed admiration for the primitive directness of Henry Berry.

"Lowry," the Reverend James Sinclair told a northern newspaper correspondent, "is really one of those remarkable executive spirits that arise now and then in a raw community, without advantages other [than those] nature gave him. He has passions, but no weaknesses, and his eyes are on every point at once. . . . No man who stands face to face with him can resist his quiet will, and assurance and his searching eye. Without fear, without hope, defying society, he is the only man we have any knowledge of down here who can play his part." [53] Thus spoke a man who hoped to find justice in a ballot box concerning one who hoped to find it between the sights of a Spencer rifle.

[52] Fayetteville *Eagle*, February 4, 1868, quoting Wilmington *Journal*; Townsend (comp.), *The Swamp Outlaws*, 28.
[53] Townsend (comp.), *The Swamp Outlaws*, 14.

5 · Jailbreaks and Undercover Work, 1869–1870

"THE LOYAL MILITIA OF Robeson County engaged, on Wednesday night [August 18, 1869], in a warm skirmish with the robbers," the Wilmington *Star* reported. "The fight occurred at 'Harper's Ferry'; and we regret to say one of the 'trooly loil' was wounded, and victory rather decided in favor of the outlaws, all of whom escaped." [1] During Reconstruction it was indeed rare to find a Conservative newspaper, such as the *Star*, expressing regrets over the defeat of a "trooly loil" company of Republican militia. But the political situation in Robeson County was even stranger. There the Republican sheriff, Benjamin A. Howell, had received the support of the Lowry band "to a man" in his campaign for his present office, the same paper reported. "The Ku Klux are not the guilty parties, but straight Republicans of the Radical stripe." [2]

The *Star*'s regrets about the outcome of the Harper's Ferry skirmish were perfectly sincere. But nevertheless, from a Conservative point of view, the incident had its happier side: for years the Conservatives had been trying to create in Robeson County some respect for law and property. As a reward for their efforts they had received denunciations and

[1] Wilmington *Star*, August 21, 1869.
[2] *Ibid.*, August 15, 1869.

sometimes worse. Now at last it appeared that the Republican Party might be taking some responsibility for this thankless task.

Even more heartwarming was the realization that "Robbersonian" Republicans were now shooting at each other, a development that would deliver this predominantly Republican county into the hands of the Conservatives for many years to come. Some Conservatives had already reached a certain understanding with the more moderate Republicans that was enabling them to recover some of the positions of influence they had held before the presidential, Black Code regimes had been dissolved.

In particular Conservative military leaders were receiving commissions from the Republican civil authorities, partly because the overwhelming majority of experienced army officers in the area were Conservatives. Another reason was that, even when the Republicans could produce an officer with practical experience, he often had little heart in the fight against the Lowrys, a campaign that his party had undertaken for broad policy reasons but which was unpopular with his constituents.

These circumstances amounted to opportunity for men such as Captain Owen Clinton Norment, who, because of his black eyes, hair, and beard, was known along the Lumber River as "Black Owen." [3] For many years the Norments had been among the most influential families of the antebellum elite; and the abolition of slavery had not wiped out their political power. As late as 1867, Black Owen's grandfather was chairman of the county court, his father was solicitor, and one of his uncles was clerk.[4] During the war he had

[3] Townsend (comp.), *The Swamp Outlaws*, 30.
[4] Birnie to Rutherford, November 28, 1867, in Freedmen's Bureau Records.

received a lieutenant's commission in a company over which one of his brothers was commander.[5]

Owen Norment, like certain other members of the ante-bellum elite, enjoyed a rather consistent personal success despite the apparent failure of the causes he embraced; he rose after each disaster to new positions of power. Immediately following the Confederate defeat at Appomattox, for example, Black Owen received a commission in the Robeson County police company at the same rank that he had held in the Confederate service. He so distinguished himself, moreover, by hunting Indians and reconstructing the county along Conservative lines that he was soon elevated to captain by the presidential regime of 1865–68. The overthrow of the Conservatives had proved a setback for him, to be sure. But not for long: the Republicans now needed an experienced officer who could hunt Lowrys without mixed feelings or sideways glances at the consequences of antagonizing the dark-skinned peoples as well as many of the plain whites. So, after two political upsets, the militia officer was back in his old position, at the head of a band of armed men, beating the bushes, hunting Indians.[6] Indeed the more things changed, the more they seemed to remain the same!

As was the case with other militia officers, Captain Norment was not nearly so well informed about how to find the Lowrys as they were concerning his whereabouts. Sometimes this could be embarrassing. On one occasion when he was attending services at Back Swamp Church, he is reported to have recognized among his fellow worshipers the face of the outlaw chief himself, Henry Berry Lowry. Yet, if there was any satisfaction in realizing that he had at last overtaken the man that he had so long pursued, it was

[5] Minutes of the Robeson County Court, August, 1860–August, 1865, pp. 250–51, North Carolina Department of Archives and History, Raleigh.
[6] Wilmington *Daily Journal*, March 22, 1870.

offset by the fact that the militia officer, unlike Henry Berry Lowry, had not come to church prepared for this particular encounter. So on this occasion the pious mood of the Sabbath was marred by the exchange of some hateful words, but nothing more deadly.[7]

Having a bitter enemy at his mercy, Henry Berry had acted on this occasion with a seeming liberality, a liberality that he himself almost certainly would not have enjoyed had the circumstances been reversed. But this was clearly no way to placate Captain Norment. The officer might well have suffered less in fact from one of the outlaw's bullets than he did from having publicly to accept the condescending generosity of a brown-skinned Indian. On more than one occasion Henry Berry endeared himself to the plain people along the Lumber by his talent for humiliating a proud gentleman.

Nevertheless, by the fall of 1869, it must have appeared to Black Owen that the day of retribution was drawing near. Bands of resolute Conservatives, such as his own detachment and that of Dr. W. J. Gilbert, were lending strength to the weak-willed county militia. By September they had succeeded in capturing eight men—six Indians and two blacks—all of whom were thought to be important lieutenants of Henry Berry. Furthermore two of the men, Eli Ewin and John Dial, were induced, apparently by a combination of threats and bribes, to cooperate with the authorities, giving information and perhaps misinformation implicating others. New arrests seemed to be in the offing.

Yet, despite these successes, all was not well for Captain Norment and his campaign against the Lowrys. If Henry Berry himself and his wife's seventeen-year-old brother, Boss Strong, were the only well-known figures who were not behind bars, it was also apparent that the band had a host of less prominent adherents who were very much at large.

[7] Origins of Lowry Band, 16.

The Wilmington *Journal* was probably exaggerating when it reported that the gang was composed of several hundred men, including all races, and that its operations extended to the towns of Raleigh, Fayetteville, Goldsboro, and Wilmington, as well as to Georgetown, South Carolina.[8] Nevertheless, the full dimensions of the Lowry band, like those of an iceberg, could not be fully measured by those parts appearing on the surface.

The authorities intensified their hunt for adherents to the band in the winter of 1869–70. Yet the Lowry foraging raids continued, often in the very neighborhoods where the militia was most active. Also the conflict was growing more bitter, with neither side showing much inclination toward magnanimity or granting quarter. The trial of the eight captive leaders was set for the spring term of the Superior Court of Robeson.

The approaching trial was a considerably less pleasant prospect for a Republican than it would have been for a Conservative: a Republican judge would have to pass sentence on some extremists in his own party for killing a Conservative sheriff, who had distinguished himself during the war by his persecution of Unionists. If he wanted to prove that the Republicans offered a clear alternative to the extralegal skullduggery of the Ku Klux type, he would have to pass a harsh sentence. But if he did, he would cost the party the very votes that had made him judge. The captain and his friends had maneuvered their enemies into such a corner that they could do little except choose which brand of poison they would prefer to take. Perhaps the Conservatives could now relax a little and let the other side make the next move.

Captain Norment especially could look with some pride

[8] Wilmington *Weekly Journal*, September 24, 1869.

on the part he had played in confronting his enemies with this dilemma. On the evening of March 19, 1870, barely two weeks before the sensational trials, he read nursery stories to his children and then joined his wife, Mary, before the fire in the living room of their plantation home. After they had chatted a while he remarked to her

in a low tone, that he had heard a noise. She replied that she had dropped a hair-pin on the hearth, and supposed that was the noise he heard. He said no, it was not that but expressed no uneasiness. In a short time he opened [the door] and stepped out leaving it open. His wife looked out at the door and saw the flash of a gun pass. Simultaneously he groaned . . . . She caught him and pulled him inside the house. He whispered to her to close and fasten the door, and hand him his rifle . . . . She did as he desired, kneeling by him supporting him in order that he might have both hands in the use of his gun.[9]

A black servant reported having seen "a woman or a man in woman's clothes, run from the road into the bushes." Other members of the household rushed away to bring a doctor to the stricken man. But as the doctor approached the Norment plantation he ran into an ambush. Amid withering gunfire he saw the mule that pulled his buggy crumple before him. He fled in terror, reaching the Norment place in safety. But, unfortunately, his precious bag, containing the medications needed for the wounded man, still lay in the abandoned buggy. Four Negro servants volunteered to go back for it. They returned with the doctor's bag a short time later.[10]

Help came too late for Captain Norment. He died shortly after dawn on the following day. But the agony of his mortal wound did not completely vanish with his death. It lingered

[9] Norment, *The Lowrie History*, 80–81.
[10] *Ibid.*, 82.

in the memory of his wife, and she poured out her anguish into a book which she wrote about the Lowry band.[11]

By nature Mary Norment was not suited to the savage blood feuds of Robeson County—few people have been. But as a local historian she championed the cause of her fallen husband. She knew a number of families who adhered to the Lowrys and may have even known several of the outlaws; and though partisan, she was not blind. Like a number of women, for example, she did not fail to note that Henry Berry "makes a handsome personal appearance when dressed up." Nor was she insensitive to his cavalier deference toward women and to his peculiar integrity; she conceded that even "those most robbed and outraged by this bandit give him credit for complying strictly to his word." [12]

But for all that, Mary Norment hated Henry Berry and his followers with the boundless hatred of one who has been injured beyond all repair. Our traditional concept of hell must owe a great deal to persons like Mary Norment, persons who have observed that life rarely treats wicked people with appropriate cruelty, that if existence is to be bearable there must be some place where evil receives its just reward. Could mere death, death from a swift bullet, mete out the full measure of retribution to men who could establish a secret hiding place in the shadow of a home, and who could

[11] One historian has asserted that Mary Norment did not actually write this book. The real author of the work, he says, was Joseph B. McCallum, presumably her brother-in-law. See Stephen B. Weeks, "The Lost Colony of Roanoke: Its Fate and Survival," *Papers of the American Historical Association,* V (1891), 474. Indeed the third edition (Lumberton, N.C.: Lumbee Publishing Co., 1909) does not bear the name of any author, although the editors state that Mary Norment "wrote the facts." In absence of some substantiation of Weeks's assertion, it seems reasonable to assume that Mrs. Norment was largely responsible for the book, much of which concerned matters of which she had personal knowledge. Furthermore subtle details of the book seem to show the imprint of a woman's personality. So if McCallum was in fact her ghostwriter, he was an uncommonly convincing one.

[12] Norment, *The Lowrie History,* 9, 12.

lurk there listening to a father reading nursery tales to his children, waiting for the proper moment to entice him to his death? In describing the death of an outlaw, Mary Norment would write that the swift bullet had merely "ended his career on earth, and sent him, a blood-stained, crime-hardened wretch, to answer before a great tribunal for the deeds committed while in the flesh." [13]

But the time had not yet come, when Captain Norment was killed, for the Conservatives to carry out the full measure of their retribution. As the trials of their leaders approached, Lowry raids and attacks increased. On the night the Norment plantation was raided, for example, there were almost simultaneous attacks in at least three other areas of the county. On March 29, 1870, two days before the first trial opened, the Conservative Wilmington *Journal*, which had long suspected that Republicanism would bring social chaos, gave an account of conditions in Robeson County which made it appear that all respect for property and authority had evaporated there:

So great is the danger that it is found almost impossible to bring the militia into service. Quiet and inoffensive men are shot at, both at their homes and on the highways, and even in the town of Lumberton few feel safe. Barns and cribs all over the county are robbed of their contents, and private dwellings are entered and ransacked with impunity, and in one or two instances robbers have been discovered under beds in the chambers of residences. For several nights recently the whole town of Lumberton has been under arms . . . . Where is now Governor Holden's desire for U.S. troops? [14]

Nevertheless the trial of two of the captives began April 1, 1870, at Whiteville, in Columbus County, where it had been transferred because of the disorders prevailing in Robeson.

[13] *Ibid.*, 142.
[14] Wilmington *Daily Journal*, March 29, 1870.

The accused were George Applewhite, a former slave; and Stephen Lowry, a brother of Henry Berry, and a former locomotive fireman on the Wilmington, Charlotte, and Rutherfordton Railroad.

The case against the men seemed to have been weakened on the first day of the trial when the chief witness for the prosecution, the Indian youth John Dial, through his lawyer, repudiated the confession that he had made earlier, saying that it had been extracted from him by force and was untrue. Of course there was still one other important witness for the prosecution, Eli Ewin, or "Shoemaker John," a Negro adherent to the band whose cooperation had also been secured by the authorities, and who, along with three other Lowry captives, was still being held at the jail in Lumberton. But on April 2, a "low white woman was criminally admitted to see these negro[15] prisoners that night, and who had an auger concealed about her person." Three of the four Lowry captives, including Shoemaker John, were able to escape through a hole that they cut in a wall.[16]

If the state's case against the Lowrys was somewhat compromised by the behavior of the chief witnesses for the prosecution, most people nevertheless assumed that the accused had killed Sheriff King, Captain Norment, and others. The trial was a short one. Republican Judge Daniel L. Russell sentenced the two men to hang, a verdict which seemed to announce that he and his party were putting law enforcement above any local partisan considerations.

The recent escape of prisoners, including a state witness, may have served to remind the authorities that, however adequate the jails at Lumberton and Whiteville might be for ordinary prisoners, they would scarcely do for Lowry captives. Indeed Henry Berry had escaped from each jail.

[15] Only one of the four appears to have been in fact a Negro.
[16] Wilmington *Daily Journal*, April 5, 1870.

Immediately following their conviction, in any event, the condemned men were transferred to the solid brick jail in Wilmington, where they were incarcerated with Calvin and Henderson Oxendine, first cousins of Stephen Lowry, both still awaiting trial there.

But even in Wilmington, though the city was outside the main base of the Lowrys' operations, an escape attempt was not impossible. The previous fall, when the Lowry captives had been held briefly in Wilmington, local officers noticed that the city jail was under observation by various unidentified men. When the police attempted to arrest the strangers, all escaped except one, who "was called upon to give an account of himself, which he attempted in no very intelligible manner." The police had no ground for holding the man for very long, even though he could show no visible means of support, gave them no name that they could verify, and told them a confused maze of contradictory stories.[17]

Realizing that the Lowrys were no ordinary prisoners, the New Hanover County sheriff took special precautions. They were to be locked in a special cell within the main cell-block of the jail. Thus even if they succeeded in getting out of their cell they would still be imprisoned by the solid brick walls of the jail itself. Furthermore he employed a special watchman to guard them. Thus during the day they were to be watched by the regular jailor, at night by a special guard. On Sunday, June 12, the night guard, Sylvester Capps, came on duty at nine in the evening. First he checked the lock on the Lowry cell and the others as well. Each was securely fastened. All was quiet on the cell-block, and he settled down for another night of watching. But the eventless night passed slowly. At two o'clock he decided to step downstairs to the prison kitchen for a few minutes.

[17] *Ibid.*, September 4, 1869.

There he met another guard who was employed as a watchman for a carriage shop in the neighborhood. The two men chatted for a while, then stepped out into the prison courtyard to smoke their pipes. The moon was shining clear and bright, the night absolutely soundless. Then Capps went back upstairs to his cell-block to check his locks again.[18]

All was silent, all locks secure. But taking a second look at the Lowry cell, he was thunderstruck. It was empty! The door was still locked. No sign of an escape hole. The Lowrys had simply vanished, perhaps while he had stood smoking his pipe in the silent, moonlit courtyard below. He sounded the alarm. No trace of the Lowrys was to be found in the neighborhood around the jail or in the city at large. But Sheriff Schenck thought he saw at a glance the key to the whole mystery. He ordered Capps, who was a Negro, arrested and charged with aiding the Lowrys to escape.[19]

A full-scale investigation of the incident, however, made it possible to reconstruct what had actually happened. If to Sheriff Schenck the Lowry escape smacked of treachery, if to Capps it seemed hardly credible, there was at least one person in the Wilmington jail who knew how the prisoners had gotten away. Willie Harper, a white prisoner, though he slept in the debtors' section, enjoyed considerable freedom to wander about the jail and keep up with what was going on. Some time back Harper had witnessed a Lowry ruse, seemingly designed to distract guards and prisoners alike, a subterfuge superbly addressed to the special circumstances of prison life. He had seen a "young lady" come to the door of the jail and inquire of the guard concerning a certain "Richardson." "Most of the prisoners were there, listening and looking at her. At the same time," Harper

[18] *Ibid.*, June 14, 18, 1870.
[19] *Ibid.*

watched Stephen Lowry "haul in the hatchet, chisel and file," by a string pulled surreptitiously through the jail window.[20]

The "young lady" who created this diversion may have been Rhoda Lowry, the wife of Henry Berry. There is a confused oral tradition, not written down until much later and containing some incorrect details, which holds that the Indian girl made the eighty-mile trip to Wilmington on foot in order to take part in an escape plan.[21] Certainly the sensation the "young lady" caused at the jail is similar to the impression Rhoda Lowry made wherever she went. Also it seems reasonable that Rhoda would have walked to Wilmington. Had she taken the train, for example, she would almost certainly have been recognized, since there were countless males in Robeson County who could identify Rhoda Lowry without the slightest difficulty and often from an unlikely distance. However, once she was in Wilmington, where she was not generally known, she could have moved about freely, readily passing for white.

Willie Harper, having seen the Lowrys sneak tools into their cell, began to observe the behavior of these prisoners closely. He saw Steve Lowry working at something. He was shaping a key for the cell door! He saw the Indian "try the key made from the tin spoon and it worked." Now that the Lowrys could unlock their cell door, they began to behave in a way that Willie Harper found very mysterious. Instead of all of them at once making a sudden bolt for freedom, they carefully watched for lapses of vigilance on the part of the guard. Then, only one of them would leave the cell, locking the door behind him, go to the floor above,

[20] *Ibid.*
[21] Claude Dunnagan, "Henry Berry's Private Six-Year War Against the South," *Male*, XI (July, 1961), 32–35, 39–45.

stay for a time but return to the Lowry cell before there was a danger that he might be missed.[22]

Having the free run of the jail, Willie decided that he would do some investigating. Upstairs he found an empty cell, one side of which was the outer wall of the prison. The Negro outlaw, George Applewhite, was in the empty cell busily scratching mortar from between the bricks. Now that Willie knew what they were up to, he thought that he had better speak to these men whose appointment with the hangman had drawn so uncomfortably close. With unbelievable stupidity he warned them, "You will get into trouble!" The Lowrys, not concerned primarily at that moment with maintaining convivial relations with the county prison staff, predicted that Harper would have some unpleasant experiences unless he held his tongue. Intimidated, he maintained silence until after the Lowrys made their escape. On June 13, about two in the morning, when their special guard went downstairs to chat with a colleague, the Lowrys acted quickly. Crawling out the hole they had cut in the outer wall on the third floor, they slid forty feet to the ground on a rope made from strips of blankets, and then hurried northward along a moonlit street.[23]

Their nearest friends or trustworthy connections were in Robeson County some sixty miles to the west—sixty miles across the thinly populated, northern parts of Brunswick and Columbus counties. This was the great piney woods, crisscrossed by junglelike swamps. If they lacked human friends in this wilderness, at least for these fugitives it was not a totally unfriendly environment, nor one to which they were unaccustomed. But between them and the comparative safety of the great piney woods flowed the broad and bridgeless Cape Fear.

[22] Wilmington *Daily Journal*, June 14, 18, 1870.
[23] *Ibid.*

Not daring to attempt a crossing of the river within the city, along the Wilmington waterfront, where they could expect to be spotted any minute, they kept hurrying northward, following the line of the river until their way was blocked by the Northeast River at a point near where it flows into the Cape Fear. But they were able to cross the Northeast, a smaller river, on the railroad trestle; and once again began following the course of the Cape Fear, which was now inclining in a northwesterly direction. At last, after putting the city well behind them, they reached a desolate spot where they were able to cross the river on a raft, possibly one they constructed themselves. But once in the wilderness they began to move slowly and with extreme caution, avoiding people and the widely scattered settlements. "We didn't get much to eat," Henderson Oxendine later remarked, though they had "knocked over a pig once and cooked it up over a fire—had no bread. It was over four weeks before we got to Scuffletown. . . . Steph. got with Henry Berry before I did. . . . I first saw Henry Berry's wife a little ways from the gate, and she told me that Henry Berry and Stephen were in the house, and I went in. I have not slept in a house since I left Wilmington jail, except once or twice in Henry Berry's, and a few times in George Applewhite's." [24]

It appeared that in the summer of 1870 the Lowry conflict was in much the same state it had been in two years before, when the Conservatives had been in control. To be sure, the Republican authorities, with substantial Conservative backing, had enjoyed a certain initial success against the band and had taken some important prisoners. But now the Lowrys were on guard against the new authorities as they had been against the old, and arrest had become less frequent. And meanwhile the principal captives had managed to escape.

[24] Wilmington *Carolina Farmer and Weekly Star*, March 24, 1871.

Yet the county leaders had learned something about conflicts of this nature. How was it that the Lowrys seemed able at times to vanish without a trace only to reappear where they were least expected—say at a church where they might chat with the militia captain in command of the men pursuing them? Guerrillas generally have no special techniques of concealment that are unknown to their enemies. The special advantage that they seem to enjoy is that of having a constituency, a considerable body of people who wish them well, thousands of eyes and ears that see and hear for them, but turn blind and deaf when the authorities ask questions.

It had become evident to some of the leaders in the campaign against the outlaws that the movements of the Lowry band, which sometimes appeared so mysterious to militia officers, were considerably less of a riddle to a great number of the plain folk of Robeson County. This suggested the possibilities of some astute undercover work. Information about the Lowrys shared by countless Indians, Negroes, and Buckskins might well, by some devious route, reach the ears of the authorities. In this connection Mary Norment relates that "in the year A.D. 1869, in the month of November John Sa[u]nders, a police officer of Boston, and a native of Nova Scotia, at the instance of some leading Conservatives in Robeson County, settled in Scuffletown, and commenced teaching the mulatto [Indian] children how to spell and read. To cover up and conceal his design he was accredited from the Republican Sheriff of New Hanover County to some of the leading Republicans in the county." [25]

Saunders had undertaken a lonely and dangerous game. On one hand it would be too risky to take local Republicans into his confidence, as they might be pro-Lowry. On the other hand, frequent associations with Conservatives would arouse the suspicions of the Indians. The contact man be-

[25] Norment, *The Lowrie History*, 95.

tween Saunders, the undercover agent, and the leaders of
the anti-Lowry campaign was the New Hanover County sheriff, Major J. W. Schenck, Jr. Schenck, who successfully
beguiled his fellow Republicans in Robeson County, was
a Yankee adventurer. Following his discharge from the Union
army at the end of the war, he had resided for a number
of years in Wilmington, where he rather amply lived up
to the general reputation that carpetbaggers had in the
South. His lively concern with dramatic schemes for making
money, combined with a certain deviousness, were qualities
which eventually might prove expensive to his ostensible
friends on the lower Cape Fear; but they perhaps explain
his early interest in the Lowrys, especially in the rewards
that the state was offering for their capture.[26]

John Saunders himself, in order to win the confidence of
the Indians, pretended to be one of the many high-minded,
Radical teachers who migrated to the South after the
war and worked selflessly with scant resources in order to
combat the educational heritage of the slave society, which
had made it a penal offense to teach reading to dark-skinned
people.

But, for a man whose actual purpose was to collect the
bounties that the state offered for the Lowrys, it was not
always easy to play the part of an idealistic zealot. Like
many genuine Radicals, for example, Saunders sometimes
found himself being bullied by local Conservatives. Yet,

[26] Schenck to Holden, October 10, 1869, in Governors' Papers, North
Carolina Department of Archives and History, Raleigh. After Schenck left
North Carolina, a Republican governor had him extradited and returned to
the state to stand trial for an alleged $34,000 shortage in his accounts while
serving as sheriff of New Hanover County. However, for some unannounced
reason, the state did not prosecute him. Wilmington *Daily Journal*, April
13, 1875; Wilmington *Post*, April 23, 1875. A possible explanation would
be that Schenck was able to reach some settlement with his sureties out of
court; and the state Republican leaders naturally wanted to avoid a trial that
would publicly demonstrate the dishonesty of one of their officeholders.

though "a large portly man, of great muscular power," the Nova Scotian sometimes found it more expedient to promote two different and contradictory doctrines than consistently to defend one. Thus, to appease irate Conservatives he told "the uninitiated that he was a veritable Ku Klux." [27]

Meanwhile, playing his double game, preaching his double creed, Saunders kept Schenck posted concerning the success of their venture. In his letters he sometimes couched his meaning in obscure language, but at other times he was remarkably candid. "I am progressing nicely," he wrote on June 3, 1870.

I spent a day and a night among them, saw several of the gang and learned that they are in the Swamp. I lecture to them tomorrow night. I have succeeded in getting the good will of all the click [sic] that I have met. It will be some days and, perhaps, a couple of weeks before I can secure them. I am in their midst and the least hasty or false step will capsize all and cost me my life. You, sir, have, I fear, no conception of the number of people implicated. There is a black policeman here, who I am making a catspaw of. He has been brought up with them. When we are ready we can indict him. When he returns I'll use him on your canvass if you need him. [To canvass in New Hanover County for Schenck's reelection?] I shall get the fellows before election. . . . I had a large attendance at my address last night in the black's meeting house and am bound to succeed.

Yours respectfully and faithfully,
J. C. Saunders[28]

A month later, before getting around to his usual request for money, Saunders wrote that he felt "more confident than before of success, but . . . it requires the greatest caution, as all here are connected. I could have gotten James Locklear and Stephen Lowery both since I have been here, but I want the whole gang, if possible, and expect to get them. Applewhite comes to his house occasionally. He is living in South Carolina, about twenty-five miles from here. In order to get my points I am living among them and began a school yesterday. I take a bottle of whiskey and go to certain houses, from whom in my way, I can learn something." [29]

Stealthily Saunders was baiting a trap, designed to capture in one grand sweep the entire band and their families as well. He seems to have persuaded the outlaws that, since the authorities appeared to be closing in upon Scuffletown, they should do as countless other Indians in the eastern United States had done. They should give up the hopeless struggle, take their families, and migrate.

But how would they get away? Once out of Robeson County their Indian appearance and the very accent on their tongues would surely give them away. Saunders, however, had given this problem some reflection too. They would have to stay discreetly out of sight during the trip, while a white friend would have to serve as their link with the Caucasian world. He was willing to serve as the Moses of their exodus, as their guide and protector.

Together they would reach the safety of Mexico, or perhaps the Great Plains beyond the western frontier. While the Indians prepared for the exodus, Saunders, for his part, arranged "to have them intercepted at some designated point in Georgia." On November 19, 1870, at least one wagon was packed, loaded with women and children, and prepared to move out under the cover of darkness. But the departure did not take place. [30]

It is difficult to say how long the Lowrys were deceived by Saunders, if indeed they ever were. He may well have underestimated the keen intelligence of the men with whom

[29] *Ibid.*
[30] Norment, *The Lowrie History*, 95.

he dealt. Certainly they allowed him to continue playing his game long after they had detected evidence of his duplicity. A student of Robeson County history, a kinsman of the leaders of the Lowry band, writes that "there came a day when some member of the band came upon a place where two men had stood and talked. There were two freshly packed tracks in the leaves . . . . They concluded Sa[u]nders had talked with an outsider there." [31]

The Indians began to keep a close watch on Saunders. They discovered that he had established a "secret camp" in the swamp near the water mill of William C. McNeill. The Lowrys did not regard the Buckskin miller as an enemy. But nevertheless they had reason to mistrust him since the marriage of his daughter Ann Eliza to John Taylor, a well-to-do turpentine distiller, a prominent Conservative, a member of the Confederate Home Guard detachment that had executed William and Allen Lowry, and a man who may have been currently active in the Ku Klux Klan. Taylor was often a visitor in the home of his father-in-law.[32]

So this was Saunders' route to the "outside"! By associating with supposedly friendly or neutral McNeills he would come in contact with their hostile in-laws, through whom he could keep in touch with the authorities. Furthermore as the Indians began to scrutinize the activities around the mill more closely, they noticed that the behavior of certain McNeills seemed neither friendly nor neutral: two sons of McNeill were visiting Saunders' camp secretly and appeared to be bringing him "advice and information." On Saturday, November 19, 1870, when Saunders' "migration" failed to

[31] Clifton Oxendine, "A Social and Economic History of the Indians of Robeson County, North Carolina" (M.A. thesis, George Peabody College, 1934), 28.

[32] Townsend (comp.), *The Swamp Outlaws*, 62; U.S., Bureau of Census, Eighth Census of the United States (1860), Free Population, North Carolina, XIII, 935; Chaffin Journal, May 30, 1865.

materialize, the police officer called a meeting of a group of young men whom he had taken into his confidence. They were to gather at the secret camp on Sunday afternoon. One of the sons of McNeill was late. As he approached the designated spot, "the young men slipped up to him and, with ghastly faces, whispered that they were surrounded and that to move would be certain death . . . . The impetuous MacNeill [sic] reached his hand toward his pistol, when four men rose up in the bushes beside him—namely H. B. Lowry, Steven Lowry, George Applewhite and Boss Strong. Henry Berry advanced . . . and took McNeill's repeater from its case, and told him to make himself at home . . . for he would be detained." [33]

But the man Henry Berry really wanted was Saunders. Even though it was already nightfall, the detective still had not appeared for a meeting which he himself had called for the afternoon. The outlaws waited. Sentinels were posted; a fire was lighted. Tom Lowry arrived with some brandy, and his brother Steve produced a deck of cards. Somebody wanted to know where Steve had gotten the cards; he replied that he had bought them at the "Scotch Fair." One of the young Scots betrayed his surprise: had this well-known Indian outlaw dared show his brown face at the Scotch Fair? "We boys go anywhere," the Indian answered. "The whole country belongs to us." [34]

As the night dragged on, there was a constant procession of messengers, arriving and departing, each reporting on some development in the surrounding country that might be of interest to the outlaw chiefs who sat around the fire face to face with their captives. What were they going to do with these men? The young McNeills, for example: how

[33] Townsend (comp.), The Swamp Outlaws, 63.
[34] Ibid., 62–63.

deeply were they involved in the projects of their brother-in-law John Taylor? Was it possible that they also had been fooled by Saunders as many Indians had? In the distance a hound dog began to bay. Someone recognized his voice; it was an outlaw dog and he had undoubtedly treed a possum. Henry Berry arose from the fire and invited Oakley McNeill to go with him to see what the dog had. As they expected, they found the dog barking under a tree in which a possum had taken refuge. In a seemingly careless gesture, Henry Berry, who always carried a rifle and several pistols, laid the supposedly loaded rifle down near the disarmed young Scot. He then climbed the tree and proceeded to shake out the possum. On the ground, the youth touched the rifle, moving it slightly. But he did not try to use it.[35] Then the two men returned to the fire together.

But Lowry treated another prisoner more harshly. Leading the man away from the fire to a secluded spot down in the swamp, Henry Berry said to him, "God damn your soul, I want you to tell me where Sa[u]nders is. He is expected here. If you don't tell me where he is and why he don't come I will kill you dead. I intend to kill you anyway when I get Sa[u]nders. You had better own right up!" The captive did not "own right up." Nevertheless Henry Berry led him back to the fire again.[36]

Just at dawn the next morning the prisoners heard an Indian voice ring out. It was the challenge of a sentry. The voice that replied was that of a white man. It was Saunders! They heard him say "I surrender." [37] Immediately Henry Berry told the other prisoners "to go and keep their mouths shut. He told McNeill that he had caught him in three

[35] Wishart Diary, October 9, 1871.
[36] Townsend (comp.), *The Swamp Outlaws*, 62–63.
[37] *Ibid.*, 63.

lies; he would let him go this time, but he had better behave himself." [38]

The question of how to dispose of the spy was settled by a council of eight outlaws: Henry Berry and Steve and Tom Lowry, Andrew and Boss Strong, Henderson Oxendine, George Applewhite, and Zack McLauchlin. While the outlaws deliberated, Saunders for his part—perhaps because he feared torture, perhaps to make an appeal for sympathy— made a faltering effort to commit suicide. "He got a knife one time," Henderson Oxendine later recalled, "and cut a vein in his wrist so he could bleed to death. But it didn't bleed a great deal." [39]

Andrew Strong favored releasing him if he would take an oath to leave the state, a condition which the Nova Scotian was willing enough to accept. "He said several times if we would let him go, he would go clean off and never bother us any more." [40] Strong's willingness to accept the oath of a confidence man and his reluctance to agree to the death penalty probably were the result of a personal experience. One of his in-laws had recently been executed by the militia and Strong himself at that time had narrowly escaped the firing squad. But most of the others, especially Henry Berry and Steve, favored a verdict of death. Perhaps seeing a flash of hope in this divided council, the police officer "appeared to be very grateful to Andrew for his efforts in his behalf, and begged him to accept his pen-knife, which Andrew at first declined to take; but, on being urged by the unfortunate man, he took it with the remark: 'God knows I pity you, for I have been in the very presence of death myself . . . , and I can understand your feelings.'" [41]

---

[38] Wilmington *Carolina Farmer and Weekly Star*, March 24, 1871. The source does not indicate to which of the three McNeills he was speaking.
[39] *Ibid.*
[40] *Ibid.*
[41] New York *Herald*, April 6, 1872.

Andrew Strong was able to persuade his companions, however, to allow the secret agent another opportunity to commit suicide, this time by taking poison. George Applewhite had some tablets that they believed to be arsenic. One was given to Saunders, who "put it in his mouth and swallowed it." The outlaws sat and waited. Three days passed and the victim seemed in no worse health for the "arsenic" that he had taken. The outlaws then decided to cast lots to determine who would shoot the prisoner. The task fell to Steve, and he did it without further delay. When the other outlaws left, Andrew Strong remained behind to bury Saunders. He reported later that he performed the burial as "decently as he could . . . . He wrapped him in his own blanket and clasped his hand." The next day he mailed to Mrs. Saunders her husband's last letter along with a photograph that had been found among the detective's effects.[42]

[42] *Ibid.*

6 · Let Scuffletown Be Devastated

ANDREW STRONG'S BEHAVIOR at the execution of Saunders does not appear to be that of a seasoned killer. Indeed at that time he may not have been one. According to his own statement he never took any part in the Lowry band's activities before 1870. The manner whereby he became involved seems to illustrate how a guerrilla conflict spreads. An individual begins by trying to remain aloof, but in troubled times can hardly avoid the association of violent men. Next he finds that others look on him as a secret partner in the cruel deeds of his relatives and friends. Finally he is attacked and takes up a cause so he might have allies.

During the war Strong had served as a conscripted laborer in the fever-ridden Confederate forts at the mouth of the Cape Fear, where the work "was of the hardest description," where the lash "was not spared." Yet, unlike many Indians, he had endured every indignity without open rebellion. As a result he returned home in good standing with the authorities. Nevertheless, he soon found that people suspected that he was involved with the Lowry band. After all, his sister Rhoda had married Henry Berry Lowry, and his younger brother Boss was considered the closest friend of the outlaw leader and had himself been declared an outlaw by the authorities.[1]

If Andrew Strong was indeed receiving a secret share of the booty taken by the Lowry band, as some people suspect-

---

[1] New York *Herald*, April 6, 1872; Norment, *The Lowrie History*, 141.

ed, it did not seem to bring much luxury and ease to his life. He worked hard as a logger, married Flora Sampson, built a log cabin on the Back Swamp, and began to rear a family. Early in 1870, however, some stolen property turned up in the possession of some black loggers with whom Strong was working. Warned of the approach of the authorities, the blacks escaped down the Lumber River on a raft. But the Indian, taking the view that he had nothing to conceal, remained at his job.

Soon a deputy sheriff came by to see him. Strong suspected that the officer might be carrying a warrant charging him with the theft. One had to be careful at such times. Sometimes Indians, or others of low social status, might peacefully submit to arrest on a verbally stated minor charge, but once they were in jail find that they were formally charged with something more serious. Just as he expected, "after a short conversation on general subjects," the deputy told him that he would have to come along with him to Lumberton. "Upon Andrew's asking him for a sight of his warrant he presented his revolver, saying this was his warrant." [2] The Indian also drew. Both men fired badly aimed shots, whereupon the deputy fled.

Strong nevertheless appeared at the next term of superior court, expecting to find himself charged perhaps with theft, perhaps with resisting arrest. To his dismay, however, he found that he was accused of the King murder. This charge had not seemed possible because of the official version of the murder. The King household had not been able to identify the six disguised men who had appeared at the plantation, though they had presumed the leader was Henry Berry Lowry. When the state finally located a positive witness, John Dial, he had said that the men had been himself, Henry Berry and Steve Lowry, Calvin and Henderson

[2] New York *Herald*, April 6, 1872.

Oxendine, and George Applewhite. It would thus seem that Strong and other persons close to the Lowrys were safe from this particular accusation.

But with the opening of the spring term of the superior court, Dial had repudiated his confession; and now the state was seeking another combination of six men. Strong said that while in jail he was visited by the county district attorney, who assured him "that if tried he would certainly be convicted, but that if he would testify against Henry Berry and Steve Lowry he would not only be released but handsomely rewarded." [3]

Strong remained in jail, unable to raise the fifteen-hundred-dollar bond required of him, unwilling to testify against his in-laws, the members of the Lowry band. Finally a Republican judge reduced his bond to two hundred dollars, which Strong raised. His temporary freedom gave him an opportunity to decide whether he wanted to go into hiding and be declared an outlaw or take his chances on being hanged for the King murder. But Strong would not be able to make his decision with detachment. His own life and the course of the Lowry conflict would take a sharp new turn due to a political event taking place in the fall of 1870.

For the Republican Party of North Carolina, the election of 1870 was a disaster from which it never fully recovered. In part this was because of the railroad scandals, which involved a number of important legislators, including the Reverend James Sinclair of Robeson. In part it was due to a reign of terror carried out by the Ku Klux Klan in more than a dozen Piedmont counties; during the twelve months prior to the election there had been three murders in Caswell County, five in Alamance, five in Orange, three in Jones, and isolated ones elsewhere. In the same general region during this time there were well over one hundred

[3] *Ibid.*

floggings and a variety of other bodily injuries, as well as extensive destruction of property, usually as the result of arson.[4]

Ku Klux terror helped deliver the thickly populated and crucial Piedmont region to the Conservatives. But paradoxically, though the Lowrys were sometimes represented as a kind of Republican Ku Klux Klan, the terror in Robeson County had exactly the same political result. It was not dangerous for anyone to vote in Robeson, unlike many counties. But there were few areas where the Republican Party was more compromised. Instead of receiving the votes of the dark-skinned peoples as a solid bloc, as had been the case in the past, the party was awarded "only the major portion" of it.[5]

In only one contest did they enjoy a measure of success; they were able to reelect Sheriff Howell. Yet, even though Howell had already moved far toward an accommodation with the Conservatives, he was never allowed to occupy the office to which he had been elected. The Republicans were a party of the poor and this was for them a particularly bad year. They were unable to raise Howell's official bond. The courts awarded the office to a Conservative, Roderick McMillan, whose bond was backed by ample money and real estate.[6]

Roderick McMillan as sheriff! There could scarcely have been a clearer signal that evil days were ahead for the Lowrys and their well-wishers. In 1867, when some Radicals had attempted to prosecute about twenty members of the Home Guard for killing William and Allen Lowry, the case was entitled *State v. Roderick McMillan et al.* During the trial

[4] Hamilton, *Reconstruction in North Carolina*, 477 and *passim*; Otto H. Olsen, "The Ku Klux Klan: A Study in Reconstruction Politics and Propaganda," *North Carolina Historical Review*, XXXIX (1962), 340–62.

[5] Wilmington *Star*, August 25, 1870.

[6] *Ku Klux Conspiracy*, II, 289.

an Indian testified that McMillan, in an effort to extract some information, "took a bayonet and jaged [sic] and stuck the point . . . in him." [7] Indeed McMillan would not be sheriff many days before he would show a lack of concern for legal niceties that was reminiscent of the Home Guard.

Meanwhile the Lowry band was scarcely behaving in a conciliatory way. On election day itself they raided the store of E. H. Paul, and the plantation of Alexander McKenzie the day following.[8] In certain of these raids one can recognize a style of operation for which the Lowrys became known, one that sometimes left the imprint of their work on a robbery in which there was no certain identification of the culprits. A band of strangers or disguised men were presumed to be Lowrys if they treated their victims with a certain courtesy, or if they seemed to be trying to minimize violence or destruction of property, or if they spared people who least could afford to be robbed. In robbing the Argyle plantation, for example, they had seized a great deal of booty as well as wagons and teams to haul it away. But, having no permanent use for wagons and teams, the robbers returned them to the victim.[9] Following a corn raid in Richmond County, it was determined that they had transported the booty to Scuffletown, "where the corn was equally distributed." [10] Or again, they robbed the presumably wealthy John McNair, but upon finding that in fact he had only fifteen dollars, they returned his pocketbook and money.[11]

But not all Lowry raids were of such a benign type. The shooting of Captain Norment seems to have been clearly a case of the deliberate killing of a man they had been

[7] Deposition of George Dial, October 19, 1867, in Investigation.

[8] Wilmington Star, August 26, 1870.

[9] Norment, The Lowrie History, 61.

[10] Townsend (comp.), The Swamp Outlaws, 50.

[11] Laurinburg Scottish Chief, April 10, 1935, quoting Laurinburg Exchange.

unable to mollify. And with them, as with their enemies, each deed of blood seemed to call for another. In place of one implacable foe, they now had at least two—John and A. C. Bridgers, both determined to avenge the death of their brother-in-law, Norment. This situation called for a visit to the Bridgers plantation, where the outlaws attempted to lure the two men out into the night by making strange noises, intended to excite curiosity or suspicion. This ruse failed, and unable to gain entrance into the house, the band opened fire on a herd of dairy cattle and went their way, leaving behind them dead and wounded cattle.[12]

Even uglier was the raid the outlaws carried out about two weeks later against the brandy distillery of Angus Leach. It appears that a considerable number of adherents to the band took part, including twelve white men. They seized a large stock of brandy; but, despite taking possession of all available vessels including "kegs, pitchers and measures," there were not enough containers. Far too much of the liquor was removed from the scene in the stomachs of the robbers, with evil consequences to the Lowrys and others. Characteristic Lowry discipline and restraint gave way to a disorderly brawl. For no known reason, Leach was attacked and injured, and one Negro employee of Leach, or of a neighbor, was beaten and another received knife wounds. Furthermore the raiders destroyed the brandy they could not carry away or drink.[13]

Perhaps the revelers reasoned that Leach would not alert the authorities, since the distillery was an illegal enterprise. He did not. He alerted his neighbors instead. They shared his loss, as he had provided a profitable outlet for their fruit crops. By the next day, October 4, 1870, a posse of about twenty men was formed, and they began to track a

---

[12] Norment, *The Lowrie History*, 85.
[13] Wilmington *Star*, October 5, 1870.

party of the raiders. The trail led to the house of George Applewhite. No sentries challenged them as they approached; and inside some fifteen men, including a number of the outlaw chiefs as it turned out, were still celebrating their reckless spree. The posse opened fire. The outlaws seized their weapons and returned fire. Then, withdrawing from the house, the band retreated into Long Swamp, firing as they went.[14]

The posse followed them into the swamp. But at sundown the pursuers ran into an ambush; some outlaws had concealed themselves "in a lot of high grass." With one man wounded and another missing, and with night coming on, the posse withdrew to higher ground. At this time they alerted the authorities. Sheriff McMillan was soon on hand with a posse recruited in Laurinburg, in Richmond County, and other places. The next morning an unusual force, consisting of men associated with the illicit brandy industry and the county sheriff with a posse from neighboring counties, advanced into Long Swamp as far as the tall grass where the last skirmish had taken place.[15]

Stephen Davis, the man reported missing, had been last seen at sundown as he had "advanced upon the outlaws in their ambuscade . . . firing on them with his revolver." They found him nearby, mortally wounded; he had "crawled into a creek in the vicinity to wash the blood from his wounds." [16] In the tall grass they found pools of blood where the outlaw chiefs, George Applewhite, Boss Strong, and Henderson Oxendine, all wounded in the first skirmish, had lain waiting for their enemies to walk into the ambush.[17]

But even with the two combined posses, Sheriff McMillan was not yet ready to fight the Lowrys in this swamp, "they

[14] *Ibid.*; Townsend (comp.), *The Swamp Outlaws*, 32.
[15] Wilmington *Star*, October 6, 1870.
[16] *Ibid.*, October 6, 7, 1870.
[17] *Ibid.*, October 6, 1870; Townsend (comp.), *The Swamp Outlaws*, 32.

being so familiar with the location." [18] A glance at the map suggested a more cautious strategy. Long Swamp, later called Jordan's Swamp, forms a cul-de-sac, which was then sealed off from the rest of Lumber River swamp system by a mill pond. There appeared to be no way the Lowrys could escape without coming out on high ground and exposing them-

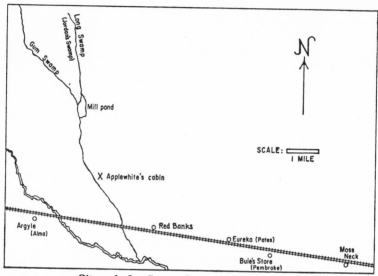

Site of the Long Swamp Engagement

selves. Why not surround the place and then close in on them? The following day, October 6, according to the Wilmington *Journal*, McMillan had one hundred fifty armed men picketing the swamp; the *Star* placed the number at "one hundred resolute men . . . on the war path." [19] Meanwhile the Wadesboro *Argus*, also Conservative, made an impassioned appeal that seemed directed toward the Scots:

[18] Wilmington *Star*, October 7, 1870.
[19] Wilmington *Daily Journal*, October 7, 1870; Wilmington *Star*, October 7, 1870.

Never, perhaps, since the days of Sir William Wallace of Scotland, was there a time when determined resistance, conquest or death was more incumbent on a people than at this time is upon the Robeson people against the Lowrys and Oxendines and other pimps of power and rapine, in the long and broad swamps of Scuffletown . . . . During the last war their deeds are fresh in the minds of all. Since then allied to the party in power, what have they not done? Noonday and midnight have been alike a terror . . . . They have been outlawed but we have little doubt but they have voted on as aforetime, unscathed by justice . . . . Never was the right arm made bare and the sword unsheathed in a better cause.[20]

While the *Argus* was thinking of "the right arm made bare and the sword unsheathed," the *Star* was considering the possibilities of some weapons that had been developed since the days of Sir William Wallace. The editors suggested that "ordinary shotguns and pistols are almost worse than useless . . . . Rifles of long range would be the proper weapons." [21] This idea would indeed become more likely before a month had passed, as Governor William Woods Holden, desperately trying to forestall impeachment by a Conservative legislature, ended the military occupation of Klan-terrorized areas and requested that federal forces be sent to Robeson. On November 12, 1870, an artillery battery was sent to that county to "aid the civil authority." [22]

But the artillerymen arrived too late to try their skill in Long Swamp. On October 8, as the authorities continued to draw tighter the net they had thrown around that area, an excited rider dashed into the village of Moss Neck. While driving a wagon he had sighted a band of about eighteen of the Lowrys. He had cut loose one of his animals and

---

[20] Wilmington *Star*, October 16, 1870, quoting Wadesboro *Argus*.
[21] Wilmington *Star*, October 12, 1870.
[22] Special Order 228, in U.S., War Department, Headquarters of Department of the East (Record Group 94, National Archives).

ridden in to tell the tale.[23] The outlaws had been seen at a point more than ten miles from the place where the band was supposed to be trapped. The sober truth was thus beginning to emerge: the Lowrys had somehow managed to slip through the net around Long Swamp, which like other nets consisted mostly of holes.

Getting out of traps was a feat that the Lowry band would accomplish a number of times. How did they do it? The Reverend D. F. Lowry, son of Calvin and nephew of Henry Berry, has said that on at least one occasion an arrangement was made between members of the band and individuals or groups who were supposed to be taking part in the Lowry hunt. Henry Berry once put on a militia uniform and joined friends in the "hunt" for himself.[24] Sheriff McMillan may have suspected that the Lowrys would use such tactics in the Long Swamp engagement, as shown by his attempts to recruit his posse from Laurinburg, Wilmington, and other places where the band had no influence, although he could have gotten more men on the spot more quickly by calling out the Robeson County regiment. In the end, however, he made use of local people, including "trustworthy and reliable colored men." [25]

The upsurgence of the Lowry conflict in early October, 1870, created a general panic in those areas most directly affected. Most people strove to avoid involvement with either side. Many persons, especially blacks and Indians, fled into South Carolina. In reaction to this migration, the Charleston *News* expressed concern that the "several hundred negroes" who "had left Robeson County . . . within the last few days, for the ostensible purpose of working on

[23] Wilmington *Daily Journal*, October 9, 1870.
[24] Interview with D. F. Lowry, September 3, 1967.
[25] Wilmington *Daily Journal*, October 7, 1870.

railroads in this State . . *may vote for Scott and Ramsier at the approaching election.*" [26] According to the *Star*, the area around Moss Neck was virtually depopulated for a time immediately after the Lowrys, having broken out of the encirclement at Long Swamp, made their appearance in that area. "The citizens in the vicinity of Moss Neck have all fled to Lumberton for protection from the outlaws, they having threatened wholesale butchery of all who came in their way. The number, being about the last of the inhabitants of that locality to come to Lumberton on the train yesterday." [27] A Lumberton Conservative, who made no pretenses to valor, wrote to his brother in Wilmington that "all able-bodied men in town have gone west in pursuit of the outlaws. It is needless to say that I start east by the first train." [28]

But not everybody could escape involvement simply by buying a ticket to Wilmington or by crossing the border into South Carolina. Had Andrew Strong done so, it is almost certain that he would have been outlawed. He was free on bond after having been charged with the King murder. On purely legal grounds the case against him did not appear very strong. The state was still holding John Dial and was still holding to the correctness of a confession which the Indian youth had since repudiated. It did not appear that Strong would be convicted unless the official version of the murder changed.

More threatening to Strong were his kinship ties, especially the involvement of his brother and sister with the outlaws. For legal reasons it was dangerous for him to flee or go into hiding. But in early October, 1870, it was probably

[26] Wilmington *Star*, October 9, 1870, quoting Charleston *News*. Emphasis in the original.
[27] Wilmington *Star*, October 11, 1870.
[28] Quoted in Townsend (comp.), *The Swamp Outlaws*, 57.

more dangerous for him to face the desperate wrath of frustrated bands of Lowry hunters.

It was the Andrew Strongs, the poor but apparently respectable people, who were driving the authorities to distraction. Bound to the Lowrys by kinship or friendship, feeling perhaps that they might someday have to avail themselves of the generosity or the avenging arms of the outlaws, these were the people who kept the band informed of every move the militia made, whose backwoods hospitality provided them with the refuge of a thousand cabins.

Quamdiu, oh! Scuffletown, abutere notru patientia? Mary Norment sighed in a burst of classical erudition ("How long, oh Scuffletown, will you abuse our patience?")[29] Yet for what offense could one convict the ordinary Scuffletonians? The Republican administration had bound itself hand and foot with its concern for such legal niceties. But Sheriff McMillan had gotten his training with the Home Guard. He and the other new county authorities would allow a little more latitude to the volunteer militia in their efforts to uphold authority and protect property.

On the night of October 5, Andrew Strong was aroused from his bed by a commotion outside. He quickly discovered that his cabin was surrounded by a band of armed men. He asked their business, and one of them had replied that "they wanted him to go along with them a little ways." He had no choice except to comply. When he had dressed and gone outside, he found that the whites were holding also another Indian prisoner, Malcolm, or "Make," Sanderson. Sanderson's position in the community was much like that of Strong: apparently a law-abiding citizen but suspected by the authorities because he had married the sister of Calvin and Henderson Oxendine, just as Strong was suspected because his sister Rhoda had married Henry Berry

[29] Norment, *The Lowrie History*, 29.

and his brother Boss, himself an outlaw, was considered the closest friend of the Lowry chief.[30]

But was it a crime to be related by marriage to the outlaws? The two Indians were led off into the night. "Before they had gone a mile one of the party . . . turned to Andrew and said, 'You'll never see morning again.'" Strong asked him "why and what he had done." It was because "he was a d——d nigger and spy for the Lowerys," the militiaman answered. "And so was Sanderson and they had determined to kill them all." Yet the prisoners did live to see another morning. The militiamen, about twenty in number, were unwilling to take the responsibility for executing the two Indians without first locating and getting the explicit approval of certain of their leaders. They were having some trouble contacting the proper authorities. To facilitate guarding the prisoners, while these efforts were being made, the militiamen tied their hands "so tightly that the blood came." To make doubly sure that there would be no escape, they stopped by the house of a white Republican farmer and "got a plow line" so the men could be tied together.[31]

In particular the militiamen seemed eager to get the approval of John Taylor before getting down to the business of forming a firing squad. This concern is puzzling. Taylor was a wealthy man and a prominent citizen, but he was not an officer in the militia. Nor did he hold any official position in the county establishment. Why did the actual commander of this band, Acting Captain Murdoch McLean, a Home Guard veteran, need the approval of this civilian, who had no official civil authority? A possible explanation is that Taylor may have been an officer in the Ku Klux Klan or some other secret society.[32]

[30] Townsend (comp.), *The Swamp Outlaws*, 80.
[31] *Ibid.*, 35.
[32] According to Steve Lowry, when the band captured John Saunders, they found on the person of the prisoner a Ku Klux Klan document, au-

But Taylor was not at home when the militia arrived at his plantation. He had gone over to the mill pond to see the miller, his father-in-law, William C. McNeill. After some consultation it was decided that they would not go there, however, until nightfall, because they did not wish "to put the McNeills in danger of Henry Berry's vengeance." Everyone sat and waited, as messages were exchanged between the militia and some persons not present.[33]

At dusk they brought the prisoners into McNeill's yard. Again everyone waited. Presently Taylor appeared on the piazza, the man who with a word could pronounce death or give back life. The bound men fell on their knees before him and begged for their lives. But in a gesture that seemed to seal their fate, "Taylor drew back with his foot half raised, as if to kick them, and he . . . said . . . 'If all the mulatto [Indian] blood in the country was in you two, and with one kick I could kick it out, I would send you all to hell with my foot.'" The militiamen remained in the McNeill yard long enough to eat their supper, and then marched the prisoners away for execution.[34]

For the place of execution Captain McLean chose the dam of McNeill's Pond. "The shooting party will be Nos. 1, 2, and 3," the commander barked. "Step out!" "Make Sanderson, who appeared to be perfectly resigned, asked if they would give him time to pray." They said they would. While they waited, the Indian, following the custom of evangelical country folk, poured out a fervent prayer, "the woods ringing . . . as he spoke of his wife and children." Finally one of the militiamen "stepped up and hit Sanderson with the butt of a pistol, saying 'Shut up you damn nig-

thorizing the assassination of James Oxendine, Patrick Lowry, and others, signed by "Sandy McIntyre, with John Taylor, witness." New York *Herald*, March 26, 1872.

[33] Townsend (comp.), *The Swamp Outlaws*, 35.

[34] *Ibid.*, 36.

ger! You shan't make any such noise as this if you are going to be shot.' " [35]

But while Sanderson had been commending his soul to God, Andrew Strong had been otherwise engaged. He had discovered some play in the plow line that attached him to Sanderson and was silently straining to loosen it further. On one side of the dam lay McNeill's Pond; on the other was Bear Swamp. Suddenly feeling himself free, the Indian bolted off the dam into the swamp. "They riddled the woods with buckshot and ball"—but Strong had vanished. The other prisoner was executed as planned. They threw his body into the mill race. Two days later a Negro recovered Sanderson's body from the swamp below the mill,[36] and the civil authorities were notified. The new Conservative coroner duly summoned a jury of inquiry and the men gravely contemplated the bullet-riddled remains of Sanderson. They then intoned a verdict that has many echoes in the findings of inquests in that region lying between the Potomac and the Rio Grande: "Death by gunshot wounds at the hands of a person or persons unknown." [37]

But the persons were not unknown to Andrew Strong. He contacted the Reverend James Sinclair, who, though having lost his seat in the North Carolina House to a Conservative opponent, was nevertheless still a local justice of the peace. Sinclair issued a warrant for the arrest of John Taylor and ordered that he be held without bail. However, as Mary Norment reports, "Mr. Taylor's friends (and he had many) were indignant at the idea of such an outrage, and immediately determined to have him released on a writ of habeas corpus." [38] They succeeded. Judge Daniel L. Russell, himself a Republican and considered a friend of the

[35] *Ibid.*
[36] *Ibid.*
[37] Wilmington *Star*, October 12, 1870.
[38] Norment, *The Lowrie History*, 93.

Negro and Indian, set Taylor free on a five-hundred-dollar bond. Judge Russell's brother Thomas had been a member of the militia band that had shot Sanderson.[39]

Now that he was free on bond, Taylor and his friends planned, first, to try to reach a "compromise" with the Indian families aggrieved by Sanderson's death; and, secondly, if that failed, to have Taylor forfeit bond and leave the county. In the months that followed one of Taylor's friends met with Martin Ransom, an Indian serving as the spokesman for Sanderson's kin. But money failed to produce its expected magic in soothing the feelings of the injured families. "After refusing to comply with Mr. Taylor's terms of compromise," Mary Norment writes, "Martin Ransom returned home, and it is supposed held a conference with the outlaws." [40] It was Henry Berry, "slow in speech" and listening much more often than he talked, who now spoke: "Well, I will kill John Taylor." [41]

Meanwhile, having failed to have the murder charge squashed, Taylor began making plans for leaving. His biggest problem seemed to be making some satisfactory arrangement for the disposition of his property.[42] Yet the matter of his personal security had become more serious now that he had failed to reach a settlement with Sanderson's kinsmen.

Fortunately for him, however, Robeson County had been "unusually quiet for some time past." The *Robesonian* suggested that "the presence of U.S. troops has something to do with this state of affairs." [43] Nevertheless caution seemed the best policy; and it was probably for this reason that he decided to move in with his wife's family, the McNeills.

[39] Townsend (comp.), *The Swamp Outlaws*, 37.

[40] Norment, *The Lowrie History*, 94.

[41] Townsend (comp.), *The Swamp Outlaws*, 37; Wilmington *Daily Journal*, October 27, 1871.

[42] Wilmington *Daily Journal*, January 15, 1871.

[43] Wilmington *Star*, January 14, 1871, quoting Lumberton *Robesonian*.

On the opposite side of McNeill's Pond from their house, less than six hundred yards away, was Moss Neck station, where federal troops were camped, one of a number of the detachments scouring the swamps for the Lowry band.

On January 14, 1871, John Taylor and Malcolm McNeill, his brother-in-law, rose from the breakfast table, saying that they were going over to Moss Neck station. They were leisurely walking along the mill dam, "talking of business matters," as they approached the spot where Sanderson had fallen before the firing squad three months before. "About two hundred yards from the Federal camp and in sight of one of the soldiers," there was suddenly a shattering blast that scorched McNeill's face. Taylor crumpled instantly dead at his feet, shot through the head. McNeill turned, and there on the dam, "not eight feet from him," stood Henry Berry Lowry. Lowry calmly removed a pistol and fifty dollars from Taylor's pockets, "drew the body to the place where he had stood when he fired, so as to be out of sight from the depot," and disappeared into Bear Swamp below the dam.[44]

Within five minutes the sergeant in charge of the squad at the depot was on the spot, and started in pursuit of the murderers, who he tracked for a half mile down the creek, where they crossed Mr. McNeill's plantation and made off through the pine woods . . . . But here the trail was soon lost, and the soldiers, not having any dogs with them, were obliged to give up the attempt. They returned to Moss Neck and immediately dispatched a request to the officer commanding the troop at Lumberton for assistance. This was promptly accorded, the officer hurrying forward at once with all at his command.[45]

Sheriff McMillan and a posse of twenty joined the federal troops in the search, but with no better luck.[46]

[44] Wilmington *Daily Journal*, January 15, 1871.
[45] *Ibid.*
[46] Wilmington *Carolina Farmer and Weekly Star*, January 27, 1871, quoting Lumberton *Robesonian*.

The Conservative press, which had all but ignored the killing of Sanderson, was electrified by the death of Taylor. The Lumberton *Robesonian,* disheartened, entertained doubts as to the possibility of suppressing the outlaws:

When it is known that these men are half Indian, possessing all the characteristics of courage, undying resentment, disregard of danger and death, together with the caution, coolness, and skill in concealment and evading pursuit, that distinguishes that race; when it is known also, that they occupy an area of country . . . covered with immense bays and swamps, many of them never penetrated by a white man, . . . it will not be difficult to understand something of the disadvantages under which the good citizens of this unfortunate community are laboring . . . . Is there no remedy? . . . Alas! It seems not.[47]

The Wilmington *Journal,* on the other hand, further from the scene and edited for a time by the state leader of the Ku Klux Klan, seemed to favor a general campaign of reprisals against Indians: "We know the officer in command of the United States troops at Lumberton will do all he can, but he is powerless in a strange country without guides and without the sympathy and aid of every citizen. . . . If one company is insufficient, let a regiment be sent. If a regiment cannot do the work, let us have a brigade, and let the Scuffletown district be burned and devastated until not even a dry twig remains rather than that the entire county suffer as it has done." [48]

But it soon became apparent that the officers in charge of the federal units did not share the point of view of the *Journal.* They were ultimately responsible to a Republican governor and a Republican national administration. They held firmly that in the campaign against the outlaws, the

[47] *Ibid.*
[48] Wilmington *Daily Journal,* January 15, 1871.

legal rights of other Scuffletonians must be observed. Because of this policy, the more enthusiastic Lowry hunters at certain times began to look on the federal troops as a liability, hampering them in their efforts to deal with the Indians. Yet when a Conservative clamor arose to remove one United States unit, a general wrote to the officer in command of federal troops in Robeson that "no matter what the citizens may say to Sheriff McMillan about the guard at Harper's Ferry it will not be withdrawn so long as I apprehend that a raid may be made on Scuffletown." [49]

The federal occupation notwithstanding, the main thrust of the anti-Lowry campaign continued to come, as it had from the beginning, from local Conservative groups, now represented by the sheriff's posse and the volunteer militia bands, of which one of the most energetic was that associated with Murdoch McLean. McLean had been a member of the Home Guard detachment that had shot Allen and William Lowry, and it had been he who had given the command "Fire!" when Malcolm Sanderson was killed. And in the months that followed Sanderson's death, as McLean led his band through the swamps in pursuit of the Lowrys, the authorities seemed to have forgotten that this execution had been carried out without the slightest legal justification. But Henry Berry had not forgotten.

On the early morning of July 17 at the McLean plantation, Murdoch McLean, his guest Archy McCallum, who was also a prominent figure in the anti-Lowry campaign, and Murdoch's younger brother Hugh climbed into a buggy and started toward the village of Shoe Heel, a mile and a quarter away. As the road entered a little grove of trees, a voice cried, "Halt!" The three turned to look, and there

[49] General Charles Hale Morgan to Captain Evan Thomas, February 17, 1871, in U.S., War Department, Records of the Army Commands, Post of Lumberton (Record Group 393, National Archives).

by the road, the men Murdoch McLean had so long sought were waiting for him.[50]

The Indians fired, killing the two McLeans instantly. Mc-Callum leaped from the buggy and fled into Shoe Heel, escaping with a few flesh wounds. The Lowrys tied the McLean horse to a tree, and Henry Berry sent a child to inform Mrs. McLean of the death of her sons. As a cart bore their bodies into the McLean yard, the anguished mother cried, "My poor innocent Hugh who never did anyone harm." [51] Why indeed Hugh, a teen-aged youth whose involvement with the conflict had probably never been greater than on this morning when he had undertaken to drive his brother and a guest to catch a train in Shoe Heel? The bullet that killed Hugh McLean probably had been intended for Archy McCallum.

In a short while Sheriff McMillan was at the McLean place with a hundred fifty men. They tracked the outlaws as far as the W. A. Sellers plantation, where they seemed to have crossed the Lumber River. But there the trail was lost. Once again the Lowrys had struck, then vanished.[52]

[50] Wilmington *Daily Journal*, July 19, 1871.

[51] *Ibid.*

[52] *Ibid.*; Fayetteville *Eagle*, July 20, 1871; undated, unidentified news-paper clipping enclosed in Morgan to Adjutant General, July 18, 1871, in U.S., War Department, Records of the Adjutant General's Office (Record Group 94, National Archives).

7 · "Slay Them Without Accusation of Any Crime"

"IF WE WERE THE citizens" of Robeson County, the *Star* exclaimed in October, 1870, "we should feel pretty well satisfied that there is no law there, and would favor Lynch law, extermination, tomahawking, anything else that would prove effective in putting to death Henry Berry Lowry and his band of outlaws." [1] In practice this view meant broadening the campaign against the outlaws into general war on the Scuffletonians, the folk who made possible the bold deeds of the Lowrys. Even the Republican governor, Holden, seemed to be moving in this direction. "It is a somewhat singular coincidence," the *Journal* noted with pleasure, "that our vigilant Governor should have simultaneously ascertained that there was peace in Caswell and Alamance," where troops were being used against the Klan, "and war in Robeson." [2]

Captain Evan Thomas, the officer in charge of the federal units that arrived in Robeson shortly after the governor had ascertained war there, shared, or was converted to, the view that the outlaws were out of reach so long as the Scuffletonians remained defiant. "The Lowrys have almost as many friends as enemies," he reported. Their friends supply them with "information of any expedition against them and resist the

[1] Wilmington *Star*, October 15, 1870.
[2] Wilmington *Daily Journal*, November 13, 1871.

civil law themselves. Taxes cannot be collected . . . nor warrants served on any of the inhabitants of this settlement." [3] Thomas thought that the commander should therefore "have power to arrest whom he pleases on suspicion. The families of the robbers ought at least be arrested"; and added that "under restrictions against infringements under civil laws as I am . . . now, I . . . can do very little toward ridding the county of the robbers and murderers." [4] Thomas, however, was denied the power to set aside civil law; and, on the contrary, he was ordered to confine himself to helping the civil authorities to uphold that law.[5] Thus federal troops may have made it easier for the local authorities to collect taxes and serve warrants. But the partisans of "Lynch law" and "tomahawking" sometimes looked upon the occupation forces as an obstacle in their efforts to subdue the Scuffletonians.

The most vigorous Lowry hunters continued to be the posses organized by the sheriff and various private bands. It was probably for this reason that the Conservative legislature—which to a great extent owed its composition to the frequency with which the Ku Klux Klan had practiced homicide in the Piedmont region during the past spring and summer—now proceeded to make that activity more profitable in Robeson County. The legislature offered two thousand dollars for the "delivery, dead or alive" of Henry Berry as well as one thousand dollars each for Stephen Lowry, Thomas Lowry, Boss Strong, Henderson Oxendine,

[3] Captain Evan Thomas to Adjutant General, December 30, 1870, in U.S., War Department, Records of the Adjutant General's Office (Record Group 94, National Archives).

[4] Quoted in Adjutant General to Thomas, December 1, 1870, in U.S., War Department, Records of the Adjutant General's Office (Record Group 94, National Archives).

[5] *Ibid.*

and George Applewhite.[6] The following legislature, 1871–72, even more generous, raised the total rewards to twelve thousand for Henry Berry plus six thousand for each of the other outlaws—except Andrew Strong, a newcomer to the list, who was worth only five thousand to the successful manhunter since no appropriation had been made for him the previous year.[7] In addition to these sums, the Robeson County board of county commissioners was offering a purse of several hundred dollars for each of the outlaws.[8]

If the legislators and county commissioners were demonstrating a marked liberality in offering rewards, the members of the Lowry band showed themselves to be of comparable mind. They offered one thousand dollars for the head of Angus McLean, a county commissioner, in 1870 and two hundred dollars each for a list of individuals they had declared "outlaws" in 1872,[9] their more modest awards resulting from the limitations of their resources rather than from a more miserly spirit. It became thus at least theoretically possible for a hunter who was enterprising and talented to have received awards amounting to a thousand or more dollars by delivering the carcasses of certain of his colleagues to the Lowrys and then to have earned well over forty thousand by bagging a half-dozen Lowrys for the authorities.

With such highly prized game stalking the swamplands along the Lumber River, it is not surprising that sportsmen were attracted from afar. A Wilmington paper published, for example, a letter from "one Abbott, formerly known as Jack Allen," who in New York was "gathering together some thirty followers, for an expedition to capture or kill Lowrey and his gang, and secure the large reward offered":

[6] N.C., *Public Laws, 1870-1871*, Chap. 68.
[7] N.C., *Public Laws, 1871-1872*, Chap. 122.
[8] Wilmington *Star*, November 22, 1870.
[9] *Ibid.*, September 19, 1872; Wilmington *Daily Journal*, November 29, 1870.

New York
March 19, 1872

Sir

Would you pleese to inform Me if Burry Lowery and his Band are yet on the war path if so i propose to offer my Services to the State as i know them all and would only like to get a chance at the Black Devils please send me a copy of your paper if the State will except me i will in site of 2 weeks have the Scalps of those NC out laws good lick to you i am Jack Allen No. 60. New chamBer New York city Street.[10]

Constructing turkey blinds was an old art along the Lumber River. As far back as anyone could remember, on rare occasions a blind was built on a path frequented by an enemy; an ambush was a primitive remedy for redressing injury to one's person or family. But now, thanks to the legislature and the Lowry band, this ancient practice was finding a feverish new life. Few persons so engaged would have conceded that they were seeking blood money. The justifications they offered rather were the traditional ones. Yet there can be little doubt that in a region where most people were desperately poor, the glittering prizes did much to open old wounds and to inflict new ones.

The richest bounty that the state offered seemed to have slipped narrowly through the fingers of some Lowry-hunters in January, 1871. On the Old Stage Road, twelve miles south of Fayetteville, they stopped a buggy headed in the direction of Lumberton. They required the occupants, two Indian men, to identify themselves and to state their business. One of the men answered that he was Sinclair Locklear; the man beside him was his brother John. They were on their way to Marion, South Carolina, where they would do farm work for one J. L. Smith. Everything seemed in order, and the buggy was allowed to move on. But before the horse could

[10] Wilmington *Daily Journal*, March 29, 1872.

take many steps, the bounty hunters, perhaps noting belatedly that the men appeared to be armed, again called on the Indians to halt. This time Sinclair Locklear leaped "from the buggy and prepared for a fight, but was quickly surrounded and disarmed." But meantime, while Locklear was being subdued and taken prisoner, the other man had lashed his horse and dashed forward "with all speed." Further down the road they found the spot, near a thick patch of woods, where he had "taken his horse from the buggy and galloped off through the woods." [11]

On the person of their prisoner and in the abandoned buggy, they found eighty-three dollars, "3 double-barrelled guns and 4 repeating pistols." Locklear, still insisting that the other man was his brother, was placed in the Fayetteville jail "on charge of robbery and being suspicioned [sic] as one of the . . . outlaws." A local paper reported, "It is now believed on good and direct authority that the one who escaped was Henry Berry Lowry." [12]

The bounty hunters had many frustrating encounters with the elusive outlaws, and sometimes their pent-up rage seemed to have burst upon an individual whose hide could bring them no profit. The Negro waiter in the Lumberton hotel told a northern newspaperman "in the presence of several white men of the town" that " 'they say they go up to Scuffletown to hunt Lowery; but I never knew them to go there without killing some innocent person.' " [13]

It has been suggested also that people who do not seem to have been closely connected with the Lowrys sometimes suffered because the "Robeson County Ku Klux Klan seldom wore disguises, the Lowery pretext covering all of their operations." [14] In particular, although the evidence

[11] Fayetteville *Eagle*, January 12, 1871.
[12] *Ibid.*
[13] Townsend (comp.), *The Swamp Outlaws*, 34.
[14] *Ibid.*, 33.

is contradictory, it appears that the men who killed Benjamin Bethea may have had motives other than capturing or killing outlaws. In the first place, Bethea was a black; and although a number of blacks and whites supported the Lowrys, they were generally less closely linked than were the Scuffletonians. Secondly, unlike the Lowrys, Bethea still had faith in the Republican Party. He probably made more enemies among the bounty hunters because of his political activities, which were a matter of record, than for any support he may have given the outlaws, which was a matter of speculation. "A violent radical," Bethea "was used by the republican politicians to disseminate their doctrines and keep the color . . . united in votes and sentiment," explained a contemporary writer. "He was what is called a praying politician, apt to be frenzied and loud in prayer and exhort wildly, and has cunning enough to [b]ring politics and the wrongs of the colored people into his prayers, so that he might be said to pray the whole ticket." [15]

According to the Reverend James Sinclair, on Friday, February 17, 1871, "Sheriff McMillan . . . ordered a Posse Comitatus to accompany him to hunt up the outlaws. . . . A portion of this posse was composed of mounted young men who roamed at large through the settlement without any responsible head to guide them. Filled with liquor and animosity against the colored race, they came to the house of one Benjamin Bethea, a freedman of good character, about dark on Saturday evening." [16] A correspondent for the New York *Herald*, however, broadly hinting that the Lowry hunt was being used in this case as the legal cover for a foray by a party of the Ku Klux Klan, says that the detachment, at the outset at least, did indeed have a "responsible head."

[15] *Ibid.*
[16] James Sinclair to Tod Caldwell, February 23, 1871, in Governors' Papers, North Carolina Department of Archives and History, Raleigh.

It was commanded by Robert Chaffin, county coroner, and numbered eighteen men. As they approached the Bethea cabin, "the proposition was sprung to take him out and kill him." [17] This proposal precipitated a debate.

Their leader was opposed. Coroner Chaffin's principal official duty, no small one in Robeson County, was to hold inquests over the bodies of persons who had died by violent or suspicious means. If he took part in the project that had been proposed, he would undoubtedly have felt some awkwardness when, in a few days, he would get to that part of his official ritual in which he recited, "Death by gunshot wounds at the hands of a person or persons unknown." But there were also others who did not like the idea. "The McQueens, and some of the more prudent turned back, afraid of Judge Russell's bench warrants." Malcolm McNeill, who the previous November had been captured and released by Henry Berry, took command of the ten men remaining, and together they rode on to Benjamin Bethea's cabin.[18]

McNeill rapped on the door. When Bethea appeared, he said, "Come out here! We want you!" Bethea, an uneducated farm laborer but aware of the political currents in the county, looked his visitors over, turned to his wife, and said, "Old woman I specs theys gwine to kill me. Mebbe I'll never come back no mo'." "Get your hat!" McNeill ordered. The next moments seemed to confirm Bethea's gloomy prediction. The men lifted him bodily out of the shanty and placed him on a horse. The yard was full of horse tracks. But nowhere to be seen were Bethea's "well known foot traces." [19]

Someone, perhaps his wife or some other member of their large family, alerted Henry Berry's men, undoubtedly feeling

[17] Townsend (comp.), *The Swamp Outlaws*, 33.
[18] *Ibid.*
[19] *Ibid.*

that this might serve a more useful purpose than notifying Sheriff McMillan and Coroner Chaffin. When the Lowrys located Bethea in a swamp four miles away, he was already dead. From an examination of his body it was apparent that he had been severely beaten before being shot.[20]

The condition of Bethea's body gave weight to an interpretation of the killing which appeared in the Wilmington *Post*, a Republican paper. Although the *Post* characterized the killers as a "band of ku klux scoundrels," it did not allege, as did the *Herald* correspondent, that they had already decided to kill him before they arrived. They shot him, the *Post* says, because "the poor man could give them no information" about Henry Berry. The lash marks on Bethea's body are perhaps testimony that the Chaffin-McNeill band had indeed been hunting Lowrys and that the black man could not or would not help them. After Henry Berry had examined Bethea's body, it was turned over to Coroner Chaffin, and the federal commander was notified.[21] As they also had done following the Sanderson murder, the Lowrys now waited to give the authorities a chance to demonstrate what would pass for official justice in Robeson County.

The Reverend James Sinclair, whom the *Journal*, with some show of partisan fervor, identified for its readers as "that dirty tool of the dirtiest portion of the dirty Radicals," acting in his capacity of justice of the peace, issued warrants for the arrest of nine members of what another Conservative paper described as "a party of young men . . . of the highest respectability who were known to have been in the neighbor-

[20] Wilmington *Carolina Farmer and Weekly Star*, March 24, 1871.
[21] Wilmington *Post*, March 31, 1875; Wilmington *Carolina Farmer and Weekly Star*, March 24, 1871; Thomas to Morgan, February 25, 1871, in U.S., War Department, Records of the Army Commands, Post of Lumberton (Record Group 393, National Archives).

hood on the night of the murder in search of the outlaws." [22]

When the case came before the grand jury, however, now firmly Conservative, that body was said to have "carefully sifted the matter and failed to find a true bill, there not being any evidence whatever, of a nature sufficient to justify the detention of any of them for trial." [23] But Judge Russell "entered a protest against the action of the jury, and issued a bench warrant for the arrest of the parties. Alarmed at the action of the court and fearing the result of a trial under the circumstances, they fled the state, and the sheriff, after a diligent search," the *Star* assured its readers, "returned the warrant with the endorsement 'not to be found,' whereupon Judge Russell issued a proclamation of outlawry against the young men, enjoining the Sheriff and all good citizens to take them *dead* or *alive*." [24] On paper at least, Henry Berry now had more enemies who had been outlawed than he had friends.

In the month following the Bethea killing, Malcolm Mc-Neill and Faulk Floyde—both under indictment for the murder but neither greatly disturbed by the "diligent search" that Sheriff McMillan was supposed to be making for them —entered into an "agreement or compact" with nine other men of like mind. "Arming themselves with navy revolvers, Spencer, Henry and Winchester guns," Mary Norment reports, they "went forth to hunt the outlaws in their swampy retreats . . . , determined to kill or be killed." [25]

These men recognized some of the weaknesses of previous Lowry hunts. It was becoming obvious, as the Fayetteville *Eagle* noted, that a "parade of soldiers or open hasty hunt by a sheriff and his posse . . . are only so many ridiculous

[22] Wilmington *Daily Journal*, March 15, 1871; Wilmington *Star*, September 19, 1873.
[23] Wilmington *Daily Journal*, March 15, 1871.
[24] Wilmington *Star*, September 19, 1872.
[25] Norment, *The Lowrie History*, 103.

and fruitless attempts at capture." [26] On the night of Bethea's death, for example, while Sheriff McMillan was busy with a large posse from Lumberton combing the swamps of the Scuffletown area, the Lowry band made an appearance within four miles of Lumberton. But by the time the sheriff's detachments had returned from the Lowry hunt, the Indians had disappeared.[27]

The eleven young men who formed the "compact," however, planned to use different tactics. Shortly before he was exposed and killed, the undercover agent, John Saunders, had revealed to the authorities—and perhaps to Malcolm McNeill and others—that certain of the outlaws returned to their homes on occasion for short visits with their families. A turkey blind built secretly near one of these houses and occupied by a small band seemed the most likely way to bag a Lowry with a rich prize on his head. But approaching one of these houses without being observed was no easy task. To avoid the countless eyes which saw for the Lowrys, one had to be well acquainted with the footpaths and trails of the area. It was probably while engaging in an exploratory foray that on April 8, 1871, as Mary Norment relates, "they saw at a distance the whole outlaw gang who, on perceiving them, made off precipitately into the low ground of the Lumber River." They did not follow.[28]

Nevertheless, on the night of April 15, they met "at the store of A and W McQueen." But "owing to sickness and other causes only five of them reported"—two McKays and three McCallums.[29] One of the "other causes" for absences may have been that Faulk Floyde and Malcolm McNeill

[26] Fayetteville *Eagle*, February 16, 1871.

[27] Thomas to Morgan, February 25, 1871, in U.S., War Department, Records of the Army Commands, Post of Lumberton (Record Group 393, National Archives).

[28] Norment, *The Lowrie History*, 104.

[29] *Ibid.*

had recently been proclaimed outlaws by Judge Russell; and, although it is debatable whether this fact would have caused them any difficulty with the sheriff, it might well have resulted in their being shot with legal impunity by some otherwise peaceful Scuffletonian farmer. The five decided that the moment was favorable to attempt an ambush of George Applewhite. It was Saturday night. On Sunday the Negro outlaw might attempt to visit his family. They were able to reach the Applewhite cabin without a mishap, and apparently without having been observed. They concealed themselves in a juniper thicket on a path leading to the house. Then, hour after hour, they waited.[30]

The previous October Applewhite had been reported dead. In tracking him into Long Swamp, the sheriff's posse had found pools of blood that he and two other wounded outlaws had left, and he was supposed to have died from his wounds. There were even reports of a strange ceremony in the overarching gloom of Long Swamp in which his outlaw comrades had honored his memory. "We learn," said the *Star*, "that the gang of desperadoes appeared at the place where Applewhite's body was found, on last Monday morning, and fired off about one hundred guns, as if in defiance, and to show that though one of their number had been slain there was still plenty left to continue the outrages on the defenseless people and to avenge his death." [31] But shortly after this splendid memorial was reported, Applewhite made one of his sudden and seemingly miraculous appearances, his wounds having healed.

Throughout the night and on into the day following, the bounty hunters lurked in the juniper thicket, always with a sharp eye out for the appearance of that black man, whose lifeless carcass might bring a greater sum in a moment than

[30] *Ibid.*
[31] Wilmington *Star*, October 20, 1870.

a black man's toil would bring in a decade.[32] Then sometime toward midafternoon they caught sight of their man. He was coming down the path toward them, alone! But when he got within twenty feet of them he saw the trap and started to run back. They fired "and brought him down," hit in the neck. He "got up and [began] to run again." Once more the manhunters fired "and brought him down again." This time they saw him reel as he fell, shot in the back. "But, notwithstanding the severe wounds he had received, he turned on his pursuers, fired his double barrel gun at them." They saw him crawling near the edge of the swamp.[33]

"Fearing the entire outlaw gang near at hand," and satisfied, no doubt, that a man who had sustained such wounds could not crawl far, the party fled from the spot and hurried to notify Sheriff McMillan where Applewhite's body could be found. The sheriff elected not to return to the place until morning. He assembled a posse and Coroner Chaffin brought along a jury of inquest. However, upon reaching the spot, they found not Applewhite's body, but rather the outlaw's children, all very much alive. They "told the Sheriff that their father said he had been struck by two balls in the mouth but had spit them out." [34] Nevertheless "copious signs of blood and other evidence of a deadly fray, were very apparent. The party followed . . . the traces of blood for some two or three hundred yards." [35] Nevertheless the posse "could obtain no clue as to his whereabouts, or as to whether he was living or dead. His wife would give no information on the subject." [36]

[32] Norment, The Lowrie History, 104.
[33] Wilmington Star, April 20, 1871; Norment, The Lowrie History, 104.
[34] Wilmington Daily Journal, April 21, 1871.
[35] Ibid., April 20, 1871.
[36] Wilmington Star, April 20, 1871.

Until July, 1871, the authorities did not bother the wives of outlaws. But in this instance, standing by Mrs. Applewhite was one of her brothers, Forney Oxendine. The only incriminating thing about this young man was that his name was Oxendine and that he was her brother. Nevertheless he was placed under arrest. Later he was charged with possession of stolen property. The basis for this charge was that one of the jurors, who had come to take part in the inquest over Applewhite's body, alleged that the visitor had appeared to be "in charge of" the house of his sister and brother-in-law, in which outlaw booty had been found.[37]

Sheriff McMillan took one other action which may have been a response to Mrs. Applewhite's unwillingness to give information about her husband. He located John Sinclair, a white man who owned the cabin in which the Applewhites lived, and warned him that if the family were "not out of it in two days he would arrest him (Sinclair) as an accomplice of the outlaws, and that he was strongly tempted to do so anyhow." [38]

Was it possible that the awe-inspiring Applewhite had once again escaped with his life? Or had the outlaws spirited away his body in order to cheat one band of manhunters of their prize, and thus avoid whetting the appetites of the others? On April 17, a *Journal* correspondent wrote that "George Applewhite was killed last night near Red Banks. A party of citizens attempted his capture which he resisted, fighting to the last." [39] But three days later the same paper reported that "Applewhite was severely, but, it is feared, not

<hr />

[37] *State v. Forney* alias *Pop Oxendine*, Superior Court of Robeson County, Fall Term, 1871, Henry Berry Lowry Papers, North Carolina Department of Archives and History, Raleigh.

[38] Wilmington *Star*, April 20, 1871.

[39] Fayetteville *Eagle*, April 20, 1871, quoting Wilmington *Weekly Journal*, April 18, 1871.

mortally wounded, and has made his escape into the swamp." [40]

A swamp is an inhospitable place for a gravely wounded man. If indeed the outlaw were still alive, somewhere—in the innumerable cabins in the valley of the Lumber or of the Little Pee Dee—he needed to have found the care of sympathetic hands, hands that might be black, white, or brown. Yet nine days later, when Sheriff McMillan located him, it was at a spot that seemed unlikely because of its very vulnerability. He was at the cabin that was ostensibly the home of Henry Berry Lowry.

Sheriff McMillan obviously did not expect to find Applewhite or anyone of importance there. If he had, he surely would have come with a full posse, instead of the band of nine men that he had called out in the early morning of April 26, 1871. Yet there were clear advantages to a small band: unlike the usual noisy military parades, a small squad could occasionally approach the outlaws; and, should they bag one, the shares of the bounty would be large.

Moving inconspicuously along the southern fringe of Back Swamp in the vicinity of the Henry Berry cabin, on this April morning, they were surprised by the sound of a banjo. Henry Berry's love of music was well known. Perhaps he had gotten together with his family at their old home. Stealthily the sheriff's party crept through the thicket. When they drew near the tiny clearing in which the cabin stood, they paused until they had spotted the lookout. It was Boss Strong. The Indian youth was "walking watchfully, armed with a two-barrelled gun and pistols." Further on, in the little clearing just before the house, the wounded Applewhite sat taking the spring air. Inside the cabin they could

<hr>

[40] Wilmington *Daily Journal*, April 20, 1871.

see Henry Berry, Rhoda, and their three children. He was playing the banjo.[41]

These were the only persons that McMillan and his men could see. Were there perhaps others in the cabin or in the surrounding thicket? With a respectable fortune in bounties before them, the sheriff's party, after a whispered consultation, decided to venture an attack. Their plan was to "fire on Boss Strong and then the others could be shot as they would attempt to escape, or the house [could] be taken by storm . . . . A deliberate shot was fired by the party, but as Strong was moving, it failed to hit him. Several shots were fired by the party, and about at the same instant, Strong dropped to the ground and crawled quickly around and into the house, as did Applewhite, when the robbers returned fire through the cracks of the house." [42]

The skirmish appeared to have reached a stalemate. For the attackers to storm the house, and thus expose themselves to proverbial Lowry marksmanship as they rushed across the clearing, no longer seemed a good tactic. On the other hand, it appeared that the Lowrys could not escape from the cabin without dangerously exposing themselves in the clearing. Thus the outcome of the conflict would quite likely be decided when one side or the other secured the help of friends. In this particular neighborhood it is possible that the sound of a gun battle on Back Swamp was the only signal required to alert the friends of Lowry, but if the deadlock was to be broken in favor of the sheriff, he would have to send for reinforcements. Leaving eight men to keep the cabin under fire and to watch the clearing, the sheriff took Frank McKay with him to recruit or summon a posse.[43]

[41] Fayetteville *Eagle*, May 4, 1871.
[42] *Ibid.*
[43] *Ibid.*

If McMillan had had some choice in the matter, he would not have picked the vicinity of Back Swamp to recruit a band of deputies. White people were not plentiful and Conservatives even less so. He stopped by Hugh G. Inman's place and drafted his two boys, Giles and Robert. The Inmans were white Republicans who had always been at least on speaking terms with the Lowrys. But could he hope for a posse made up of the kind of racists who had carried off Benjamin Bethea?

Somewhere around Buie's Store or Red Banks they recruited or summoned a man named Thompson, who had just moved in from Bladen County, and one other. McMillan put these four men under the command of the seasoned Lowry-hunter McKay and sent them back to reinforce the siege of the Henry Berry cabin. Meanwhile the sheriff caught the westbound train, which had just come in, as far as Shoe Heel, a community in which there was some heartwarming duplication of membership between the McCallum clan and the Ku Klux Klan and where it was fairly easy to recruit large and reliable posses.[44]

In a remarkably short time Sheriff McMillan had assembled a respectable posse of fifteen or more men, and they rapidly covered the twelve miles between Shoe Heel and the scene of the skirmish. They could well expect that when they arrived, the party holding the outlaws at bay would have increased to thirteen men, since there had been plenty of time for Frank McKay to have joined them with the recruits from Buie's Store and Red Banks. With Shoe Heel alerted, they could also be sure that there were as many militiamen and federal soldiers on the way as seemed to be needed.[45]

[44] *Ibid.*; Wilmington *Daily Journal*, April 28, 1871; Wilmington *Star*, April 28, 1871; Lumberton *Robesonian*, February 26, 1951, quoting Lumberton *Robesonian*, December 11, 1919; Norment, *The Lowrie History*, 111.
[45] The account which follows is based on reports in the Wilmington

But, upon coming within a short distance of the Lowry place, where they should have already been hearing some gunfire, they received a rude jolt: coming down the road to meet them was the other posse. The men were visibly shaken. Three of their companions they were carrying—one dead, two gravely wounded. These men related a terrible tale.

The eight men that Sheriff McMillan had left at the Lowry cabin had continued to exchange volleys with the outlaws, fire that seemed to inflict no injuries on either side, but nevertheless served to keep their enemies securely pinned while help was on the way. Momentarily they expected McKay to arrive with some recruits, and the sheriff still later with a sizable posse. Yet at about eleven-thirty the outlaws stopped returning their fire. It was hardly possible that the defenders were all dead. Perhaps it was a ruse or maybe they needed to use their ammunition more sparingly. The besieging party remained vigilant and continued to pour lead into the cabin. But suddenly they were surprised to hear a barrage of gunfire down in Back Swamp, perhaps a mile distant.

It was then that they grasped the actual situation: there was absolutely no one in this cabin on which they had so generously been expending powder and ball! They checked in the cabin and indeed the Lowrys had disappeared. Then, perhaps guessing that the McKay party was in trouble, they ran in the direction of the gunfire they had just heard. Down in the swamp they found McKay lying wounded. One of the recruits was also wounded and another lay dead.

Sheriff McMillan was soon there. All told, he had at least twenty-five able-bodied men, and more on the way. But there were some uncertainties in the situation that had not been apparent a short while before: Lowry appeared to have

---

Daily Journal, April 28, 1871, the Wilmington *Star,* April 28, 1871, and the Fayetteville *Eagle,* May 4, 1871.

gotten at least seven people out of the cabin in broad daylight without being seen. Of these, certainly one had been
wounded and three had been his children—Sally Ann, four
years old; Henry Delany, two; and Neelyanne, no more than
a few months.[46] Also, of the three or four places where
one might have crossed Back Swamp, how had he known
where to prepare an ambush that would take McKay? It
was not clear either what had happened to the outlaws after
they fired their last barrage. Perhaps these uncertainties combined to make it appear that Back Swamp might be an
inhospitable place to spend the oncoming night. So "after
consulting fully, it was thought a little delay and organization would be more successful than immediate pursuit, and
all dispersed for the present." [47]

How had the Lowrys in fact gotten out of the cabin? A
short time before the skirmish of April 26, federal officers
and soldiers had raided the Henry Berry place. Their search
had revealed "a trap . . . concealed in the floor, the hinges
hidden or mortised beneath. This trap afforded admission
to a sort of mine or covered way, which ran under the surface about sixty yards to the swamp" [48] "through which he
had so often made his escape." The "officers and soldiers . . .
sacked his house and dug up the underground passage leading from it." [49]

For this reason, in April, 1871, the authorities did not believe that the Lowry cabin was a tenable refuge for Henry
Berry or any of his important lieutenants. When Sheriff
McMillan had visited the cabin, therefore, he had a squad
of only nine men. But now the Lowrys had once again mys-
teriously escaped from the same cabin. Consequently a

[46] New York *Herald*, March 26, 1872.
[47] Fayetteville *Eagle*, May 4, 1871.
[48] Townsend (comp.), *The Swamp Outlaws*, 58.
[49] *Roanoke News* (Weldon, N.C.), May 28, 1873, quoting Raleigh
News, quoting Lumberton *Robesonian*.

thorough investigation was held, which revealed "a small false closet or buttery by the chimney, acting as a concealed door." Because they had only eight men watching the house, the members of the sheriff's posse had concentrated their attention on the windows and doors of the three sides with possible exits. But meanwhile, beside the chimney on the lightly guarded and apparently blind south wall, a secret door had opened and the Lowrys had stolen away into the swamp. It was recognized at the time that had McMillan had an extra squad, this particular Lowry ruse would not have worked.[50] But there still would have been a question whether, with an extra squad, he could have approached the place undetected.

How was Henry Berry able, within a half-hour of escaping from the cabin, to prepare an ambush on the route that McKay was going to choose across Back Swamp? If the men who ambushed the McKay party were indeed the same ones who thirty minutes before had been defending the Lowry cabin, it is possible that Henry Berry shrewdly guessed what his enemies were planning and by chance picked the route that they would use. What appears more likely, however, is that the outlaw chief acted upon information received by way of the Back Swamp "grapevine telegraph." The entire neighborhood had been alerted since nine. And when Sheriff McMillan and McKay went from house to house looking for likely recruits, they could not avoid advertising their plans. The only thing remaining for the friends of the Lowrys to do was to figure out the route that the posse would probably take and get word to Henry Berry.

In any event, Frank McKay and his recruits had been hurrying along to take part in the siege of the Lowry cabin. They had gotten as far as the place where their path led down into Back Swamp. But there, in the cool shadows

[50] Fayetteville *Eagle*, May 4, 1871.

under heavy foliage, lurking men had been expecting them. In a single barrage of gunfire, three of their number were cut down. When the smoke had cleared, Giles Inman, an eighteen-year-old recruit from a Republican family, lay dead. A few days later, Henry Berry contacted Hugh G. Inman, the boy's father, to tell him that he was sorry he had killed his son Giles.[51]

[51] Norment, *The Lowrie History*, 112.

8 · The Lion in His Nature

IN 1872 SOME INDIANS from the Great Plains may have volunteered their services to the Lowry band. The Lowrys, however, would probably have had some questions as to the potential value of these particular recruits from the West. At that time much of North Carolina was being scandalized by the Indians who performed in Deerfoot and Pierce's Wild West Show. "I have witnessed many performances, but never one so disgraceful," exclaimed an indignant "victim" in a letter to the *Star*. "I would respectfully warn the ladies, particularly, to beware of them. I give this hint knowing that none of our respectable ladies, after this intimation of the character of the concern, will attend." [1]

But many people were even more shocked by some of the unscheduled performances that these uprooted and commercially exploited circus Indians were said to have rendered on occasions in hotels and on trains. At Rich's Hotel in Laurinburg they were reported to have "stolen everything they could lay hands on." And when their train passed through Lilesville the following Saturday night, they were "all drunk and yelling like demons. We learn that two of the Indians belonging to the Company deserted at Shoe Heel and it is reported that they expressed the intention of joining the outlaws in the swamps of Robeson County." [2]

---

[1] Wilmington *Star*, August 13, 1872.
[2] *Ibid.*

There were other reports suggesting that the Lowry band had a sufficiently far-reaching prestige to attract an occasional volunteer. In July, 1871, following a skirmish with the Lowry band, the militia captured a white stranger who gave his name as Theade Dailey. "Dailey is a villainous looking character," the *Journal* remarked, "and although he refuses to state why he is in the Scuffletown district, there is but little doubt that he [is] endeavoring to join the outlaws."[3]

The wide publicity that was given to the dramatic feats of the Lowrys sometimes prompted other bandits to make use of the awe-inspiring reputation to confuse or intimidate their pursuers. This stratagem may be seen in an episode taking place April 20, 1872, in Columbia, Kentucky. Just at noon, on that fine spring day, five horsemen rode abreast down Buskesville Street in Columbia, a small market town in the south-central bluegrass country. The streets were very nearly deserted and few people were to be seen in the stores. Many stores in fact were not even open. At this season farmers were busy in their fields, and in town business was dull. Many shopkeepers had closed their doors and gone home for their noon meal.[4]

When the horsemen were about five blocks from the public square of the town, three riders reined their mounts to a halt. They waited until their two companions had gained a lead on them of about one hundred fifty yards and then they too rode on. The advance party rode up to the city bank, dismounted, and went inside. A moment later the three others rode into the square. One of them also stopped at the bank, dismounted, and held his horse as well as the horses of the men who had just gone inside. The other two remained on their mounts, riding around the square, keeping a vigilant eye on everything.[5]

[3] Wilmington *Daily Journal*, August 19, 1871.
[4] Louisville *Courier-Journal*, May 16, 1937.
[5] *Ibid.*

But the bank was not so deserted as one might have supposed. The cashier was chatting with four other gentlemen when the robbers walked in with drawn guns. They instantly realized what was taking place. It was not easy for two bandits to watch every move made by five persons. Catching a gunman off guard for a second, W. H. Hudson suddenly kicked him into the fireplace. A desperate scuffle began between the gentlemen and the robbers, and the cashier was shot to death. As soon as firing began in the bank, the two mounted lookouts began galloping "around the square, keeping up a continuous fusillade and shooting at every head they saw." One of them shouted, "This is the Lowry Gang from North Carolina." Moments later two bandits emerged from the bank carrying several hundred dollars. They leaped on their horses and all five left town at a headlong gallop. The entire affair had lasted just five minutes.[6]

Who were these bandits? Certainly the real Lowrys at this time were more than five hundred miles from Columbia, Kentucky, and were otherwise engaged. Even though a posse tracked the Columbia robbers across three Kentucky counties, their identity was not very firmly established. From various sources it appears, however, that four of the five men were Jesse James, Frank James, Bob Cole Younger, and Jim Cummings, all members of the James band of Missouri.[7]

In eastern North Carolina, on the other hand, it was sometimes difficult to determine whether a particular raid was carried out by genuine Lowrys or by more conventional thieves. The robbery of the McLeod plantation, in Cumberland County, for example, resulted in two members of the family being killed and two more wounded, and was reported to be the work of the Lowrys. The *Robesonian*,

[6] *Ibid.*
[7] *Ibid.*

however, which followed the deeds of Henry Berry's men rather closely, thought that "the Lowrys had nothing to do with that awful tragedy." [8]

In 1872 a group of disguised men, identifying themselves as Lowrys, robbed William C. McNeill. One of his sons was a bounty hunter, but other members of the family appeared to have continued to live in peaceful relations with the Lowrys. The next day, Henry Berry came to within a hundred yards of McNeill's and sent word that he would like to meet him in Moss Neck. "He wanted to tell him that he did not do it." McNeill nevertheless was not convinced; he "refused to see him or have anything to say to him." [9]

One clearly bogus Lowry raid, however, created a greater sensation in Robeson County than did many of the genuine activities of the band. It attracted a great deal of attention because it was organized by Albert C. Moody, a gentleman who was socially prominent in the community; and because the Republican Party, which greatly disliked Moody, attempted to exploit the incident politically.

Albert Moody was from a family that was important in the political life of neighboring Marion County, South Carolina. Moody's marriage, however, had made him a substantial figure in Robeson as well. He married the daughter of High Sheriff Reuben King, who may have been the wealthiest man in the county.[10] Following the assassination of King by the Lowrys in 1869, the high sheriff's fortune was divided between the families of his two daughters, his only children, of which the Moodys received roughly half.

The Moodys lived at the mineral water resort Red Springs; but, as he was a man with extensive property and active in

[8] Lumberton *Robesonian*, March 25, 1874.
[9] Norment, *The Lowrie History*, 79.
[10] U.S., Bureau of Census, Eighth Census of the United States (1860), Free Population, North Carolina, XIII, 896, Slaves, North Carolina, IV, 50.

public affairs, the demands of business frequently required
that he be in Lumberton, the county seat.[11] Sometimes
Mrs. Moody accompanied him when he rode in his buggy
from Red Springs to Lumberton. Sometimes he went alone.
It is probably from the frequent trips that Moody made
between Red Springs and Lumberton that one can trace
the origins of his undoing as a county dignitary. Four miles
out of Lumberton on this road stood a "double-pen log
house," with a separate log cabin, some distance behind it,
that served as a kitchen. The family living there consisted
of a widow, Mrs. Winnie MacDaniels, and her four children,
a teen-aged boy and girl and a boy and a girl who were still
small. Moody was not such an old and settled family man
that he failed to notice, as his horse had trotted by, that the
elder of the MacDaniels girls, Mary, was quite attractive.

Circumstance had erected high fences between Albert
Moody and this lovely girl. He was middle-aged and married;
she was sixteen. He was socially prominent; she was a Buckskin Scot. He was a leading Conservative; her family and
kin were Radical Republicans.[12] Yet no society has ever
been able to build barriers high enough to contain man's
spiraling thoughts. There is reason to believe that sometime
in the spring of 1871 Moody's imagination achieved for him
that which life had denied. Suppose he were taken prisoner
by the Lowry band. Suppose they should drag him, their
captive, to the cabin of those Buckskins, the MacDaniels.
Then, as a coarse joke, Henry Berry or some other member
of the band would force him, quite against his wishes, to go
to bed with Mary. Under such circumstances, who could
possibly point to him with a finger of blame?

[11] Except where otherwise indicated, the following account is taken from
State v. Albert Moody, Notes of Justice of the Peace James Sinclair, June 3,
1871, in Henry Berry Lowry Papers, North Carolina Department of Archives
and History, Raleigh.
[12] Fayetteville *Eagle*, July 6, 1871.

During the seven years that they had been active, the Lowry band had never done anything even remotely resembling this. Nor were they likely to. Henry Berry's chivalrous attitude toward women was well known.

Moody's fantasy concerning himself and the Lowrys would probably not have caused anyone any difficulty if he had not once gotten too much to drink. On the evening of May 15, he found himself driving aimlessly through the darkened streets of Lumberton, having for company only two bottles of whiskey and some brandy. It was under these circumstances that he rashly decided to jettison miserable reality and make a vision happen. The real Lowrys would not do. They were likely to treat Moody, as a prominent member of the county establishment, in some disagreeable way. But one could perhaps organize a Lowry band that would behave better. At the Lumber River bridge he met a youth named John Brown who had just the right skin color.[13] He invited the young man to ride in the buggy with him, where he plied him generously with liquor, all the while unfolding to him a fascinating scheme for playing Lowry gang. Brown would be "John Lowry," a brother of Henry Berry,[14] and Moody would be his prisoner. But how could you have a one-man Lowry band? Moody had given this problem some reflection. The Lowrys rarely sent an entire party into a house. Ordinarily the rest of the band would guard the approaches to a house while one or two went in. "Mr. Moody told me," as Brown later recalled, "to tell the women that

[13] Yet it is by no means certain that he was in fact an Indian. The name *Brown* does not seem to exist among Lumber River Indians, nor, so far as can be determined, has it ever existed. The Reverend D. F. Lowry has suggested that this Brown may have been an Indian who had changed his name. (Letter from D. F. Lowry, July 22, 1970.) Also in Robeson County one meets individuals who look like Indians but are not so regarded. The name *Brown* was not uncommon among the whites.

[14] In reality, though Henry Berry had nine brothers, none of them was named John.

the balance of the crowd of robbers were close at hand." [15] Also, that he might better play the part of "John Lowry," Moody supplied his young guest with a pistol.

It was about eleven o'clock when they reached the Mac-Daniels cabin. The family had already gone to bed. Mrs. MacDaniels was especially frightened by the arrival of strangers at this hour because her older son was not at home. He was spending the night with some cousins who lived a half-mile away. Moody told his captor to take care of his horse, as he walked through the front gate. As Mary remembered later, "they came to the door and knocked for a half hour and cussed and said Damn you open the door for there is somebody in there for I hear you and we got scared and opened the door and Moody came in and said Come in Mr. Lowry. He then said to my mother You don't know this gentleman. His name is John Lowry being Henry B. Lowry's brother. Look at his fine pants and high pluten bosom shirt he stole from some gentleman." [16]

"Moody pretended to be scared to death" of the youth, who was interpreting his Lowry role as that of a wild tyrant, brandishing his pistol "pretty freely," and threatening "to shoot Moody several times." Brown demanded something to eat. Mrs. MacDaniels replied that she had nothing to eat on the place except one chicken and she did not want to kill it. But the youth, warming up to the role of despot, did not want to eat chicken anyway. He ordered her to bring honey. She pleaded that she had none. But, as she later related, "he said he knew I did have honey and wanted me to get it." "Let her alone about the honey," the prisoner commanded his captor. Then, turning to Mrs. MacDaniels, Moody advised her that "she had better kill the chicken for she knew

[15] *State v. Albert Moody*, Lowry Papers.
[16] *Ibid.*

how the Lowrys were," and he added that he would pay her for the chicken.[17]

Mary went out to the kitchen to help her mother cook the chicken. Moody evidently thought that the preparation of the supper—an event that had resulted from the big commotion that "John Lowry" had raised about being hungry —was causing a long delay in the crude practical joke that the Lowrys were going to play on him. In any event he sent "John Lowry" out to get Mary. The youth found her by the well, where she was drawing water. The way she remembered it, he "had a pistol in his hands and said I must go to Moody. My mother objected to this and said I must stay with her but . . . Lowry replied that whenever a Lowry says go, go. I was afraid he would shoot me. I went to Moody and sat by him . . . on the bench by the fire . . . . [Later] I was trying to get away from Moody but he would not let me. . . . [He] did nothing to me, but he said things . . . that are too bad to tell." [18]

This "scuffle between Moody and the girl" was interrupted by Mrs. MacDaniels and "John Lowry," who required his prisoner to come out to the kitchen and join him for supper. After they had eaten supper and returned to the main cabin, which had no illumination except the fire on the hearth, "John Lowry" walked into the room with a pail of water and poured it on the flame. For the rest of the night darkness filled the cabin. But if alcohol had imbued the youth with a willingness to play Lowry, it had done nothing to improve his talent for that role. He rushed around shouting orders, making threats, confounding the darkness with confusion. At one point Moody found himself in bed with Mary's little brother, John. But somehow he managed to convey to his captor his dissatisfaction with this particular arrange-

[17] *Ibid.*
[18] *Ibid.*

ment. Then there were more threats and commands and he soon found himself in another bed that turned out to be occupied by the girl's mother, who informed him that "if he did not quit she intended to hollar as hard as she could." [19]

In the midst of this all-encompassing gloom, where was Mary to be found? "Lowry" went outside to look for her. Moody waited patiently enough, for a time, for his captor to return, but finally he went out to look for "Lowry." He eventually found him. The youth had reached his saturation point for alcohol and was lying passed out "by the table near the passage" that led out to the kitchen. Then, taking considerable liberty with his role as prisoner, the white man began "trying to wake him telling him to get out of there as Henry Berry had sent them word to get away from there as they would all be taken." [20]

At some point, although it is not certain when, seeds of doubt were planted in the mind of Mrs. Winnie Mac-Daniels. There could be no doubt that she and her family were victims—but whether they were victims of a Lowry raid seemed open to question. After Moody had gotten "Lowry" in his buggy and driven away, she consulted with the families of her kinsmen living in the neighborhood. Upon their advice she located the Republican justice of the peace, the Reverend James Sinclair, and swore out a warrant for Moody, charging him with assault with intent to commit rape. Moody, failing to reach a money "compromise" with Mrs. MacDaniels, was convicted before the Reverend Mr. Sinclair.[21] While his case was under appeal, however, he forfeited his bond and left the county, probably to return to Marion County, South Carolina. Later Brown was also

[19] *Ibid.*

[20] *State v. John Brown*, Robeson County Superior Court, Spring Term, 1872, Henry Berry Lowry Papers, North Carolina Department of Archives and History, Raleigh.

[21] *State v. Albert Moody*, Lowry Papers.

indicted, but the final disposition of his case appears to have been lost.

In the spring of 1871, genuine Lowry raids were attracting nearly as much attention as the bogus one that Moody had carried out. On April 29, the Lowrys raided a plantation in Richmond County, seizing mules and a wagon, which they loaded "with corn and drove in style to Scuffletown, where the corn was equally distributed." [22] Then to end the affair with a grand Lowry flourish, though in this instance it entailed some risk, they went back to the scene of the robbery in Richmond County in order to return to the planter his mules and wagon.[23]

"At this moment the outlaws rule the county," the Reverend James Sinclair wrote to Governor Tod R. Caldwell in May, 1871.[24] A month earlier the Reverend Mr. Sinclair had not given such a note of urgency to his comments on the local scene; his own community, Lumberton, was one of the few places in Robeson County where the authority of the courts seemed unchallenged, where a warrant could be issued without fear that the civil officer who served it might be shot from a turkey blind. Not since the winter of 1864–65, when Confederate power had been tottering on its last legs, had the Lowry band dared enter Lumberton, the county seat and principal town. Protected by a company of federal soldiers, this community seemed to be one place where Henry Berry would not show his brown face.

But on May 10, 1871, shortly after midnight, a large band of armed men made its way through the darkened streets of the town. They were led by Henry Berry, Steve Lowry, Boss Strong, and George Applewhite, whose wounds of three weeks ago had seemed sufficient for convening a

[22] Townsend (comp.), *The Swamp Outlaws*, 50.
[23] Fayetteville *Eagle*, May 11, 1871.
[24] Sinclair to Caldwell, May 16, 1871, in Governors' Papers, North Carolina Department of Archives and History, Raleigh.

coroner's inquest. Arriving before the fortresslike county jail, they "entered the enclosure by means of a key which unlocked the gate." Most of their force were left around the gate to protect the retreat of the party entering the jail in case the federal troops were alerted. Then the "jail doors were forced open by means of augers and other tools with which the adventurers were well supplied . . . . In this way Henry Berry, Steve Lowry, Boss Strong, and George Applewhite made their way to the cells in which Tom Lowry and Forney Oxendine were being held. The irons were struck from the limbs of the prisoners, and all retired together through the gate, which they locked securely behind them." By the time the soldiers were galvanized into action, the Lowry band and the liberated prisoners were parading through Scuffletown in triumph.[25]

The prestige of the Lowrys never stood higher than it did in the spring and early summer of 1871, and conversely there was never more confusion and demoralization in the anti-Lowry camp. What was the role of the federal units, for example? Their commander had orders, whenever a posse was summoned, "to march your command to Scuffletown and take such positions as may serve to protect all the people against whom writs [of arrest; warrants] have not been issued and to remain there until the posse has disbanded and dispersed." [26] The federal forces thus took no initiative against the outlaws and typically arrived at the scene of a raid after the Lowrys had delivered their blow and disappeared.

But the militia and the sheriff's posse were not doing much either. "Since Judge Russell outlawed nine young men . . . for the murder of . . . Ben Bethea," wrote a federal

[25] Wilmington *Daily Journal*, May 11, 1871.
[26] Morgan to Captain Evan Thomas, February 5, 1871, in U.S., War Department, Reports of the Army Commands, Post of Lumberton (Record Group 393, National Archives).

officer who shared the views the Conservatives held toward
the Lowrys, "I have been informed by Sheriff McMillan
that the citizens say they will not obey any call made by the
Sheriff for posses to hunt Lowry and his gang. I have heard
several express the same determination myself." [27] The most
active of the semiofficial bands, furthermore, the so-called
"compact of young men," announced in June that they
were "exhausted" and were withdrawing from the Scuffletown region.[28] Yet at least one member of the compact
would remain behind: Francis Marion Wishart, known to
his friends as "Frank," would bring a vitalizing new energy
to the campaign against the Lowrys.

Frank Wishart was no stranger either to swamps or to
fighting. He had grown up in what was later to become
Wishart's Township in eastern Robeson County, a community which was then unusually inaccessible and primitive. The politics of this neighborhood may have had some
influence on the future Lowry fighter. The people were
white and poor. Though many of them, including Frank,
became Republicans after the war, they would not show the
kind of sympathy for the Lowry band that Republicans
would show in areas where Indians were more numerous.

Before the war Frank's father, Eli Wishart, who may have
been more prosperous and better educated than many of
his neighbors, had been elevated to the squirearchy, receiving
according to custom an appointment from the governor
for life.[29] Besides his duty of settling disputes among his
neighbors, Squire Wishart now had the right to a seat in the
county court, which was not only the governing body of

[27] Thomas to Morgan, April 1, 1871, in U.S., War Department, Records
of the Army Commands, Post of Lumberton (Record Group 393, National
Archives).

[28] Norment, *The Lowrie History*, 105.

[29] Minutes of the Robeson County Court, August, 1860–August, 1865,
p. 170, North Carolina Department of Archives and History, Raleigh.

the county, but also tried the more important law cases. Ordinarily Buckskin squires, a number of whom would later become Republican leaders, had little influence at the county court, which tended to be dominated by wealthy slave-holders. But Squire Wishart appears to have been an exception. He was made overall commander of the militia, two of his sons eventually became colonels, and others connected to the family held lesser offices. All told, the Wisharts came to hold almost as many commanding positions over the military arm of the court as such wealthy families as the Norments and Kings held over the court itself.[30] The Wisharts may have had their differences with the old slave society, yet few families had been more active in its defense.

Though it was chiefly by success in the profession of arms that his family had attained its prominence, Frank Wishart, like many another combatant, had gotten more than his fill of this profession before the Civil War was over. Once in 1865 he had remarked to a fellow officer in Lee's Army of Northern Virginia that if indeed he ever got home alive he "would bid adieu to muskets and swords forever." [31] As had been the fate of many such resolutions, this one did not last forever. But it did last for five years, and during this time he married Lydia Pittman and established himself as a small storekeeper at Shoe Heel, a village surrounded by a large Indian population that was under the influence of the Lowry band.

Like Nat and Hector McLean, Neill McNeill, and others from the Buckskin level of the squirearchy, Frank Wishart joined the Republican Party. Though the party after 1868 controlled both the state and federal governments, Republicans in the Lumber River region were caught in an agonizing

[30] Lawrence, *The State of Robeson*, 11–12.
[31] John M. Waddill to Francis Marion Wishart, July 12, 1871, in Wishart Papers.

dilemma: their state and national leaders, including Radical leaders, had rejected a philosophy of revolutionary legitimacy in favor of one of constitutional legitimacy. Their policy, therefore, was not one of consolidating their power, of carrying out their program by making whatever constitutional changes might be necessary to achieve these ends. On the contrary, their policy was one of consolidating only so much of their power and carrying out only so much of their program as would be consistent with the Constitution of 1789, as broadly interpreted by Alexander Hamilton. These more limited objectives were quite sufficient for the business leaders now running the party.[32] In practice this policy meant among other things a limited, inhibited, legalistic response to Ku Klux terror, and—with a measure of inconsistency— the military suppression of the Lowry band.

The demand by state leaders that local Republicans join in an armed assault on the Lowrys must have appeared to Republicans along the Lumber River as tantamount to a demand that one use his strong right arm to amputate his left. As a result, in overwhelmingly Republican Robeson County, Mary Norment was able to find one—but only one —Republican "of any distinction who could or did rise superior to party politics" to join the campaign against the Lowrys.[33]

Faced with the uncooperative attitude of local Republicans and the ineffectiveness of federal troops when used against guerrillas, the state leaders had turned to local Conservatives to lead their campaign against the Lowrys. The results had been embarrassing. The Conservative Party had a Ku Klux wing which sometimes tried to turn the campaign into a war against Indians and blacks. The Bethea killing

---

[32] Alfred H. Kelly, "Comment on Harold M. Hyman's Paper," in Harold M. Hyman (ed.), *New Frontiers of the American Reconstruction* (Urbana: University of Illinois Press, 1966), 52–53.

[33] Norment, *The Lowrie History*, 105.

was an indication as to the lengths to which this policy could lead: a group of men, who were probably members of the Ku Klux Klan, had used a campaign initiated by a Republican governor to murder a Republican activist who probably had little or no connection with the Lowry band. But even a campaign led by local Conservatives was showing signs of faltering, as the "compact of young men," announcing that they had become exhausted, departed suddenly for unannounced destinations.

It was at this point that Frank Wishart stepped forward, the only Robeson County Republican "of any distinction" to take part in the campaign against the Lowrys. If this step posed any dilemma for him, at least it was the kind of dilemma that he had faced all his life. His family had not thought highly of the old slaveholding elite. Yet this attitude had not prevented the Wisharts as militia officers from hunting down blacks and Indians; and by so doing they had gained recognition and advancement. After the war at least one member of the family would climb the same ladder. A grateful governor gave Frank Wishart overall command in Robeson County, commissioning him captain (the rank he had held in the Confederate service), and within a year raising him to full colonel.[34]

Thus it would seem that by this appointment a process of change, set in motion by the Civil War and Reconstruction, had come full circle. Colonel Eli Wishart, as commander of the antebellum county militia, had once brought as much security and peace to the plantation big houses along the Lumber River as he brought fear to the cabins. Now another Colonel Wishart, his son, occupied the same position.

[34] Wishart Diary, August 18, 1871; Wilmington *Daily Journal*, October 27, 1871.

Colonel Frank Wishart's approach to the Lowry campaign was basically the Conservative idea of subduing the Scuffletonians, rather than limiting oneself to capturing the outlaws. But unlike some Conservatives, he was not contemptuous of legal formalities such as obtaining a warrant in order to arrest a person or to search a house. On the contrary he used warrants liberally, although some of them were not issued on very substantial legal grounds.

In another respect Wishart may have had a certain moderating influence on the campaign: much of the cruelty and violence toward the Scuffletonians resulted from the fact that the militia imbibed liquor more readily than they did the elements of military discipline. Colonel Wishart struggled mightily, though with limited success, to bring sobriety and discipline to the militia. In his efforts to minimize violence, however, he never arrived at the Republican ideal of supporting evenhanded justice for all, whether friend or foe of the Lowrys. He included on his militia roster the name of Malcolm McNeill, who for four months had been outlawed for the murder of Benjamin Bethea. He did not get around to arresting McNeill, however, for more than six weeks and then only after he had been indicted for another murder.[35]

For Wishart's July campaign, the authorities planned to raise a force of at least one hundred fifty men. They therefore called upon the militia companies of each of the fifteen townships for at least ten men. In one instance the response was quite good: Saint Pauls reported with twenty-five men. Burnt Swamp Township also responded with more men than the minimum requirement—but Wishart must have scrutinized this twelve-man squad with some care, for it

[35] Roster enclosed in Roderick McMillan to Wishart, July 18, 1871, in Wishart Papers; Wishart Diary, September 6, 1871.

was composed entirely of Indians.[36] Britt's Township was able to draft nine men and therefore came very close to achieving its quota. The enthusiasm which one of these recruits showed for the venture, however, seemed to leave much to be desired: "H. Cribb put on a woman's dress to keep from coming . . . when he was summoned, was found between two of Elias Stone's girls in bed . . . made to get up and brought anyway." [37]

In some townships the entire militia, when summoned to take the field and fight the Lowrys, appeared to have taken to the swamps and hidden from their officers instead. Lumberton could thus locate but three men while three other townships did not report any at all. In at least one community the resistance was reported to have been active and may have had political overtones. Sheriff McMillan received a half-literate letter from a recruiting officer who doubted that all the men he had summoned would actually report. But "if they don't . . . I will act as you say nock don or drag out It don't differ with mee . . . . They are trying to keep out of my way but I am as sharpe as they or . . . . Old Allen Walters followed me Rond last weak and told the men not to go . . . . He is all and all with Som of theas Lagers Blacks [Union League] I think such men ort to be reported to headquarters." [38]

Thus by one means or another the authorities provided Wishart with some one hundred seventeen men for his July campaign, the most concerted single effort ever made against the Lowrys. These men were organized into detachments, which, having been drawn from the county militia, were sometimes referred to as "township companies," despite the

[36] Township roster enclosed in H. McE. McMillan to Wishart, July 18, 1871, in Wishart Papers.

[37] Wishart Diary, July 15, 1871.

[38] Illegible signature to Roderick McMillan, July 14, 1871, in Wishart Papers.

fact that they ranged in size from three to twenty-five men. Not many of these men, however, were so eager or so qualified to fight the Lowrys as was their commander.

Colonel Wishart prepared himself well for the campaign. He drew a map of the Scuffletown region on which he was able to locate obscure footpaths and swamp trails not appearing on ordinary maps. He even indicated the names of the persons living in isolated cabins. He was determined to discover the secret of the Lowry magic, their ability to appear at a point where the authorities were weak only to vanish again before adequate forces could be brought to bear upon them. In an effort to solve this riddle, he had studied the reports prepared by John Saunders, just before the Lowrys had killed the police agent. Wishart had also spent many wakeful nights at lonely spots where he might observe the movements of the Scuffletonians and receive the reports of his undercover agents. "Scout left at dark," he scrawled in his small pocket-sized notebook. "Another cold long night without blanket fire or water . . . . Spy has not reported. Uneasy. Train blows at Red Banks. Quiet. [Morning:] Stir among the citizens of Scuffletown. All seem to be busy." [39]

Some of this experience is certainly reflected in the orders that Wishart gave his men. One of his directives "to the Commanders of Back Swamp, Sterling Mills & Britts Townships" instructs,

Take a list of your men . . . and should any of them disobey orders take him under arrest . . . . You will arrest and detain all persons who may come in contact with you unless you know them to be *all right* . . . . Be careful not to fire on any one until you know who they are (as some detachments will be continually moving about). You will not allow any of your men to trouble

---

[39] Wishart Notebooks, notations made apparently during the night of March 14, 1871, in Wishart Papers.

private property or plunder houses. Try and post yourselves to be convenient to water and be sure to keep a good look out. Keep quiet as possible and talk as little as you can help & keep concealed.[40]

Yet despite Colonel Wishart's concern for discipline, this offensive, like the previous ones, was not without outrageous episodes. From a sworn statement that Mary Catherine Oxendine made before the Reverend James Sinclair, we have an account of the way a militia raid appeared to an Indian girl. The band, which was apparently the Smith's Township detachment, searched her father's house and farm without a legal warrant, the commander "ordering all locks to be broken." It seemed that the militia failed to find any adult male Indians on this farm. Perhaps they were hiding in the swamp. Or perhaps, as the raiders undoubtedly suspected, they were away with their weapons in support of the Lowry guerrillas. The militiamen never seemed to be able to locate the persons for whom they were looking. But if we may believe Mary Catherine Oxendine, some of the commander's requited wrath was turned upon a noncombatant; he struck "her a violent blow on the side of her head with the stock of his gun." [41]

Colonel Wishart may have winked at the rough tactics used by the Smith's Township detachment. His strategy appears to have been to carry out a series of inflammatory actions that would provoke the Lowrys and their adherents into an open confrontation with the militia. For guerrillas this could mean suicide. The raid on the Lumberton jail, for example, would have resulted in their annihilation had they not had the advantage of surprise. What would happen if the wives of the outlaws were placed in that same jail?

[40] Order of July 7, 1871, in Wishart Papers.
[41] *State v. John S. McNeill*, Superior Court of Robeson County, Fall Term, 1872, Henry Berry Lowry Papers, North Carolina Department of Archives and History, Raleigh.

Perhaps the Lowrys, if sufficiently provoked, might try again in July a procedure that had worked well in May. But this time the authorities would not be caught off guard. Since the outlaw wives, like other noncombatants, had generally been enjoying immunity, it would be simple enough, for a few hours at least, to capture any of them. But once the word got around that Colonel Wishart was after the women, they might become as hard to locate as their husbands. The tactic that he employed, therefore, was to send out the township detachments separately, on July 10, 1871, with orders to bag all the outlaws' wives, as well as some other prominent Indians, all to be seized as nearly as possible at the same time.

It worked. Furthermore, for a time at least, it appeared that the larger purpose of the move was also being realized— that the Lowrys were being drawn into an open confrontation with the militia. Indeed, during the days Rhoda was held prisoner, Henry Berry carried out a number of the bold feats that were to make his name a legend. But clearly this undertaking did not work out in the way that Colonel Wishart planned it. Perhaps he did not anticipate that the Lowrys would strike back so quickly, while the militia was still broken up into township units, widely separated, out beating the bushes for Lowry women. Scarcely any of these units by itself was a match for the Lowry band when its members were spoiling for vengeance.

Wishart himself was with the Smith's Township detachment, which two days before had outraged the Oxendine clan. Though originally they had only ten men, they had acquired several others. Bad things sometimes happened to persons suspected of being favorable to the Lowrys, but an Indian was often given an opportunity to prove his loyalty to the authorities by going with Lowry hunters as a recruit or guide. In this way the Smith's detachment had acquired the services of two Indians, one of whom was James

Seizure of Rhoda Lowry

Lowry, a cousin of Henry Berry's. The detachment seized some important hostages, including Rhoda Lowry and Mrs. George Applewhite, and together with the guides and prisoners made their way out to the railroad. They headed east along the tracks for the militia headquarters, which was located at the little settlement around Buie's Store, where the town of Pembroke now stands. At the edge of the village, only three hundred yards from headquarters, "they were suddenly fired upon by Lowry and his gang, who were concealed behind an ingeniously constructed ambuscade." [42]

Six men were cut down—one killed instantly, two mortally wounded, and three others with wounds from which they later recovered. Among the latter was Henry Berry's cousin James, who like other Indians newly armed and officially enrolled in the militia, had failed to defend himself when fired upon by his kinsmen. When the whites questioned them about this behavior, the two Indians had said "their gun caps failed to explode or some such excuse." [43] A Lowry now had Lowry bullets in his leg and hand. [44]

[42] Wilmington *Star*, July 12, 1871.
[43] Fayetteville *Eagle*, July 13, 1871.
[44] Wishart Diary, July 10, 1871.

Even though certain detachments had not yet returned
to headquarters, the militia appears to have already had
more men in the area around Buie's Store than the Lowrys
had. Yet they had been somewhat disorganized by their
surprise and by their losses, and they were reluctant to
attack the Lowrys in well-concealed positions. This circumstance gave Henry Berry a chance to turn the tables on
Colonel Wishart. It was now the Lowrys' turn to try to
provoke the militia into making a disastrous attack. When
the militia made no effort to assault their ambush, they
withdrew from it, ran through the woods, and came out
on the railroad at a place that was three hundred yards
further removed from the village than the spot where they
had made their initial attack. There they "commenced cheer-
ing and firing with their long range guns." [45] But Wishart
would not allow himself to be provoked. He would soon
have well over a hundred men on hand. He probably guessed
that the main objective of the Lowrys was to disperse the
militia detachments again and set free the hostages. In any
event he herded his hostages into headquarters and placed
them under secure guard.

Meanwhile the Lowrys, who were perhaps beginning to
feel uncomfortable because of the militia detachments con-
verging on the Buie settlement, withdrew a mile or more
to the south, to Harper's Ferry on the Lumber River, the
spot where they apparently were trying to lure the militia.
When Wishart's men finally arrived at the place, they soon
discovered why: the Lowrys had previously constructed
there "a raft of timber with logs piled up near the edges
of the raft for protection, after the manner of a fort or
floating battery." From their positions on the south bank of
the river and by means of this movable battery, the Lowrys
now could make it costly for the militia to cross the river.

[45] *Ibid.*

With evening approaching and "owing to the patches of swamp and to the fact that the robbers were in greater number than usual and scattered along the woods well protected," the militia were ordered out of the Lumber River low grounds, back to their headquarters on the railroad.[46]

In the meanwhile the combined Alfordsville and Thompson detachments, totaling perhaps eighteen men, on their way back to headquarters, stopped for a short respite at Wire Grass Landing on the Lumber River. Had they arrived a short while earlier, they would scarcely have chosen this particular place to enjoy the cool of the evening after a long and arduous July day, because they would have heard the shooting that had been going on just up the river at Harper's Ferry. The officer in charge of the two detachments was Captain Charles McRae, who, besides being commander of his township company, operated a small store in the village of Alfordsville. He may have been no more eager to fight than were some of his men, four of whom were Indians. The patronage of the Lowry clan was not something to be despised by an Alfordsville storekeeper. Even the inseparable friends Boss Strong and Henry Berry were not total strangers at his store.[47]

On that morning, July 10, Captain McRae and his two detachments had been given the assignment of capturing Flora Strong, Andrew's wife. This they had accomplished early in the day. It had not been safe to have such an important hostage in their midst, however, so they had turned their prisoner over to another detachment to be taken to headquarters. Still, Captain McRae and his men had been in no hurry to get back to Buie's Store and receive another assignment. But now in the stillness of the evening the militiamen were aroused by the sound of voices, carried over the water from up the river toward Harper's Ferry. They heard the splash of a paddle and realized that a boat was coming down the river toward them. Cautiously they concealed themselves and got their weapons ready to fire. Just beyond a sharp bend in the river they heard the sound of wading in the water and concluded that one or more persons had left the boat. Then, their eyes fixed upon the bend in the river, they saw a canoe glide into view. It was occupied by a lone individual. They recognized him. It was Henry Berry Lowry!

Breathlessly they waited for him to come within range. Then they opened fire. In a flash Lowry flipped over the side into the water. But taking his rifle from the floor of the boat, he began returning their fire, sighting over the edge of his craft and tipping it slightly to conceal his body from their view. Then to their consternation, instead of swimming back upstream out of range, he began swimming toward them, using his canoe as a shield, firing as he came with an accuracy that had already become legendary.

Henry Berry Lowry Engages Eighteen Militiamen

The four Indian recruits leaped up and started to flee, but Captain McRae ordered them back to their positions. They obeyed. The militia poured volley after volley into the river, but the Indian's canoe continued to advance. One militiaman and then a second one—Duncan McCormick and Charles Smith—were wounded. The supply of ammunition was running low. The shadows in the Lumber River low grounds were growing long and black. At last Captain McRae ordered his men to withdraw from Wire Grass Landing, an engagement that has never done much to promote the doctrine of white superiority in Robeson County.[48]

When Captain McRae and his men arrived at Buie's Store, the railroad stop that served as militia headquarters, they found that Colonel Wishart had assembled there a group of prisoners, the harvest of a day of raids. Included were the wives of four outlaws, Henry Berry, Steve Lowry, Andrew Strong, and George Applewhite. Also captured were Andrew McMillan and his wife as well as Aaron Revels. All had been arrested on warrants charging them with "aiding and abetting the outlaws."[49] The militia was thus able to deliver the prisoners to the authorities "in triumph," according to Mary Norment.[50] They were placed securely

[48] Morgan to Adjutant General, July 18, 1871, in U.S., War Department, Records of the Adjutant General's Office (Record Group 94, National Archives); Wilmington *Star*, July 12, 1871; Wilmington *Daily Journal*, July 12, 1871; Fayetteville *Eagle*, July 13, 1871; New York *Herald*, April 6, 1872; Wishart Diary, July 10, 1871; Norment, *The Lowrie History*, 106–107. The sources disagree as to how many militiamen Henry Berry drove away from Wire Grass Landing, and therefore as to the magnitude of his victory. I have chosen the figure eighteen, the number Colonel Wishart noted in his diary, intended only for his personal record, on the day of the skirmish. The same figure is given in the somewhat confused account appearing in the Fayetteville *Eagle*. General Morgan, who was presumably in Raleigh at the time, reported the number as twenty-two to the adjutant general. The New York *Herald* correspondent, who was probably likewise far from the scene of the skirmish, reported it as twenty-three. Mary Norment, writing three years later, gave the figure as ten.

[49] *Ku Klux Conspiracy*, II, 288.

[50] Norment, *The Lowrie History*, 106.

in the Lumberton jail, where their presence, another Conservative hoped, could enable the militia "to get a sight of the outlaws." [51]

Would Henry Berry reply with another bold raid on the Lumberton jail? On this occasion, as so often was his custom, he seemed in no hurry to give his answer. On Tuesday, Wednesday, and Thursday there was nothing but a disconcerting silence from the Lowry camp, while on the other side, "armed citizens were collecting from all directions to overrun Scuffletown and scour the whole country for the outlaws and all of their aiders and sympathizers. The excitement is intense." [52] The outlaws, however, had vanished.

But early on Friday morning, July 14, as the feverish hunt continued, Henry Berry, his brother Steve, and his brothers-in-law Andrew and Boss Strong, appeared suddenly at the plantation of John McNair. So far as anyone could tell, the four men were completely alone. But so was the McNair family. The Indians said simply that they had come for breakfast, and a meal was promptly served to them. When they had finished eating, Henry Berry turned to his intimidated host, a gentleman with extensive lands and property,[53] and said,

Mr. McNair I want you to gear up and go to Lumberton, where they have put my wife in jail for no crime but because she is my wife; that ain't her fault, and they can't make it so. You people won't let me work to get my living, and I have got to take it from you; but, God knows, she'd like to see me make my own bread. You go to Lumberton and tell the Sheriff and County Commissioners that if they don't let her out of that jail I'll retaliate on the white women of Burnt Swamp Township. Some

---

[51] *Ku Klux Conspiracy*, II, 288.

[52] Wilmington *Eagle*, July 13, 1871.

[53] U.S., Bureau of Census, Eighth Census of the United States (1860), Free Population, North Carolina, XIII, 945.

of them shall come to the swamp with me if she is kept in jail, because they can't get me.[54]

The outlaw leader then dictated a note that he wanted McNair to deliver to Sheriff McMillan and to the Presbyterian minister who headed the local organization of the Republican Party:

Robeson County N C July 14th 1871
To the Sheriff of Robeson County & C L Sinclair
We make a request, that our wives who were arrested a few days ago, and placed in Jail, be released to come home to their families by Monday Morning, and if not, the Bloodiest times will be here that ever was before—the life of every man will be in Jeopardy

Henry B Lowry
Stephen Lowry
Andrew Strong
Boss Strong[55]

Lest John McNair should return home accompanied by the militia, the Lowrys left the McNair place shortly after he did. Steve probably went to arrange a safe rendezvous with McNair to learn the result of their ultimatum but the

[54] Townsend (comp.), *The Swamp Outlaws*, 16–17.

[55] For some reason the name of Boss Strong, who was unmarried, appears on the ultimatum to release the wives of the outlaws, while the name of George Applewhite, whose wife was being held, does not. The foregoing version of the ultimatum comes from a manuscript in the Wishart Papers, which is probably the original. It is addressed to McMillan and Sinclair on the outside fold and may be in the handwriting of Mrs. John McNair. Mary Norment quotes a more striking but probably less authentic version of the same document:

   Mr. James Sinclair: If our wives are not released and sent home by next Monday morning there will be worse times in Robeson County than there ever have been yet. We will commence to drench the county in blood and ashes.

	his		his		his
H B Lowrie	X	Steve Lowrie	X	Andrew Strong	X
	mark		mark		mark

Norment, *The Lowrie History*, 108.

rest of the outlaws appeared at the home of another affluent planter, James D. Bridgers, the father of Mary Norment. They had come for their noonday meal. If the militia and the bounty hunters, including two of Bridgers' sons, were following their usual practice, they were at this moment searching for the outlaws in the cabins of the poor. But on this particular day the Lowrys were having their meals in the dining rooms of the rich. Mary Norment concedes that, while dining at her father's place, the Lowry leaders "conducted themselves very quietly." But after they had finished eating, they heard the sound of music and singing outside. "Steve . . . came up picking his 'banjo' and singing, seemed in excellent spirits." The meeting with McNair was arranged. They would soon know what the authorities were going to do.[56]

McMillan's reply, if we may believe Mary Norment, was a firm one. "He told Mr. McNair to inform the outlaws that the people of Robeson were not to be tampered with in this way, and driven by mere threats . . . , and the white men of Robeson [will not] become branded as cowards."[57] But the next day he appealed for help from the militia of Bladen and Columbus counties and wrote Governor Caldwell for a "good supply of ammunition and other equipment for one hundred men." He also asked the governor to "represent our condition to the federal government" and "secure . . . a strong detachment from the U.S. army. Cavalry I think would render most effective service."[58]

Colonel Wishart also was opposed to yielding an inch on the question of the hostages. "I would see them in hell before I would release them," he growled; and he had some

[56] *Ibid.*, 85.
[57] *Ibid.*, 108.
[58] Wilmington *Star*, July 16, 1871; Roderick McMillan to Caldwell, July 15, 1871, in U.S., War Department, Records of the Adjutant General's Office (Record Group 94, National Archives).

sarcastic words for those gentlemen whose reaction to the Lowrys was less heroic and more accommodating than his own. "There is some of the d——t men in Robeson County that God ever made: Eat dinner at James Bridgers. Fiddled a while. Froliced. Met John McNair below there to get the news from Lumberton." [59]

But despite the firmness of the McMillans and the Wisharts, Robeson County was in a state of panic. Even from the safety of Wilmington the *Morning Star* warned that now especially the whites should be on guard against Henry Berry, that the arrest of Rhoda "has aroused the lion in his nature." [60] He was not a man of many words but the few words that he had spoken were ringing in many ears. Especially disturbing was his statement that, if his wife were not set free, some of the white women of Burnt Swamp Township "shall come to the swamp with me"—though it would be difficult to say who was more alarmed by the handsome outlaw's threat, the men of that township or Rhoda Lowry.

But if the possibility that Henry Berry might carry off the white women of Burnt Swamp Township was causing panic, the more immediate prospect—that Colonel Wishart and his enrolling officers would carry off the able-bodied men of fifteen townships—was causing a general stampede. The Wilmington *Journal* noted "the refugees from Robeson, now crowding in surrounding counties to avoid a summons." [61]

As a result when Wishart ordered out a township "company," he rarely got enough men to form a squad at full strength. "Township reports very badly," he noted in his diary. "Called out Smith's, Shoe Heel, Sterling, Burnt Swamp. Mustered thirty-two men and eighteen guns, all

[59] Wishart Diary, July 14, 1871.
[60] Wilmington *Star*, July 15, 1871.
[61] Wilmington *Daily Journal*, July 22, 1871.

told." [62] And on the day the Lowry ultimatum expired: "Rations out and the men in confusion. I have the hardest time of any poor devil [that] ever was in the world. . . . Howell ordered to Cobb Mill [with] thirty men [and] seventeen guns. About 10 o'clock the firing commenced heavy and all the running God ever let men do was done." [63]

On the same day, July 17, 1871, there was a meeting of the civil authorities. As Mary Norment reports, "quite a number of the old grey-haired citizens of Robeson County went to Lumberton and held a consultation with the Sheriff and county commissioners, and the conclusion arrived at was that taking all things into consideration, it was probably best to release the wives." [64] This decision was carried out by the civil authorities without even consulting the commander of the militia. "Give up to H. B. Lowry," the colonel exploded the next day, when he heard of the decision. "Fare well Robeson County!" [65]

On July 18, 1871, the westbound train came to a halt at the Indian village of Red Bank. Among the passengers who got off were the wives of the outlaws.[66] They had left their homes a week ago as prisoners, dragged through the midst of a gun battle. How different was their return!

[62] Wishart Diary, July 15, 1871.
[63] Ibid., July 17, 1871.
[64] Norment, The Lowrie History, 108.
[65] Wishart Diary, July 18, 1871.
[66] Wilmington Star, July 20, 1871.

9 · "To Desperadoes They Bear But Little Resemblance"

As THE LOWRY hostages were being taken to jail in Lumberton on a Wilmington, Charlotte, and Rutherford train, a correspondent for the Fayetteville *Eagle*, who was traveling on the same train, had seen some of the Lowry band "rush from the woods a few miles below Buie's Store as if prepared to attack the train." But they "did not fire as their wives were near the car windows." [1]

Was this really the reason? The day before, the Lowrys had shot six members of a posse in an effort to free the prisoners. Did they have to shoot at the windows? Would not a few rounds fired through a locomotive boiler send geysers of white vapor spiraling skyward and bring the train rattling to a halt? Could they not have stopped the train simply by obstructing the track or removing a single rail? In this strange conflict there was no feature more curious than the relationship between the Lowry band and the WC&R railroad, the company that had once employed Steve Lowry as a locomotive fireman. [2]

The WC&R ran through the heart of the district known as Scuffletown, or the Settlement, having stops in some five villages controlled or influenced by the Lowrys. Yet, although a few days of conflict in 1865 between Generals Sherman

[1] Wilmington *Eagle*, July 13, 1871.
[2] New York *Herald*, April 6, 1872.

and Johnston had put this road out of operation for several months, by curious contrast the company was able to operate through almost a decade of guerrilla conflict without having a single train stopped, a single passenger molested, or railroad property damaged by the Lowrys. There does not appear even to have been an interruption in the regular published schedules of the WC&R. If in the swamps on both sides of the WC&R the Lowrys knew how to practice a sorcery that enabled them to vanish and reappear according to the needs of guerrilla conflict, at the same time it appeared that the owners of that railroad were able to protect their right of way by a magic spell, the secrets of which were best understood by some solid Conservative businessmen in Wilmington.

But it was not only along the railroad right of way that these gentlemen seemed to know how to perform dark wonders. One could also observe evidence of their power in the town of Raleigh, at saloons where members of both the legislature and the railroad lobby gathered for drinks. There was a definite softening of some of the deepest and most divisive prejudices that had previously marred the character of these lawmakers; and, as for railroad appropriation bills, the reddest of red-necked racial enthusiasts were able to see eye to eye with the blackest of the black Radicals. The most unreconstructed of Rebels—one possessing a dubious fortune in Confederate securities—could stand shoulder to shoulder with carpetbaggers who had arrived in North Carolina on the baggage trains of Sherman.

Robeson County perhaps more than any county in the South stood in need of some benign influence, having more than a just share of those things which are centrifugal or divisive, of those human distinctions that often provide men with an excuse for behaving like hyenas. Along the Lumber River one distinguished three shades of skin color—black, white, and brown—as well as four shades of political opinion —turkey-blind Republican, ballot-box Republican, moderate Conservative, and Ku Klux.

The administrators of the WC&R were not able to harmonize the discord they found in Robeson County to the same extent they had been able to reconcile the prejudices that existed in the legislature. But somehow they were able to prevent those burning differences, which inflamed people's minds and stoked guerrilla war on both sides of the tracks, from ever igniting a single fat lightwood railroad trestle or from causing distracted men to heat iron rails in the middle and bend the ends around trees, as had been done during the days when Sherman had fought Johnston.

How was this immunity accomplished? A newspaper correspondent has written that the WC&R and the Lowry band had an agreement "which prevents the former from allowing armed passengers in pursuit of the outlaws on their trains, and prohibits the outlaws from visiting the trains with hostile purposes toward passengers."[3] Does it not overtax the imagination to suggest that owners of the WC&R had an agreement with the outlaws that both sides observed rather scrupulously?

A sampling of the correspondence of some railroad men has revealed no reference to such an agreement. But these were the years of the railway scandals. It is said that one never pronounces the word *rope* in the house of a man who has been hanged. In the surviving letters that railroad men wrote during these years there is often a similar reluctance to use the word *railroad,* and the letters collected by their loyal and judicious descendants are full of innocuous personal matters.[4] Yet from other sources it would appear that

[3] *Ibid.,* March 22, 1872.
[4] The Hugh MacRae Papers, for example, in the Duke University Library, are full of railway news before 1868 and after 1872, but references are scarce for the period of the scandals.

a businesslike understanding with the Lowry band would not necessarily have been the most dubious transaction undertaken by the WC&R during Reconstruction.[5] Certainly both the railroad and the Lowrys behaved as if an agreement existed. Colonel S. L. Fremont, general superintendent of the road, is reported to have explained the very limited cooperation that he was giving the anti-Lowry campaign on the grounds that if he allowed armed bounty hunters on the trains it would endanger the safety of the railroad, and that the Lowrys "could toss a train almost any day." [6]

So long as a passenger paid his fare and conducted himself peaceably, the WC&R conductor did not concern himself with the man's race, his sympathies, whom he may have killed last night, or how much his head might be worth. Thus the Lowrys were able to use the trains themselves. But on at least one occasion, they had to allow the most hated of all bounty hunters, the renegade Indian James Donahoe-McQueen, to travel the entire length of Scuffletown unarmed and hence unharmed.[7]

Because of this arrangement, passengers on the WC&R had an opportunity to view both sides of the conflict, if not impartially, at least with a degree of safety that is rare in the midst of a contest of violence. In a series of leisurely stops, one might have an opportunity to chat in one village with a leader of the Lowry band, with a heavy price on his head, and in the next village with a militia officer commissioned to take dead or alive the same man. On one occasion,

[5] N.C., *Report of the Commission to Investigate Fraud and Corruption Under Act of Assembly, Session 1871–1872* (Raleigh: James H. Moore, State Printer and Binder, 1872), 316–18 and *passim*; Charles L. Price, "The Railroad Schemes of George W. Swepson," in Hubert A. Coleman and others (eds.), *East Carolina College Publications in History: Essays in American History* (Greenville, N.C.: East Carolina College, 1964), I, 45–46 and *passim*.

[6] Townsend (comp.), *The Swamp Outlaws*, 11.

[7] New York *Herald*, March 22, 1872.

Stephen Lowry and Colonel Frank Wishart—at the time the most important figure in the anti-Lowry campaign—found themselves traveling in the same car, sat together, and conversed for a while. But, although the two men took leave of each other cordially enough, as the other passengers noted, each got off at a different stop.[8]

If a passenger were a stranger, and unaware of these delicate circumstances, he could make a serious blunder. There is a report that one such gentleman, leaving the train with the other passengers at Moss Neck, inquired aloud, "Where does this rascal, Lowery, keep himself?" An Indian standing nearby answered, "Well, sir, if you'll step this way I'll show him to you." A moment later the astonished traveler found himself face to face with a heavily armed and "sombre-looking" individual. "This is Henry Berry Lowery," said the other Scuffletonian. "Yes," said the outlaw leader, "and we always ask our friends to take a drink with us." The passenger replied, with all the assurance he could muster, "I'll take a drink if you'll let me pay for it." "Oh, yes, we always expect our friends to treat us." [9]

But not always: on February 14, 1872, at Moss Neck, the Lowry band treated the passengers on both the east- and westbound trains with sweet cider.[10] Henry Berry was not a man who was ready in speech, and in fact he rarely spoke at all. His actions, however, sometimes seemed to express ideas. Standing around on the railroad platform drinking sweet cider with the passengers may have been his answer to the legislature, which during the past week had increased the bounty on him to twelve thousand dollars and the bounties of his chief lieutenants to six thousand each.[11]

On one occasion the passengers reported that Henry Berry,

[8] Wilmington *Daily Journal*, May 4, 1872.
[9] Townsend (comp.), *The Swamp Outlaws*, 18–19.
[10] Wilmington *Star*, February 15, 1872.
[11] N.C., *Public Laws, 1871–1872*, Chap. 122.

"bold and defiant," had mingled with the crowd at the station. He was carrying his banjo, they noted, "with which, we suppose, it is his custom to regale himself when in camp." [12] A month and a half later, when the train stopped at Moss Neck, the travelers were astonished to see the leaders of the Lowry band having a picnic lunch at the edge of McNeill's Pond. Such actions, so a *Star* reporter thought, showed "the utmost contempt of the civil authorities." [13]

The WC&R seems to have been generally successful in keeping armed bounty hunters from using its trains. It did not, however, and probably for legal reasons could not, prevent United States troops from using them. Nevertheless, the company may have winked at the efforts of black members of their crews to warn the Scuffletonians if there were soldiers aboard. "A movement among the negro train hands will be observed as the locomotive approaches the stations of Scuffletown." And then "when the troops pursued the scoundrels they could hear a peculiar bark like that of a cur precede them, and die away in the distance . . . . It was passed from shanty to shanty to put Lowery on the qui vive." [14]

The WC&R's acquiescence in the legal necessity of moving federal soldiers does not appear to have threatened either the Lowrys or the relations of the company with those particular customers. Much of the prosperity of Wilmington depended upon the financial success of this rail link with Piedmont North Carolina, and that city's newspapers were not eager to see the WC&R embroiled in the Lowry conflict. Thus, when one of the locomotive engineers on that line reported that some band, whom he supposed to have been the Lowrys, had fired on his train between Buie's Store

[12] Wilmington *Star*, April 18, 1871.
[13] *Ibid.*, June 2, 1871.
[14] Townsend (comp.), *The Swamp Outlaws*, 55.

and Camp Seymour, the *Star* replied that "we have been
informed by a friend living in that vicinity that the shooting
is supposed to have been done by some outsiders and not
by anyone connected with the Lowry band. . . . being at all
times willing to 'give the d——l his due,' we cheerfully accord Lowry and his associates in crime the benefit of this cor-
rection." [15] The neutrality of the railroad gave the Lowry
conflict an unusual character, one in which many of the
leaders on each side knew each other by sight and even had
occasional conversations. It created special opportunities for
newspapers to report both sides of the struggle.

Local newspapers for the most part did not make use of
this potential, confining their reports chiefly to pronounce-
ments by Robeson County authorities. The editors of the
New York *Herald*, on the other hand, saw the possibilities
of producing some sensational journalism by sending a reporter to cover the conflict from the Lowry camp. At different times the *Herald* used three reporters to cover the
Robeson County scene. The most important of these was
A. Boyd Henderson, who in March, 1872, spent several
weeks among the Scuffletonians. Even upon his arrival in
Wilmington, however, on his way from New York to Robeson County, Henderson learned something about the limitations on the immunity enjoyed by travelers on the WC&R.
When he attempted to buy a ticket from Wilmington to
Moss Neck, the clerk at the window had answered, "My
God! stranger, you are not going to stop there!" [16] People
felt free to use the trains, but a stranger should not wander
far from the station at those stops between Lumberton and
Shoe Heel.

Henderson bought his ticket to Moss Neck, despite the
advice of the clerk. But the WC&R conductor nevertheless

[15] Wilmington *Star*, September 28, 1871.
[16] Townsend (comp.), *The Swamp Outlaws*, 70.

persuaded him to remain on the train until they reached Shoe Heel, where he would not only find better accommodations, but also where he would find it easy enough to get in touch with the Lowry leaders.[17] At Shoe Heel he wrote a letter to Henry Berry and dispatched it by way of some Lowry sympathizers. After several days he was contacted by Lowry agents who took him to visit the mother of Henry Berry, Steve, and Tom. The old Indian lady, he thought, "boasts her maternity of the bold outlaws . . . as proudly, perhaps, as did the Roman mother of the Gracchi." [18]

Henderson was never able to interview Henry Berry, though for a time he was a guest at the outlaw chief's home and on one occasion attended church with Rhoda and the children.[19] While at the Henry Berry place, he was contacted by three of the outlaws—Rhoda's brother Andrew Strong and her brothers-in-law Steve and Tom Lowry. They required him to take a terrible oath that would absolve them from moral responsibility if they should kill him for attempting to betray them. He agreed under these circumstances not to "accuse them on the Day of Judgment." [20]

They then led him blindfolded, "in some places wading almost waist deep in water," to inspect a cache of weapons, where he saw "thirty or forty shotguns." Upon returning the same way, Henderson had lunch with the outlaws. "Steve bought a couple dozen of eggs from a woman near by who boiled them for him, and we went to the store at Moss Neck to eat them . . . . In addition to eggs we had ginger cake, cheese and wretched whiskey." After the meal, "Andrew 'picked' the banjo, played on the violin and sang . . . to an appreciative and enthusiastic audience. Steve sings very well, and the peculiar airs which he was accompanied on the

[17] *Ibid.*
[18] New York *Herald*, March 21, 1872.
[19] *Ibid.*
[20] *Ibid.*, March 26, 1872.

banjo were novel and exceedingly pleasant." [21] They then took the correspondent to the quarters that they had arranged for him during his visit. He was to stay in the home of Thomas Chavis, a well-to-do Indian living three miles from Moss Neck. The outlaws left Henderson at the Chavis place, cautioning the host to feed him well and to let him go to bed early as he was "clean done worried out," and that Steve would pay the bill.[22]

But Henderson was employed by the *Herald*, a paper which, though not neglecting to report the fame of men, nevertheless recognized that racy accounts about their infamy would sell more papers. In almost any good article in that paper the readers could look forward with some pleasure to having their Victorian sense of propriety jarred, if ever so gently. But where was Henderson going to find that essential scandalous element in the lives of these straightforward, churchgoing, family men, the outlaws?

Yet the hint of things that are odious may not be totally absent where journalistic imagination is sufficiently present. Having published in the *Herald* a wire he had sent his wife, "I am with the Lowerys, perfectly safe," [23] Henderson began to insinuate to thousands of *Herald* readers that, in his relations with the lovely wife of the fearful Henry Berry, he might be growing imprudent. "A little after dark" one evening, shortly after his arrival at the Chavis place, he "returned to Henry Berry's house, in pursuance of his wife's invitation to spend the night there," although he admitted in the same article that Rhoda and the children had slept on the floor so that their guest could have the only bed in the cabin.[24] Henderson was indeed being imprudent. It was fortunate for him that this cynical bit of vulgarity with which

[21] *Ibid.*
[22] *Ibid.*
[23] Quoted in Wilmington *Daily Journal*, March 17, 1872.
[24] New York *Herald*, March 26, 1872.

he supplied the *Herald* did not come to the attention of the kinsmen of Henry Berry and Rhoda, who surrounded him. They would not have been amused by this particular way of repaying the hospitality of the Scuffletonians.

Yet the observations made by Henderson must have raised some important questions concerning the nature of the turmoil in Robeson. Anyone reading his reports—or, for that matter, anyone who frequently used the WC&R railroad —must have entertained some doubts as to whether the authorities were right in viewing the Lowrys as common criminals. If Colonel Wishart and Steve Lowry could peacefully share a seat in a railway coach, what useful purpose was being served by the armed bands that stalked each other in the swamps? If the WC&R could make an agreement that created a narrow ribbon of peace and security cutting through the turmoil, why could not the authorities make an agreement that would end the conflict, which, with stops and starts, was now dragging on into its seventh year?

By 1871 it had begun to appear to many people that the time had come for the men who were "lying out," tortured by yellow flies and mosquitoes, to sleep once again in their beds; for the exiles, whether they had fled before Henry Berry's wrath or Colonel Wishart's recruiting officers, to return home again to their own fields and kin; for a man to be able to travel any path that he might choose without fear that just beyond some fatal turn he would find himself standing before a turkey blind; for houses to be filled with lamplight in the evening and the shutters thrown open wide without any thought of a lurking assassin.

To country people, watchdogs were of tremendous importance, if one was to go to bed with peace of mind and sleep without fear. Yet by 1871 there were few warning barks to break the frightful stillness of the night. Dogs were used for tracking. They inhibited the movements of spies and scouts. Any dogs that escaped the Lowry band were not likely to have survived Colonel Wishart's men. Surely the time had come when people could once again enjoy the security provided by dogs.

As early as the fall of 1870 a peace plan was proposed by Dr. Richard M. Norment. One would hardly have expected Dr. Norment to favor compromise with the Lowrys. It had been only six months since his brother, the militia captain, Owen C. Norment, had been mortally wounded by the Lowrys. As a physician he had attended his brother during the last, terrible hours of his life. One might reasonably expect that such an experience would have won another convert to the faction favoring the devastation of Scuffletown.

But sometimes Dr. Norment acted in ways that one might not expect. During the winter of 1865–66, for example, when many people fled because of a smallpox panic, he had remained behind. Abandoned by his helpers, he had continued caring for afflicted freedmen and Scuffletonians, burying the dead with his own hands.[25] The smallpox had passed; but the people along the Lumber River continued to suffer from a disease that was even more pernicious, and for which man has never been able to devise an inoculation. Each year it took lives; and those who survived did not escape its marks: one could observe definite lapses of rationality, some deformation of conscience, and in severe cases the loss of all humanity.

The best treatment for this affliction, Dr. Norment thought, was to "petition the governor to issue a proclamation offering pardon and protection to those outlaws on condition that they within a prescribed time come in and take an oath to support the laws and abstain from further dep-

[25] Richard M. Norment to William Henry Harrison Beadle, March 10, 1866, in Freedmen's Bureau Records.

redations." [26] He thought that the petition should be circulated quietly in Conservative circles, where on the local level, at least, there was some sentiment for compromising the conflict. Though Dr. Norment would himself later become a Republican, at this time he preferred to exclude the Republicans from the effort. Despite their eagerness for peace, he was afraid that they would use negotiations with the Lowrys as a means of improving their political position.[27] Much of the strength of the plan consisted in the fact it had originated with a member of one of the two or three most influential Conservative families in the county.

What was the outcome of Dr. Norment's prescription for peace? Six months after the beginning of this quiet campaign among the party elite, the Wilmington *Journal*, widely regarded as the official voice of the state Conservative organization, made some hostile remarks about a peace petition in Robeson County, which it said had been inspired by Henry Berry Lowry and the Republicans. Lowry, that paper said, "in view of the utter demoralization at present existing in the ranks of the Republican party in this State, has in consideration a retirement from public life. To effect this a pardon is necessary, and to obtain this pardon it is said that he is causing a petition to be circulated among the people of Robeson." [28] A few days later the Fayetteville *Eagle* repeated the same idea in almost the same words.[29] The party controlling the legislature had spoken.

The defeat of Dr. Norment's plan foreshadowed the outcome of every subsequent effort at a negotiated settlement. Virtually all Republicans favored some kind of compromise, the conflict being their political liability; and in Robeson

[26] Richard M. Norment to William Stokes Norment, September 20, 1870, in Historical Collection of the Lumberton *Robesonian*.
[27] *Ibid.*
[28] Wilmington *Daily Journal*, February 26, 1871.
[29] Fayetteville *Eagle*, March 2, 1871.

County so did many Conservatives. But, outside the immediate area of turmoil, Conservative leaders had no intention of letting their rivals escape easily from their dilemma. They had no desire to hand Robeson County back to the Republicans. And a triumphant "What about the Lowrys?" might be offered as a retort for the mention of any number of dramatic feats that the Klan was carrying out between the Potomac and the Rio Grande.

The state leaders of the Conservative Party had an answer of their own to the turmoil in Robeson. They thought that with more federal troops, with more state aid to the local militia, with higher bounties offered for the Lowry leaders, peace could be won through the military triumph of Conservative whites rather than through negotiations with brown-skinned Scuffletonians. Moreover when a local ballot-box Republican declined to cooperate with this plan, the *Journal* suspected the worst: "To prove that there is something of an affiliation between the Radicals of this section and the . . . gang [of] . . . murderers and outlaws, Nat McLean . . . *refused to sign* a petition to the Governor of the State, asking for arms and ammunition for the people in the campaign against the Lowry gang." [30]

The *Journal* helped discredit Dr. Norment's plan for a settlement by attributing its inspiration to Henry Berry Lowry. The next important move toward an accord, however, did indeed come from the outlaw chief. "Henry Berry Lowry, accompanied by some five or six of his gang, appeared suddenly at the residence of Mr. John McNair," who had helped them negotiate the freeing of the hostages a month before. "Lowry was evidently on a peace mission as he stated that he would not hereafter molest anyone in Robeson County, provided he was left alone. He desired

[30] Wilmington *Daily Journal*, July 21, 1871.

Mr. McNair to notify the authorities at Lumberton of this fact." [31]

The following day they visited other plantations, where they made essentially the same proposals, having breakfast at the McRackens' and lunch at the Pattersons'. During the afternoon they appeared at the home of James D. Bridgers.

Several of the neighbors were collected together assisting Mr. Bridgers in a job of working. Here they remained for a considerable time discussing the situation, and giving their views . . . .
They expressed themselves as tired of their present mode of life, and anxious to return to the duties and peaceful pursuits of good citizens, if they could do so safely. They proposed if the citizens would unite in a petition to the governor and procure for them a pardon . . . , they would leave the state within three days, never to return; but unless this was done they would remain, and expressed full confidence of being able to maintain themselves for ten years.
They expressed contempt for the militia. [32]

For the federal troops Henry Berry also had a message and a characteristic way of delivering it. A group of six United States soldiers, who were bivouacked near Prospect Church, were walking along a path toward the house of "an old woman who sells 'tangleleg' whiskey, [and] who has been receiving frequent visits from the 'boys in blue.' " Suddenly a man "sprang from the bushes, armed to the teeth, and confronted them, startling them with the information that he was the redoubtable Henry Berry Lowry."

He told them they were fools if they came to Robeson County with the expectation of killing or capturing him, for it would never be done. He had lately received a message from the Lord that he had 12 years yet to live, and further informed the astonished "men of Mars" that he had singled out some of their

---

[31] *Ibid.*, August 16, 1871.
[32] Wilmington *Star*, August 18, 1871, quoting Lumberton *Robesonian.*

comrades upon whom he intended to wreak his vengeance . . . .

A few days after . . . an officer of the militia received a message from Lowry, stating that he had visited their camp the night before and inspected their arms to see if they were in proper condition. As proof of this assertion he stated that he had left his "card," which would be found attached to one of their guns. Upon examining their weapons the name Henry Berry Lowrey was found inscribed upon the breach of one of them.[33]

Despite his opposition to freeing the hostages, Colonel Wishart was not opposed to a peace that resulted from the removal of the outlaws from Robeson. The Lowrys therefore approached him also and through him North Carolina Adjutant General John C. Gorman. Wishart's diary records the progress of these negotiations:

August 27, 1871, Sunday. Had an interview with Henry Berry Lowry's emissary on terms of peace. I am to meet him unarmed and talk with him about matters in general. I have a hope of accomplishing his removal from this place. He was seen talking to two of the [United States] soldiers [with]in three hundred yards of their camp . . . .

August 28, 1871, Monday. . . . Heard from Lowry today. Very anxious to meet me on terms of peace. Tomorrow morning I am to meet them. Duff Cummings is the man that pilots me. Must I go or not? I will [go even] if I am killed . . . .

August 29, 1871, Tuesday. Rainy. Duff [has] come this morning soon, waked me up. Said all was ready. . . . Started through the woods up the railroad. At [a culvert] below Red Banks in the Big Bay, Henry Berry, Boss, Steve, and [illegible] were all sitting beside the road, armed.[34]

He arranged for them to meet Gorman, who was spending five weeks in Robeson County, during which he had visited, he thought, "nearly every house in the outlaw domain, and took special pains to inform myself as to the feelings and expressed opinions of the people." After agreeing to a meet-

[33] Wilmington Star, September 7, 1871.
[34] Wishart Diary, August 27, 28, 29, 1871.

ing with the outlaws, Gorman wrote that he was instructed to "go unattended through a swamp some three or four miles from camp."

It was possible that they would meet me, and . . . without informing any but Col. Wishart of my intention, I proceeded thither, unarmed except with a repeater . . . . When I first saw them they were sitting on a log awaiting my promised presence. They were all heavily armed, Henry Berry . . . with a Spencer rifle, and a double barrelled gun, while within his belt were five repeaters. The balance of the gang had two double-barrelled guns, and three to five repeaters. All of them, I believe, also carried a bowie knife . . . . They were exceedingly respectful to me during the interview, and stated that their object in wishing a conference was to know if it was possible for me to grant them some terms. They . . . stated that if they were allowed, they would depart from the territory of the United States . . . . Some of the crimes alleged against them, they denied, and complained that from the first, they had acted on the defensive.

Before leaving them, they assured me that they would not ambush or shoot any of the troops under my command, except they should be "cornered," in which event they intended to die game. They also promised that they would not physically injure any citizen except in defense of themselves, but said they were bound to eat, and as they were not allowed to work, they would be forced to make requisitions upon the farmers for supplies . . . .

For desperadoes and murderers, which they undoubtedly are, they bear but little resemblance.[35]

But General Gorman was a Republican. He and the whole administration of Governor Caldwell were almost helpless before the Conservative majority in the legislature; and the Wilmington *Journal* had already pronounced that party's verdict: "We hope that this peace overture will not, however, procure the gang any indemnity from pursuit at the hands of the white people. Their hands are too red with

[35] Letter dated October 16, 1871, published in Wilmington *Daily Journal*, October 27, 1871.

some of the best blood of the county to allow them to walk in peace there." [36]

As for Republican efforts to compromise the question, the same paper remarked bitterly that "it is rumored that Henry Berry Lowery and James Sinclair are both aspirants for the Radical congressional nomination. When we vote that way we'll go it blind." [37] Thus although Dr. Norment, Colonel Wishart, and other local people of both parties would continue in good faith to try to negotiate a settlement, the political situation in the state was such that each attempt was doomed to failure.

The federal administration, however, appeared to have been more impressed by the peaceful gestures of the outlaws than it was by the intransigency of the North Carolina legislators, who, though a large number of them owed their election to Ku Klux terror, were nevertheless unctuously insisting that the full rigors of the law be applied to the Lowrys. By October 15, 1871, the last federal troops were withdrawn from Robeson County.[38] The next day, in a characteristic gesture, Henry Berry appeared before Oakley McNeill, the brother of a bounty hunter, and presented him with a raccoon that the Indian had just shot. The animal had been treed by McNeill's dog; and, according to custom, the game belonged to the owner of the successful dog. The two men chatted about dogs and hunting, and then Henry Berry said "good morning" and disappeared again into the swamp.[39]

Meanwhile the outlaws faced a dilemma. They had told General Gorman that they "would be forced to make requisi-

---

[36] Wilmington *Daily Journal*, August 16, 1871.

[37] *Ibid.*, December 14, 1871.

[38] General Charles Hale Morgan to Adjutant General, October 15, 1871, in U.S., War Department, Records of the Adjutant General's Office (Record Group 94, National Archives).

[39] Wilmington *Star*, quoting Lumberton *Robesonian*, n.d.

tions upon farmers for supplies." But there is no record of their having done so before December, 1871, and even then the "contribution" that they politely "levied" on a planter consisted of only three pieces of cured meat.[40] Perhaps they felt that more extravagant foraging would spoil efforts that were being made to obtain for them pardons or safe conduct beyond the borders of the United States.

Yet, on the other hand, in the absence of some conciliatory gesture by the legislature, they could hardly settle down to ordinary jobs, the repetitive routine of which would present the bounty hunters with an opportunity for a quick profit. As generous Robin Hoods they had not been unwelcome guests in the cabins of the poor. But with no plantation wealth to share, they had become a burden to their kinsmen and friends. They had no way to compensate their hosts for risking the retribution of the authorities.

The difficulties of trying to subsist as law-abiding outlaws came to an end in February, 1872, when the state lawmakers gave a definitive answer to all peace negotiations by appropriating money for increasing the bounties on the outlaws.[41] A week later Henry Berry replied with a raid on Lumberton. Yet so different was this from the Lowry raids to which people had become accustomed that the *Star* entertained doubts as to who was responsible.[42] This was certainly no "levy" of "three large pieces" of cured meat, a free meal, or a wagonload of corn to be distributed among the needy. Indeed there must have been few lawbreakers in American history that conducted successful robberies for so many years for such modest return. But this raid was lucrative.

On the night of February 16, the robbers entered a livery stable, seized a horse and dray, drove to the store of some

[40] Wilmington *Star*, December 23, 1871.
[41] N.C., *Public Laws, 1871–1872*, Chap. 122.
[42] Wilmington *Star*, February 18, 1872.

prominent merchants, Pope and McLeod, loaded about a thousand dollars' worth of merchandise and a safe containing about twenty-two thousand dollars, and left town.[43]

Yet, though this was by far the most remunerative raid that the Lowrys ever undertook, it marks the end of the Lowry band. One possible motive for the raid, in fact, may have been to obtain enough money to make a successful escape from the region. Indeed a short time later Henry Berry disappeared from view, amid conflicting rumors as to what happened to him. Did he abscond with this fortune, abandoning his family and friends? If he did, it appears strange that no word of censure seems to have escaped any of their lips during the three-quarters of a century that followed. Whatever Henry Berry did, whatever may have happened to him, his reputation among the plain people of Robeson County remained undamaged.

[43] *Ibid.*; Wilmington *Daily Journal*, February 18, 1872; Townsend (comp.), *The Swamp Outlaws*, 40.

10 · To Die Game

IF THE POPE AND MCLEOD robbery marked the practical dissolution of the Lowry band, the losses had begun nevertheless some fourteen months earlier with the death of the young white outlaw Zachariah T. McLauchlin. There is no clear evidence that he was involved with the band, except in the last few months before his death, although he had long been suspected by the authorities because of his association with Indians and his obvious sympathies.

In 1867, for example, when the Freedmen's Bureau had investigated the wartime killing of Scuffletonians by the Home Guard, McLauchlin had testified on behalf of the Lowrys about events taking place when he had been about sixteen years old.[1] This action may have influenced the way the authorities during the next two years would construe the evidence against him. In 1869 Captain Owen C. Norment and others searched the farm where he lived with his mother, a Scottish-born widow, but they found no Lowry booty. The youth was nevertheless arrested and while he was held, a white girl identified him as one of a group of disguised men who had robbed a plantation where she had been a guest. However, he showed a Lowry-like ability to escape from jail. On this occasion he escaped; when he was recaptured in the fall of 1870, he and Tom Lowry again escaped. About this time a search of his mother's farm revealed a trunk said to contain some Lowry booty.[2] The

[1] Hearings, 16, in Investigation.
[2] Wilmington *Star*, October 11, 1870; Wilmington *Daily Journal*, October 11, 1870; Norment, *The Lowrie History*, 83, 98–99.

authorities declared him an outlaw and offered four hundred dollars to anyone who might kill or capture him.[3]

But, despite the protection of Henry Berry, he was not able to survive long the relentless manhunt of the authorities. On the night of December 16, 1870, as McLauchlin lay sleeping beside a lonely campfire, he was shot to death by Henry Biggs, another white youth who said that the young outlaw was trying to entice or force him to join the Lowry band. Biggs collected the official bounty for his companion's body and fled the county.[4]

The Lowrys made at least one effort to avenge McLauchlin's death. They learned that Henry Biggs was working in a lumber mill at Abbottsburg in Bladen County, which lay well to the east of their area of operations. They nevertheless attempted a raid but were detected near the Bladen-Columbus county line. A warning went out, a local posse was alerted, and Biggs escaped.[5] But a year later Biggs wrote Henry Berry a letter asking to come home, saying that he had been a conscripted rather than a voluntary Lowry-hunter: "i have bin forsed out after you but if that time Roles Round again i will leave the country first[.] i want you to answer this so i can come back." [6] Henry Berry probably never received this letter.

Only one member of the Lowry band, Henderson Oxendine, was ever captured and executed. This outlaw had been captured and condemned to death for the murder of Sheriff Reuben King, but had escaped from the Wilmington jail, along with Steve Lowry and George Applewhite. He had been wounded in the fighting around Long Swamp in the fall of 1870, and was finally recaptured

---

[3] Wilmington *Star*, November 22, 1870.
[4] *Ibid.*, December 18, 1870.
[5] *Ibid.*, February 4, 1870.
[6] Quoted in New York *Herald*, April 6, 1872.

on February 26, 1871, in a trap that had been set for George Applewhite. According to the Wilmington *Star*, the "leader of the gallant party who effected the capture . . . learned a few days ago that the wife of George Applewhite . . . was about to be confined in child-bed, and supposing that her husband would consequently be lurking about the home, he went quietly to work and formed a party of reliable men. . . . the party proceeded to the house of George Applewhite," where they surrounded the house and lay in ambush from about ten in the evening until dawn.[7]

The bounty hunters had guessed correctly. Not only had Applewhite risked a visit to his wife, but so also had two of her brothers, including the outlaw Henderson Oxendine. However, shortly after nightfall, the husband had prudently decided to leave. But the brothers decided to spend the night. Sometime during the night Henderson was alerted to the danger. "I got up," he said, "took my gun and walked through the house." It did not take him long to evaluate the situation: the house was completely surrounded. There was no path of escape left open. In apparent resignation he went back to where he had been sleeping and got back into bed beside his brother "Pop," or Forney.[8]

At dawn the bounty hunters sprang their trap.

They suddenly closed around the [house] and demanded admittance. Finding their efforts to gain admission in this way futile, the party broke down the door and rushed in. In the front room they found no one but the sick wife of Applewhite, with two or three small children. Proceeding to the back room, however, they recognized lying quietly in bed, and apparently fast asleep, the stalwart form of Henderson Oxendine, and by his side his brother "Pop" . . . , the former wearing a repeater in his belt, and having a double barrelled gun standing near the

---

[7] Wilmington *Star*, February 28, 1871.

[8] Wilmington *Carolina Farmer and Weekly Star*, March 24, 1871.

head of his bed. They offered no resistance, but quietly surrendered.[9]

But the sentence that had been passed upon him previously for the King murder was not carried out. Since that trial, John Dial had repudiated his confession, upon which the conviction had been based. Instead, Oxendine was indicted for the murder of Stephen Davis, who, as a member of a posse, had been killed on October 4, 1870, in a gun battle with the outlaws. The authorities took no chances of allowing the prisoner to escape. He was "kept heavily ironed and the jail guarded day and night" by United States soldiers, "armed and uniformed." The Lowrys attempted no rescue, though on the day that Oxendine was arraigned someone made a "diabolical attempt . . . to burn the town of Lumberton." A fire was discovered "in rear of the store of Willis P. Barnes," which "occupies a central position. The fire was put out in the nick of time." [10]

Apart from the problem of security, the most important difficulty the authorities had was to find a jury sufficiently impartial as to give a measure of dignity to the trial. Some candidates were reluctant "in answering direct questions as to their qualifications." "One old man of the African persuasion," the *Journal* noted, "was dismissed because he declared the prisoner 'not guilty.' " [11]

Though he was defended only by court-appointed lawyers, one of whom was also assisting the prosecution, and having no visible prospect before him except death, the appearance of the young Scuffletonian impressed even the correspondent for the *Journal*, a paper edited by a former state leader of the Ku Klux Klan.[12] He wrote, "His face is not a bad one

[9] Wilmington *Star*, February 28, 1871.
[10] *Ibid.*, March 10, 1871; Wilmington *Daily Journal*, March 11, 1871.
[11] Wilmington *Daily Journal*, March 11, 1871.
[12] Hamilton, *Reconstruction in North Carolina*, 461.

—the features express a great deal of determination, but do not bear the marks of debauchery. His whole bearing during the trial was [one of] calm and self possession. Perhaps he thinks his hour has not yet come—possibly he is reckless of consequences." [13]

Friends and foes of the Lowrys might disagree as to whether justice was swift in the Oxendine case. But certainly punishment was. March 17, 1871, was fixed as the day for his execution, just nineteen days after his arrest. The calm demeanor that the prisoner presented before his enemies was to some degree deceptive. When the Methodist preacher came to see him, he asked for help with a letter that he wanted to send to Calvin, his brother, who had been held for almost two years in the Wilmington jail awaiting trial for the King murder. To Calvin he confided, "You know what it is to be deprived of your liberty, but you have never known the agony I have endured for the past few days." [14]

Calvin had never known what Henderson had had to endure, nor did the condemned Scuffletonian give many other people reason to suspect it, as he "walked with a firm and steady step to the foot of the ladder ascending to the gallows." Winter had broken and the spring showers had come down in torrents throughout most of the morning. This had not, however, discouraged the great "concourse of people" who had come to witness the execution. "At an early hour in the morning, every housetop in the vicinity of the jail was crowded with eager spectators, and several persons perched themselves upon the limbs of neighboring trees that overlooked the gallows, and there, for two or three hours preceding the execution, patiently sat, exposed to a drenching rain." The prisoner opened a Methodist hymn book and began "to sing, in a clear, unfaltering voice the

[13] Wilmington *Daily Journal*, March 11, 1871.
[14] Wilmington *Carolina Farmer and Weekly Star*, March 24, 1871.

hymn commencing, 'And shall I yet delay.' " He then sang "Amazing Grace! How sweet the sound." "At the close of this hymn, the prisoner looked anxiously around upon the audience a moment, and then stood with bowed head and handkerchief to his face, as if in prayer, for a few seconds, when he handed the book and his handkerchief to the Sheriff." Frank Marden, a northern bounty hunter, then "ascended the scaffold, and proceeded to pinion the hands and feet of the prisoner . . . who met his fate with astonishing fortitude. . . . The black cap was drawn over his face, and precisely at 12:30 . . . the trap fell." [15] The multitude in the jail yard, on the housetops, and on the limbs of the surrounding trees had come to find out how a member of the Lowry band would die. They now had the answer.

The executioner of Oxendine was a bounty hunter, and, although Oxendine was the only member of the Lowry band to be executed publicly, he was by no means the only one to die at the hands of a bounty hunter. One of the more successful of these was James McQueen, who in his youth used the name Donahoe. Having "small eyes which he has the trick of dropping the instant he is looked at," [16] he was the illegitimate son of a Scottish father and an Indian mother. His mother had reared him in Richmond County as a Scuffletonian. But upon becoming a man he had moved from Richmond to Robeson County, changed his name from Donahoe to McQueen, began to speak with a Scottish instead of an Indian accent, and rejected his Scuffletonian upbringing. But though he became more Scottish than most Buckskins, he had not forgotten all he had learned about the habits of his mother's kin; and he applied his knowledge as a bounty hunter.

In the first place, since guides were not to be trusted,

[15] *Ibid.*, quoting Lumberton *Robesonian* extra of March 18, 1871.
[16] New York *Herald*, March 26, 1872.

one must learn to be his own guide. It was not easy for a stranger to do this, even for the half-Indian McQueen. But he began "going from house to house and telling the people that he wished to buy a tract of land, and would sometimes examine tracts that were offered for sale, and then decline purchasing on the ground the price was too high; sometimes he would offer to lease from some farmer a one-horse farm, etc. In this way he became acquainted with the people of Robeson and . . . he found out also the roads and by-paths of Scuffletown." [17] So it was that he prepared himself for his real mission, the manhunt.

On March 7, 1872, about midnight he left the village of Shoe Heel, alone "with rations for a day or two and well armed with a long-range rifle and one or two good repeaters." [18] Not all bounty hunters could have done what he did that night. Without being detected, he found his way along forest and swamp trails until, just before dawn, he arrived before the cabin of Andrew Strong, on Back Swamp. Like many other families by 1872, the Strongs were vulnerable: their dogs had long since become casualties of the conflict. In the moments of darkness remaining to him, McQueen concealed himself well in some thick bushes about two hundred yards from the cabin. Then, like an Indian in a turkey blind, he sat still and waited, hour after hour, as the day wore on.[19]

On this occasion at least, McQueen's vigil did not end in disappointment. Just before nightfall he caught sight of the Strong brothers walking toward the house. Andrew was in his late twenties, and Boss, Henry Berry's best friend, was still a youth hardly out of his teens. They were greeted by their mother and by Andrew's wife Flora. It was Friday.

[17] Norment, *The Lowrie History*, 117.
[18] New York *Herald*, March 21, 1872.
[19] *Ibid.*, quoting Lumberton *Robesonian*.

They had risked a weekend reunion. McQueen could hear the sounds from inside the cabin. The family were having their supper. Then a stillness settled over the place. This was the moment that McQueen was waiting for.[20]

He crept from his hiding place and crawled to the cabin door. The bottom corner of the door had been cut out to allow the cats to go in and out of the house. Through this opening McQueen could see inside. Flora and her mother-in-law had withdrawn to the chimney corner and had lit up their pipes. The two brothers lay stretched out on the floor before the hearth talking.

At length Boss drew from his pocket a small harp, upon which he commenced playing a tune, and McQueen taking advantage of the sound of the music to drown any slight noises he might make in bringing his rifle into position, threw himself flat on the ground, and, placing the muzzle of his gun at the small opening . . . , took deliberate aim at the bare head of Boss Strong, which lay at a distance of about three feet from the door, and fired. The ball took effect, and the outlaw shrugged his shoulders once or twice, as if making feeble efforts to lift himself up, then he became perfectly quiet and lay motionless, apparently quite dead.[21]

Inside someone extinguished the light and closed the cat hole. McQueen quickly withdrew into a dark corner formed by the cabin wall and the exterior part of the chimney. There he waited in the shadows, hoping to see Andrew Strong step from the cabin door. Boss's body would be worth six thousand dollars, that of Andrew worth five thousand more. Flora came out finally and looked around, but Andrew did not appear. At last McQueen stole away and hurried back to Shoe Heel.[22]

[20] *Ibid.*
[21] *Ibid.*
[22] *Ibid.*; Wilmington *Daily Journal*, March 12, 1872.

When Colonel Wishart and the posse arrived at the Strong place about ten the next morning they found that "the game had escaped." But they found Flora and the fallen youth's sister, Rhoda Strong Lowry, scrubbing what appeared to be bloodstains from the cabin floor. Rhoda had also brought her sister-in-law a dog. The young women said that Andrew Strong and Steve Lowry had taken Boss away. "Where?" the whites wanted to know. The women professed not to know. "It is to be regretted," the *Journal* remarked, that McQueen "could not have secured the head and thus claimed and obtained the price set upon it by the authorities." [23]

The Indians did nothing to facilitate matters for him. In fact they spread reports that people had seen Boss alive. The *Robesonian* published a report that Henry Berry had "quietly left the country," that Boss Strong was "badly wounded, and as soon as he was able to travel the rest of the band will follow their chief." [24] The legislature was reluctant to pay a huge bounty to McQueen if there was any possibility that the youth might make another one of his sudden, and seemingly miraculous, appearances. After a year of controversy, however, with no firmly verifiable reappearance of Boss Strong, the legislature appropriated the six thousand dollars to the bounty hunter.[25]

Throughout 1872 there were continuing attempts to solve the Lowry question. In general the Republicans tried to do so by convincing Indians that justice was more likely to be found in the courts than it was in the avenging weapons of the Lowrys. The Conservatives, on the other hand, thought that the problem could best be solved by annihilating the Lowry leaders and restoring respect for authority and prop-

[23] New York *Herald*, March 21, 1872; *ibid.*, March 21, 1872, quoting Lumberton *Robesonian*; Wilmington *Daily Journal*, March 12, 1872.
[24] New York *Herald*, March 25, 1872, quoting Lumberton *Robesonian*.
[25] Wilmington *Daily Journal*, March 6, 1873.

erty. Judge Daniel L. Russell was taking a typical Republican approach when he had the case of Calvin Oxendine moved to Smithville in Brunswick, a community outside the area of turmoil, where the Lowry question did not cause much excitement.

Retrying Calvin Oxendine in Smithville made it possible to panel a fairly impartial jury and to conduct a trial that might win the respect of the Indians. But it did not make it any easier for the state to obtain a conviction. In the first place the state rested its case on a confession by John Dial that he, the Oxendine brothers Calvin and Henderson, and others had murdered Sheriff King. Now in the less charged atmosphere of Smithville, Dial repudiated that testimony, which, except for some timely jailbreaks, would have sent three men to the gallows. The story he now told, corroborated by Negro jail employees,[26] was that while in jail "he had been visited by a party of white men, who told him he would be killed unless he would testify against Steve and Tom Lowery, and that if he would, he would receive a reward of $2,500 and be sent north, where the state of North Carolina would pay for a two-year course of instruction at a good school." [27]

Secondly, Duff Cummings and other Indians testified that they had seen Calvin and Henderson Oxendine on the afternoon of the murder. They had seen the brothers working, cutting turpentine boxes in a pine forest many miles distant from the King plantation. Finally, a Buckskin Scot testified that he had "known Calvin all of his life; they had grown up together; had worked and played with him as a boy and said 'no gentleman in this house bears a better name than Calvin.' " [28] Calvin Oxendine was set free. His

[26] *Ibid.*, April 12, 1872; New York *Herald*, April 15, 1872.
[27] New York *Herald*, April 6, 1872.
[28] Wilmington *Daily Journal*, April 12, 1872; New York *Herald*, April 15, 1872.

trial had created more mystery about the King murder than it dispelled. But one thing it made clear: a person accused of a Lowry band killing might call upon friendly witnesses from all three races.

The month following the acquittal of Calvin Oxendine, Colonel Frank Wishart was killed in what appeared to be a further effort to find a peaceful solution to the conflict, but which resulted only in adding a new name to the death toll and further increasing the mistrust between the friends and the foes of the Lowrys. The circumstances of Colonel Wishart's death clearly pointed to treachery, though partisan sources do not agree as to which side was conducting honest negotiations and which was guilty of treachery.

Colonel Wishart arranged to meet Steve Lowry and perhaps others near Lebanon Presbyterian Church on May 2, 1872. The purpose of the meeting, according to the *Journal*— a purpose which that paper would never have supported— was to have arranged a compromise which would "benefit the country by causing the outlaws to leave in some manner." [29] Such efforts had failed repeatedly because the state organization of the Conservative Party opposed compromise on the question. In attending this meeting, Colonel Wishart was placing his trust in the Lowry reputation for integrity, as he and General Gorman had done on a number of occasions the previous summer. "But alas!" the *Journal* lamented. "He never returned alive. He was either cowardly murdered from ambush, or shot down in the conference to which he had been betrayed. Between twelve and one o'clock that day two or three negroes working in the woods near the scene of the murder, heard four distinct reports of firearms. About four o'clock the same day Mr. William Sellars, while riding by this point, found the body of Colonel

[29] Wilmington *Daily Journal*, May 6, 1872.

Wishart lying in the road, and completely riddled with buckshot." [30]

An Indian local historian, on the other hand, basing his account at this point on the oral tradition of his people, writes that the talks were to take place between Colonel Wishart and Steve Lowry. But as a special precaution, "Steve had Andrew Strong to go to the meeting place and conceal himself so that he, Steve, would have protection while he was talking with Wishart." The account continues, "Wishart and Lowrie met according to the agreement. They were apparently unarmed. They talked over their differences and finally decided to separate. As Steve turned to go, Wishart drew a revolver, which he had concealed, and shot at him. At this point, Andrew Strong shot Wishart." [31]

Sometime after she heard the news of her husband's death, Lydia Pittman Wishart opened the family Bible to the flyleaves where vital records were kept. Under the heading *Deaths*, she made the following notation: "May 2, 1872, Francis Marion Wishart, killed by the Lowerys. 'Oh, God, to whom all vengeance belongs, avenge his death, and speedily.' " [32] But, if vengeance belongs rightfully to the Almighty, it is nevertheless a prerogative which in Robeson County often has been usurped by the kinsmen of the person slain. It is possible, of course, that the colonel's younger brother, Aladon Strong Wishart, and his nineteen-year-old half brother, Robert Evander Wishart, believed that they were facilitating divine justice when they, together with James McKay and James Campbell, formed a team for another manhunt.

[30] *Ibid.*, May 4, 1872.
[31] Oxendine, "A Social and Economic History of the Indians of Robeson County," 34, citing interviews with B. W. Lowry, May 26, 1934, and James W. Oxendine, May 21, 1934.
[32] Wishart Bible, Wishart Papers.

According to a son of the slain militia officer, the way his uncles secured the necessary information for avenging his father's death was by going to an Indian community and "secreting themselves in a church loft by day, and prowling by night." Since the Scuffletonians had few dogs left, they could approach many cabins and overhear the conversations taking place within.[33] In this way they learned that Thomas Lowry was planning to attend a political meeting at Union Chapel on Saturday morning, July 20, 1872. They correctly calculated the route that he would take for reaching the chapel, and prepared a turkey blind at the ford of Holly Swamp, a small branch of Raft Swamp where ironically almost at the same moment Steve Lowry and Andrew Strong were building an unsuccessful turkey blind at a point where they expected Sheriff Roderick McMillan to pass.[34]

At about eight in the morning, Tom Lowry came down the path through Holly Swamp. With him was a white friend, Furney Prevatt. The two men were arguing. Prevatt was trying to persuade the Indian to turn back, that it was not safe for an outlaw to attend the meeting at Union Chapel. But Lowry was insisting firmly that he would nevertheless attend. The men lurking in the turkey blind opened fire on Lowry. Both men turned and fled, but the Indian, "after receiving terrible wounds . . . ran into the swamp a distance of about one hundred yards, pursued by the party."

When they came up with him he tried to draw his pistol to fire on them, but was too far gone to carry his intention into effect, and fell back a corpse. He had a Spencer rifle in his hand . . . which was clutched so tightly that the party had to loosen the fingers, one by one, by main force. Then they put him on a hastily improvised litter and bore him thus about half a mile, when they met a wagon on the way to a political meeting, to

[33] W. C. Wishart, Commentary on Diary, 13.
[34] Wilmington *Star*, July 24, 1872.

which it was said Lowry was also bound . . . . The party got possession of the wagon, placed the corpse into it and carried it to Lumberton. It was then fully identified . . . after which it was delivered to his wife, who had followed the remains of her husband to Lumberton.[35]

Tom Lowry's funeral was preached the following afternoon at New Hope Chapel in the village of Eureka (now called Pates). It was reported that "nearly the whole of the residents of the Scuffletown section were present at the funeral, many of whom were armed." He was buried in Back Swamp Grave Yard beside many of his ancestors. His killers were paid $6,200 in state and county bounties.[36]

There were now only two outlaws left, the others having either been killed or having disappeared from the scene. Yet Steve Lowry and Andrew Strong still continued somehow to elude their enemies. Their efforts to strike back at their pursuers, however, now seemed more pathetic than awe-inspiring. In September, 1872, for example, they issued a "proclamation of outlawry" against a list of bounty hunters. But, whereas two years before, they had been able to offer a five-hundred-dollar reward for certain members of the board of county commissioners, they now could offer only two hundred dollars each for enemies who were dogging their very footsteps.[37] The authorities were offering more than six thousand dollars for each of them.[38]

Yet the bounty hunters were not meeting with quick success. The logic behind offering a bounty is in the view that each thing of value also has its price. From year to year the rewards offered for the outlaws had been increased until at last they had reached a sum which, to poverty-stricken Scuffletown, must have appeared to be a princely fortune.

[35] *Ibid.*, July 23, 1872.
[36] *Ibid.*
[37] *Ibid.*, September 19, 1872.
[38] *Ibid.*, November 5, 1872.

At what price would they sell the heads of the men who found refuge in their cabins? It appears that, though the money offered by the authorities was drawing manhunters from afar, the outlaws were never without the kind of protection that the plain people had furnished them for almost a decade.

That they enjoyed the support of friends and kinsmen is the key to the riddle of how they could constantly appear in public, but somehow beyond the range of the bounty hunter's rifle. Thus we learn that "Stephen Lowrey and Andrew Strong . . . were present among a large congregation that assembled at the burying ground near Buie's Store . . . Sunday last to hear the funeral sermon . . . by Reverend N. M. Ray. The congregation numbered about five hundred, and these men mingled freely among them without molestation or restraint." [39] Despite the weakness of their situation, they continued to make public appearances.[40]

They continued to show their old talent for disappearing and making a seemingly miraculous reappearance at the spot where they were least expected, a talent that long confounded the militia as well as the bounty hunters. Indeed they could appear in some unlikely places:

Stephen Lowrey attended a justice's court at Union Chapel Church, in Burnt Swamp township . . . on Saturday last [November 2, 1872] and spent the day witnessing a trial in which two whites were concerned. . . . The outlaw carried in his hands a Spencer rifle and wore in his belt around him several large pistols. He seemed perfectly at ease during the trial, at the close of which he invited some members of the bar and others to join him in a glass of sweet cider, there being a barrel on the ground. Subsequently he requested a private interview with Colonel W. Foster

[39] Wilmington *Daily Journal*, May 25, 1872, quoting Lumberton *Robesonian*.
[40] Wilmington *Daily Journal*, May 4, 1872; Wilmington *Star*, August 16, 1872.

French, one of the counsel in the case, before the court, when he proposed to purchase a small tract of land belonging to Colonel F[rench], in the Scuffletown region. The Colonel informed him that he could have no transactions with an outlaw, when Lowrey said he expected as much, but thought there would be no harm in making the proposal. He evinced considerable feeling when informed of the reported capture of George Applewhite, in Georgia.[41]

Yet Steve might well have spared himself any concern about what had happened to his friend. A man who, when "struck by two balls in the mouth . . . had spit them out" and returned fire, was certainly not to be disposed of easily.[42] Either the report of his capture in Columbus, Georgia, was false or the indomitable outlaw again cheated the gallows with another jailbreak.

Twice he had been reported shot to death. Once while severely wounded he had been forced to hide in Cumberland County and subsist only on watermelon and other fruit.[43] Yet Applewhite, alone among the outlaws, not only would survive the conflict but, following his recapture in 1875, would be granted immunity under the Amnesty Act of 1873. This measure, written by the Conservatives to protect the Ku Klux Klan, was nevertheless interpreted by Republican judges on the North Carolina Supreme Court to protect Applewhite.[44]

Applewhite was thus allowed once again to take up his old occupation working as a bricklayer; and with the trowel, as with the Spencer rifle, he enjoyed a high reputation for skill.[45] But he had an important advantage over Steve Lowry

[41] Wilmington *Star*, November 7, 1872, citing Lumberton *Robesonian*.
[42] Wilmington *Daily Journal*, April 21, 1871.
[43] Norment, *The Lowrie History*, 99–100.
[44] N.C., *Public Laws, 1872–1873*, Chap. 181; *State v. Applewhite*, 75 N.C. 206 (1876).
[45] Goldsboro *Carolina Messenger*, July 5, 1875; W. C. Wishart, Commentary on Diary, 13.

and Andrew Strong. As a black man, using the name "William Jackson," Applewhite could range far and wide, and there was little to distinguish him from millions of other Negroes.

The other outlaws, however, had a more restricted base of operations. Once out of Robeson County, their Scuffletonian speech, appearance, and manner tended to draw attention to them. At the same time, as long as they remained among their own people they enjoyed a certain security. Despite the high rewards that were being offered, the *Robesonian* reported that "Stephen Lowrey and Andrew Strong, attended a social party in Scuffletown one night last week, and were the objects of marked attention." [46]

It was the Christmas season. Spirits were relaxed and jovial. But Andrew Strong relaxed too much. Christmas Day, 1872, found him drinking, separated from Steve Lowry, and apparently careless about his own security. Andrew and some friends were invited to the home of Duff Cummings for Christmas dinner. After they had eaten, he, his host, and friends visited the store of John E. Humphrey at the village of Eureka. Employed there was William Wilson, a white clerk about whom the Lowrys had received unfriendly reports. Nevertheless Strong laid down his rifle and stood around outside the store joking with his friends, none of whom appear to have been armed. No one was paying any attention to the clerk in the store. But Wilson was stealthily drawing a double-barreled shotgun from its place of concealment. He crept up behind Andrew, taking deliberate aim at the back of his head, and fired both barrels, killing him instantly. He then stood over the fallen Indian, "gun in hand and gave notice that he would shoot the first man who attempted to rescue the body." [47] Then "a wagon

[46] Wilmington *Star*, December 19, 1872, citing Lumberton *Robesonian*.
[47] Goldsboro *Carolina Messenger*, January 6, 1873.

and team were procured, and Mr. Wilson and two or three friends immediately set out for Lumberton to deliver the body to the Sheriff." He collected the two-hundred-dollar county bounty at once.[48] A short time later he collected the five-thousand-dollar state bounty.[49]

The death of Andrew Strong had been accomplished with apparent ease. The killer had gotten away alive and the authorities had paid him his bounty without delay. The hunters grew bolder, vigorously pushing the search for Stephen Lowry.[50] Nor were the bounty hunters to be cheated by the Amnesty Act, passed March 3, 1873. Reading the act, one might think that a blanket pardon to persons who, as members of semipolitical armed bands, had committed deeds of violence during the war and turmoil of Reconstruction, might benefit Steve. But the last section of the act contained these words: "the provisions of this act shall not be construed to extend amnesty . . . to Stephen Lowery"—the only individual mentioned in the law (Applewhite and Henry Berry were overlooked, apparently, because of the repeated reports of their deaths).[51]

As the hunters closed in on Steve during 1873, there may have been fewer doors open to him, fewer persons willing to risk the retribution of the authorities to help him. His friends circulated a petition asking the governor to pardon him. But, as had been the case in earlier such efforts, a Republican governor was not willing to risk the wrath of a Conservative legislature in a move that might serve to unify his party in one county; the official voice of Conservatism, the pro–Ku Klux *Journal*, had warned that "no respectable white man will affix

[48] *Ibid.*

[49] Wilmington *Daily Journal*, January 5, 1873; Clarence E. Lowrey, *The Lumbee Indians of North Carolina* (Lumberton, N.C.: Clarence E. Lowrey, 1960), 48–49.

[50] Wilmington *Daily Journal*, January 21, 1873.

[51] N.C., *Public Laws, 1872-1873*, Chap. 181.

his name to such a petition." [52] The effort came to nothing. Meanwhile Steve Lowry withdrew into a thin, shadowy existence. No longer did he appear at public gatherings, surrounded by swarms of friends; rather he is reported to "have kept pretty close to the swamps." Once he had been "stout and robust, but has become pale and thin of late," [53] and in his pockets he carried "all kinds of roots," [54] perhaps as a backwoods remedy for some ill, possibly even as food.

For more than a year Steve clung to his solitary half-life. Then one February evening a wagon train came to a halt in a field on the plantation of John McNair, and the wagoner prepared to camp for the night. Country folk gathered around the wagons, curious to know what interesting wares the stranger had brought with him from the red hills of Randolph County. All three races were there. It was the kind of gathering that the country people loved, as the cheerful blaze, the wagoner's copious stock of liquor, and their own abundant supply of songs all combined to drive away the gloom of a winter night. [55]

In the cold shadows where Steve was hiding, he heard the sound of merriment, and he crept toward the light and the warmth. There around the fire he found friends and old acquaintances. Chicken was served and a large turkey was roasting over the fire. [56] Sometime after midnight three young whites, one of whom was a Republican, "rose and bade Steve good night, saying that they were going home." As the hours slipped by, it fell Steve's turn to render a song. Seated before the fire, he handed his rifle to a Negro boy who stood beside him, and picked up a banjo. As Steve bowed his head to tune the instrument, one of the Indians

[52] Wilmington *Daily Journal*, December 2, 1873.
[53] *Ibid.*, February 24, 1874.
[54] *Ibid.*, February 26, 1874.
[55] *Ibid.*, February 24, 1874.
[56] Norment, *The Lowrie History*, 141.

"crept near him, so as to more readily get his fill of the music."[57] Then he "threw his head back," the firelight shining upon his face as he began to sing.[58] But his shining face provided the lurking bounty hunters with the target that they had been waiting for. The night air was ripped by a deafening barrage of gunshots. Steve slumped dead before the fire. Another Indian fell wounded beside Steve and the camp became a scene of wild panic as people fled in all directions. The three young whites rushed from their hiding place. They seized Steve's body, brought up a cart, loaded it, and hurried away to Lumberton, where they were able to catch a train that took them beyond Lowry vengeance.[59] A few days later the authorities awarded the young men more than sixteen hundred dollars each for the bullet-riddled body of the man they had bade a pleasant good night.

[57] Wilmington *Daily Journal*, February 24, 1874.
[58] Norment, *The Lowrie History*, 142.
[59] Wilmington *Daily Journal*, February 26, 1876.

11 · The Man Who Became Bulletproof

STEVE LOWRY HAD died singing. Henderson Oxendine had stood singing before the gallows during the last moments of his life. Boss Strong died while playing a tune for his family. Others had died more prosaically: the white outlaw Mc-Lauchlin had been shot on a winter night as he lay sleeping by a lonely campfire, Tom Lowry had fallen before the turkey blind of the Wisharts, and Andrew Strong had turned his back on a clerk in a store. Applewhite, veteran of one and perhaps two jailbreaks, survivor of two pointblank barrages of gunfire, and—what for a black man sometimes could be as fatal—a full-scale encounter with the court system, was able to return to his peaceful craft.

But what about the arch-outlaw Henry Berry? He seems to have made no public appearances after February, 1872. Yet no enterprising bounty hunter applied for the twelve thousand dollars that the legislature was offering for him. The fate of Henry Berry is evidently considered to be of some importance, for the question has been debated for about a century.

According to the view which the authorities took of them during Reconstruction, Henry Berry and his followers were simply local bandits. Yet where was there another band of local highwaymen whose hides were estimated to be worth almost fifty thousand dollars? In the territory lying between the Potomac and the Rio Grande was there such a shortage of violent men and armed bands during these troubled years? How expensive it would have been had they all been honored with the kind of bounties that were placed on the Lowrys! Was it simply the violent methods of the Lowrys that shocked the dominant party? These were precisely the methods of the Conservatives themselves. When they had some choice in the matter, they often selected violent means for achieving their objectives.

It is hard to believe, therefore, that Henry Berry and his followers would have been accorded such special treatment had they not had some special significance in the eyes of the dominant group. The Lowrys practiced violence, but it was not of the common variety that was currently shattering the fragile Reconstruction democracy imposed by the victorious northern Radicals on the former southern elite. On the contrary it seemed aimed at the very foundations of the social order that the Conservatives were erecting to replace the Reconstruction experiment. There were at least two founding principles of the new, solid, one-party South that the Conservatives were building on ground located somewhere between slavery and democracy: the sanctity of white property rights and the docility of dark skin. These were the very mudsills upon which this society was being founded. In the whole South one could scarcely have found a less edifying embodiment of these ideals than was provided by the Lowry band.

Dark-skinned people were expected constantly to reiterate their acceptance of their place by means of prescribed rituals, governing their daily relations with whites, in which they acted out their own inferior status. But along the Lumber River Henry Berry had made it imprudent for men who had property and white skin to speak "in any disrespectful way" of himself or his followers, most of whom had neither.[1]

---

[1] *Ku Klux Conspiracy*, II, 300.

If Henry Berry was "slow in speech," nevertheless, his talent for acting out ideas had considerable importance in a land where most people could not read words that were written and only half believed many of those that were spoken. It seems doubtful whether, with a river of ink, Radical newspaper editors could have challenged the social distinctions that the Conservatives were laboring to perpetuate, any more sharply than Henry Berry did when he led a band of armed men, black, white, and brown, into a plantation dining room, where they sat with calm dignity while their proud enemy cooked breakfast for them, and while the militia combed distant swamps searching for them.[2]

Clearly such a man had to die. But could one meager death possibly redress the balance for this kind of career? If we may believe all that appears in print, Henry Berry had to atone for his deeds in life not simply with one but with many terrible deaths. A report appearing in early March, 1872, stated that he had drowned "while fishing in the Lumber River."[3] Two weeks later the Conservative *Robesonian* revealed that "it is now positively asserted that the report circulated two or three weeks ago that H. B. Lowry has met his death at the hands of his brother Tom is true."[4] The same paper reported two months later that "it is known here as a well established fact that HBL is dead—that he was shot and killed by his brother Stephen" on February 17, 1872.[5] The New York *Herald* correspondent, A. Boyd Henderson, who traveled extensively through Robeson County during the month after Henry Berry's disappearance, interviewing outlaws and their families, gives another version:

[2] Wilmington *Daily Journal*, March 11, 1871; Wilmington *Star*, July 15, 1871.

[3] New York *Herald*, March 7, 1872.

[4] *Ibid.*, March 25, 1872, quoting Lumberton *Robesonian*, March 21, 1872.

[5] Wilmington *Daily Journal*, May 25, 1872, quoting Lumberton *Robesonian*.

From evidence the most reliable when connected with a well-connected chain of circumstances, I am able to give you a correct account of the death of this robber chief.

Between February 13 and 16, in company with his *fidus Achates*, Boss Strong, Henry Berry Lowery was ranging in country in the neighborhood of Moss Neck in search of some person who he had been informed was hunting him, while Steve and Tom Lowery were stationed at a rendezvous on the Lumber river. . . . They discovered in the bushes a new-made "blind" (a place of concealment or ambush made by intertwining the branches of the thickly grown bushes). It was not then occupied and Henry Berry, believing it had been recently made by one of his pursuers, who would shortly return to it, ensconced himself in it, while Boss made a blind for himself a short distance off, covering the road. But a few minutes after they had placed themselves in their respective positions the report of a gun was heard from Henry's hiding place, and when Boss, who waited to hear a word from his chief or an answering shot from an enemy, cautiously approached the spot[,] Henry Berry Lowery lay on his back, . . . the whole front of his head blown off. The broken ramrod and the missing wiper showed that he had been trying to draw a load from his gun.[6]

A difficulty of the Henderson account is posed by the dates he gives. If these events indeed took place February 13–16, 1872, as Henderson says, they would seem to be poor preparation for the Pope-McLeod robbery on February 16, one of the best-planned and -executed raids that the Lowrys ever carried out.

Mary Norment, writing in 1875, was familiar with the Henderson reports as well as material that had been appearing in the *Robesonian* (many issues of which have since been lost). She reports that on February 17, 1872, the day following the Pope-McLeod raid, "between daylight and sunrise," the whole band went to the house of Thomas Lowry.

[6] New York *Herald*, March 26, 1872.

Being fearful of pursuit, [they] built up a fire near the [corn] crib of Tom Lowrie and commenced to fixing their firearms . . . while attempting to draw a load out of his double barrel gun, the gun slipping in his hand, the hammer of one of the barrels struck against the sill of the crib and the gun went off taking effect in Henry Berry Lowrie's face . . . . He died almost instantly. . . . A party . . . went to the saw mill of Mr. Archibald Buie for lumber, which had to be sawed. . . . Jesse Oxendine (being a carpenter) was called in and made the coffin, the other outlaws standing guard all the time. . . . On the following night, near midnight, the remaining outlaws took up the body of the dead robber chief and carried it off and buried it, where, in all probability, no white man will ever find out.[7]

Mary Norment was a conscientious historian and her connections in Robeson County were extensive. But she was very much a part of the Conservative camp, and this fact to a great extent determined her sources. If Conservative information about the Lowrys had been accurate the conflict would scarcely have lasted ten years.

In general if a person was a foe of Henry Berry, he was likely to believe one of the various accounts of his death. Friends of the great outlaw, on the other hand, tended to be partial toward some story of his escape from Robeson County, and within a few years there was a wide selection of escape narratives from which to choose. There were, of course, notable exceptions to this rule. Sinclair Lowry, who was never an outlaw, is reported to have stated at a Republican convention in 1872 that his brother Henry Berry was dead, as was Boss Strong. Indeed "he had visited their graves." [8] Yet Steve Lowry and others denied that either of the men was dead, though he conceded that Boss was "hurt powerful bad." [9] When asked the whereabouts of his

[7] Norment, *The Lowrie History*, 127–28.

[8] Wilmington *Daily Journal*, April 21, 1872.

[9] New York *Herald*, March 21, 1872.

brother, Steve is reported to have said that Henry Berry had "gone over the swamp to look after Boss Strong." [10] Other members of the family have emphatically denied that Henry Berry was dead.[11]

The friends of Henry Berry have shown quite as much redundance in composing ingenious new versions of his escape as his foes have in superfluously re-killing him. A story appearing in 1872 had him escape from Robeson County "in disguise";[12] another one, nine years later, smuggled him out in "a tool chest." [13]

Certain of the escape narratives allege connivance in the escape plan by General Gorman, who negotiated with the Lowrys and became an advocate of compromise. Mary Norment and others suspected that he made some secret arrangement with the outlaws, aimed at relieving the embarrassment of his own party, but which would be unacceptable to the Conservative majority in the legislature. "The true men of Robeson . . . believe to this day," she wrote, "that the Adjutant General . . . was in collusion with the outlaws." [14]

Not only Mary Norment but also a nephew of Henry Berry believes that the outlaw leader received some help from the state adjutant general. The Reverend D. F. Lowry gives two reasons for this belief:

1st. When Gen. Gorman came with a militia and demanded an equal number of men in Robeson County to join him to hunt the outlaws . . . they searched for about 3 months and dis-

---

[10] *Ibid.*, March 25, 1872, quoting Lumberton *Robesonian*, March 21, 1872.

[11] Oxendine, "A Social and Economic History of the Indians of Robeson County," 36.

[12] Wilmington *Daily Journal*, March 16, 1872.

[13] Wilmington *Review*, May 21, 1881.

[14] Mary C. Norment, *The Lowrie History, as Acted in Part by Henry Berry Lowrie, the Great North Carolina Bandit, with Biographical Sketches of His Associates, Being a Complete History of the Modern Robber Band in the County of Robeson and State of North Carolina* (Weldon, N.C.: Harrell's Printing House, 1895), 104.

banded, not having apprehended a single outlaw. Here is the secret: Gen. Gorman on his arrival went over to the home of Henry B[erry] and told his mother to tell H. B. to meet him at Mossneck Swamp at first dark—stating that he, Gen. Gorman, knowing the situation, did not intend to hurt him. H. B. met him and Gen. Gorman put a uniform on Henry Berry and H. B. helped to search for the outlaws—finding none of them. This is a true story because my brother, Billy, who lived to be 100 yrs and 3 months, told me and I will be 90 at my next birthday. Bro. Billy told me Henry Berry helped him . . . hive bees more than one time on Sunday.

Therefore Bro. Bill knew Henry Berry and had met him several times with a militia uniform with a crew of soldiers and that Henry Berry would sign them by shaking his head at them to say nothing.

2nd. When [I was] quite young an aged Indian, Mr. Marcus Dial, told me that he saw Henry B. standing in the woods above Wash Lowries on Sunday A.M. and Henry called Dial to him and said that Gen. Gorman was leaving from Pates with his militia and he had asked me (Henry B.) to go along with them and he would bandage several men around their faces in order to hide a spot on H. B.'s face so that the general public would not know H. B. He then asked Mr. Dial what to do about it. Mr. Dial told me that he said to Henry B. by all means I would go with them. Mr. Dial told me that he was at the station when the militia were being loaded and a dozen or more had white bandages on and he had never seen Henry Berry again.[15]

Dr. Earl C. Lowry, who had investigated at some length the circumstances of his granduncle's disappearance, has written that "Henry Berry made and executed a perfect plan for his escape."

He told his wife how unreasonable it would be for him to remain longer and left her some money, bidding her goodbye. The next day he spent with his mother, sitting on the porch,

---

[15] Letter from D. F. Lowry, March 2, 1970.

most of the day shooting robins. He also left her some money.
. . . Tom Lowry shot a rabbit, removed its brains and dashed
them out at Steve's home. A gun fired off. Henry Berry removed
most of his arms and fled. A dummy of straw was placed in the
pond back of the home of Steve and it was reported that Henry
Berry had been killed by his own gun. Many of the curious
came there and saw the dummy but none but his mother was
allowed to see the head. Lumber was obtained from a sawmill
for the stated purpose of building a coffin in which to bury
Henry Berry. Jesse Oxendine was employed to build the box.
With the box the remaining members of the gang went from
a point near Union Chapel to the home of Peter Dial, near
Harper's Ferry, where the boards were removed and made into
a cart. No trace of the burial was ever found, and the dummy
was unstuffed and its straw thrown into a pond.

Armed with two small pistols and dressed in a Federal soldier's
uniform, Henry Berry Lowry boarded the train as it pulled out
of Pates. His trusted body guard, Andrew Strong stood guard
at a box car. . . . At Moss Neck another member of the gang
waited at the station platform "in case he was needed." [16]

According to this version, Henry Berry served for four years
in the United States Army and was discharged in Norfolk,
Virginia.[17]

Along the Lumber River Henry Berry had had for a long
while the reputation for appearing in places where he was
little expected, but the spot where he was reported to have
turned up in 1873 seemed more unlikely than usual. A con-
tributor to the *Robesonian* suspected that the reports of his
death were but "a cunning Indian ruse . . . to cover his retreat to the far North West." There was something familiar
and sinister about the individual who had inspired the
Modoc Indians on Lost River, near the California-Oregon
line, to fire on United States troops and retreat into the lava
beds of that section: "In 'Capt. Jack,' chief of the Modocs,
behold Henry Berry, leader of the Lowry Band!" The writer

[16] Raleigh *News and Observer*, May 9, 1937.
[17] *Ibid.*

could even imagine the soft-spoken and cavalier Scuffletonian adopting the primitive customs of tribalized Indians, "displaying to the gaze of his victorious band the scalps of the officers and soldiers, who while in Robeson County, sacked his house and dug up the underground passage leading from it, through which he has so often made his escape when soldiers were in pursuit of him." [18]

If this writer transports Henry Berry to California to play Indian chief, two frank admirers of the great outlaw smuggle him to the same state in order to play cowboy. In their novel *The King of Scuffletown*, John Paul Lucas and Bailey Groome have him escape the encirclement of his enemies and reach California, where he becomes a conventional cowboy hero of popular fiction, surviving many dangerous encounters with bad men, and performing feats of arms to equal those that he had once carried out on the Lumber River. In his old age he returns home to Scuffletown, completely vindicated and acclaimed by everyone.[19]

What in fact did happen to Henry Berry Lowry? So far as verified, uncontradicted historical facts are concerned, in February, 1872, he might as well have been swallowed up by the winter mist that rises from the quagmires of Back Swamp. There the marked trail ends and Henry Berry enters the twilight world of hearsay and legend. But perhaps this is the most important part of the story—because legends are more indestructible than men, even men like Henry Berry. So long as he appeared from time to time in the flesh, there was always the possibility that he would be seized, humiliated, and used to prove once again that if you are poor, have dark skin, or lack status, you will certainly pay dearly for rebellion.

[18] *Roanoke News* (Weldon, N.C.), May 28, 1873, quoting Raleigh *News*, quoting Lumberton *Robesonian*.

[19] John Paul Lucas, Jr., and Bailey T. Groome, *The King of Scuffletown: A Croatan Romance* (Richmond, Va.: Garrett and Massie, 1940).

Henry Berry became less vulnerable after 1872. There was no general agreement as to just where he was. But, whether one placed him in New York, Mexico, Indian territory, or some secret spot where he lay buried beside Boss Strong, one thing appeared certain: he was now quite beyond the reach of Sheriff Rod McMillan's longest rope. If the bounty hunters could not strike him down then, they would never be able to get him now.

Nor did the man who became bulletproof appear so vulnerable to the devastation of time as did others of his generation, whose faces, with the erosion of passing years, became furrowed ever deeper until one by one they were swept away, leaving scarcely a trace in the memory of the living. Even in the 1930's Indians were still insisting that Henry Berry Lowry was very much alive,[20] as befitted one whose image had remained so young and heroic. To be sure he would then have been moving from his eighties into his nineties. But it is hard to recall dates and to calculate the sum of the years. Deeds are what people remember, and Henry Berry was still the golden Scuffletonian youth who broke down the wall of the Whiteville jail to return home to his bride, the shackles still on his arms.

There are other things people do not remember. Forgotten is the hardened guerrilla fighter, who, having slain two brothers, could without apparent remorse send a child to tell their mother that "Murdoch and Hugh were dead, and that she had better come and get their bodies." [21] Instead one remembers his courtesy, that he would give a friendly family a few minutes' advance warning of his arrival so that they would not be frightened by the sudden appearance of armed men.

[20] Oxendine, "A Social and Economic History of the Indians of Robeson County," 35–36; Raleigh News and Observer, May 9, 1937.
[21] Wilmington Daily Journal, July 19, 1871.

Forgotten too is his silence, that he sat and listened as others talked. Now eloquent words are sometimes attributed to him, in which he gives voice to ideas that he once expressed through bold deeds. Stories are told that he was able to rout advocates of racial discrimination by a devastating appeal to the Scriptures. So magnetic was his personality, it is said, that at "St. Anna church one day he had practically the whole congregation down by the swamp while the minister exhorted to practically empty pews at the church. He said that there was no reason why Indians should not vote and hold office. He demanded restoration of their privileges. At first he had only a small following in his beliefs because of fear." [22]

It is not possible to summarize here all the lore that has accumulated around the name of Henry Berry. But it may be said that one thing is certain: he made a difference in Robeson County. He gave the Indians, with all their diverse origins, the sense of being a people. From just what tribal origin one was not quite sure, whether Lumbee, Cherokee, Croatan, or descended from the survivors of the unsuccessful English colony on Roanoke Island during the 1580's. But one people they certainly are—united by ancient bonds of kinship, friendship, and above all the towering image of Henry Berry, who, living or dead, imparted some of his personal qualities to the thousands of brown-skinned people living along the banks of the Lumber.

The Indians have drawn strength from a mighty legend. As a result their subsequent history has been somewhat happier than that of the Negroes, during the years following the failure of the Reconstruction experiment in democracy, when there emerged a new, one-party South, based on restricted suffrage and repression. No one ever succeeded in putting Indians in what the Conservatives called their place,

[22] Raleigh *News and Observer*, May 9, 1937.

that is, the half-free status that Indians and nonslave Negroes had held before the war.

Following a political revolt in 1878 that sent a Greenback candidate to Congress from an adjoining district, the Democrats, as the Conservatives were now called, sharply reversed their policy toward the Indians. Now they began making concessions to the Indians and soliciting their votes. This softer policy bore fruit in 1885 with the passage of an act that officially recognized them as Indians, thus abolishing their "free persons of color" status, under which they had been humiliated since 1835.[23]

There were, of course, definite limits to how far the Democrats were willing to go in extending rights to Indians. This was particularly true after 1900, when the threat of agrarian revolt began to fade. The Democrats did not believe that the Indians should have the same rights as whites, but merely that they should have more rights than Negroes. At this time the dominant party began to lay considerable stress on the legal doctrine "separate but equal," with some special emphasis on the former. In most parts of the South these gentlemen felt that, with the legal creation of two racial castes, the achievements of Anglo-Saxon civilization could be made secure. But in Robeson County the official policy of treating Indians as a middle-status group produced a weird triple and even quadruple jim crow, perhaps the most elaborate caste system ever developed in the United States.

In some of the newer and more up-to-date public buildings there were installed, side by side, separate drinking fountains for black, white, and brown; and also, with some further duplication of plumbing, six rest rooms to accommodate three races and two sexes. But when the racial school systems were being developed, a special shade of brown was discovered that the authorities felt should justify a

[23] N.C., *Public Laws, 1885*, Chap. 51.

special school system. So with three official races they were able to create four racial school systems. Unlike the blacks, the Indians never lost their right to vote, but they were segregated and subjected to many kinds of discrimination. Above all they remained poor, many of them completely landless.

Yet the story of Henry Berry does not end with the failures of Reconstruction. As his image has grown, even the hardiest of his detractors have given up the field. Whole generations have been shaped by the tales of his exploits. It is only by understanding this tradition that one can explain incidents such as those that took place in January, 1958. At that time the Ku Klux Klan, well established in neighboring counties of South Carolina, was making a concerted effort to reconstitute its organization in Robeson, where there had been no demonstrations by hooded men in almost thirty years. The Atlanta office of the Klan insisted that the Knights had no quarrel with the Lumbees (as Robeson County Indians were now generally called) and indeed urged some of them to attend a demonstration they held in a black neighborhood in Lumberton. Indians received this declaration with a certain skepticism, perhaps recalling some earlier deeds of the Klan along the Lumber River, but nevertheless a number attended the Lumberton meeting.

A young air force veteran who accepted this invitation is reported to have remarked that they had "said some awful things about the Negroes," and that "the Negroes should have done something about this." [24] But it soon became apparent that the local people of Ku Klux persuasion, just as had been the case during Reconstruction, had some "awful things" to say about Indians as well as about Negroes, notwithstanding the wishes of the national organization to pit brown against black.

[24] Detroit *Times*, January 20, 1958.

The Knights expressed special concern for the well-being of the whites. As a measure of their good faith, they dug into some sordid scandals that marred the relations between certain individuals of this community, but which were sufficiently petty to have been largely ignored; and converted these into public issues which were bitter, divisive, and irrelevant. As Lewis Randolph Barton, an Indian local historian remarked, "They care no more for the white race than they do for the Indians or Negroes. . . . They care only about themselves." [25]

As a warning to an Indian family who had recently moved into what had been an all-white neighborhood in Lumberton, on January 13, 1958, hooded Knights burned a cross near their home. On the same night a cross was burned near Saint Pauls in the driveway of a white woman who was supposed to be having an affair with an Indian man.[26] Interest was thus created for an address by the Grand Wizard, the Reverend James W. Cole, to be delivered at an open-air rally to be held near Maxton (formerly Shoe Heel), on the evening of January 18.

In one sense the dramatic episodes that the Klan had carried out during the past week were a complete success. Interest in the rally was clearly high. Some twenty-five hundred people attended.[27] But on that night the Ku Klux found out that in Robeson County there was a clan of an entirely different sort—the Lowry clan, the thousands of men and women claiming descent from a common ancestor, a patriarch looming large in the eighteenth-century dawn of recorded history along the Lumber River, a clan that was not only more ancient but which also embraced far

---

[25] Lumberton *Robesonian*, January 30, 1958.
[26] *Ibid.*, January 16, 20, 1958. The Saint Pauls affair was incorrectly reported in the press to have involved a white man and an Indian woman.
[27] Lumberton *Robesonian*, January 20, 1958.

more lusty fighting traditions than the Ku Klux Klan.

Henry Berry's young kinsmen attended the Ku Klux rally: Braboys, Chavises, Cummingses, Hunts, Locklears, Lowrys, Oxendines, Ransoms, Revels, Sampsons, and others, many of them veterans of the armed forces. The result was what a *Robesonian* reporter called "the shortest Ku Klux Klan rally in history." [28] Another newsman gave this account:

> The Indians let the Klansmen set up their microphone and a single electric-light bulb; they let about 100 Klansmen assemble around the truck. Then they began to move forward, roaring: "We want Cole!" (The Rev. James W. Cole, self-styled grand wizard of the Klan.) Cole stayed precisely where he was—behind the truck. The Lumbees began firing their guns in the air; a sharpshooter shot out the light bulb.
>
> There was pandemonium in the darkness; the guns spat flame into the air; the amplifying system was torn apart; auto windows were shattered by bullets. The Klansmen, themselves well armed, decided to run for it; there was the roar of automobile engines.
>
> Then the sheriff's deputies fired the tear-gas bombs. When the gas cleared, the Lumbee raid at Maxton was over. The Indians had won.[29]

After a fifty-mile flight, which carried him a prudent distance into South Carolina, the Grand Wizard paused to issue a fighting statement to the press: the Klan would return to Robeson County—though, when questioned, he conceded that he did not anticipate a return in the near future. A short time later he reportedly received a telegram with the message "Deepest Sympathy" and signed "General Custer." [30]

The young Indians who routed the Klan had been nurtured on the stories about the exploits of Henry Berry and his men. Some of them undoubtedly could have related

[28] *Ibid.*
[29] *Newsweek*, LI (January 27, 1958), 27.
[30] Lumberton *Robesonian*, January 20, 23, 1958.

what had once happened at Wire Grass Landing—when Henry Berry, alone, came swimming down the Lumber River, using his canoe as a shield, firing over the edge as he came, until at last a detachment of eighteen militiamen, panic-stricken by his boldness and marksmanship, had fled from their position. And, having heard this tale, one can imagine that these Indians may reflect with some pride that "this is the kind of people we are."

12 · The Lowry Conflict
and Reconstruction

Is THE STORY of the Lowry conflict in the final analysis simply a catalog of local deeds of violence? During Reconstruction there were observers in both political camps who believed that if the Lowry band made any impact on political events it was indeed in precisely the opposite direction from what the Indians wanted. They split the ranks of the Republican Party in Robeson County and thus made it possible for a Conservative minority to control this large county. They were an embarrassment, furthermore, to the state organization of the party; and a Conservative historian cited their activities as a justification for the violence of the Klan.[1] It is possible that they hastened the demise of the Republican Party in Reconstruction North Carolina.

But to say that they hastened the downfall of the North Carolina Republicans is not to say that they helped *cause* it, an event that was in fact inevitable once a larger political process got underway. The Radical ideas that had once inspired Union soldiers were no longer needed when the antebellum power structure had been smashed and a new one established. The Whiggish business leaders, now as firmly in control of the Republican Party as that party was in control of the nation, were beginning to develop a queasy feeling about their earlier commitment to civil rights. One by one

---

[1] Hamilton, *Reconstruction in North Carolina.*

they now began to lay aside their Radical ideas, as a band of small boys at a secret smoking session might one by one lay aside, unfinished, their third cigar. The Lowrys split and embarrassed the Republicans because they opposed the party's dominant policy of piecemeal accommodation to the new, avowedly racist southern power structure.

The Lowrys clearly made an impact, as we have seen, on the home territory of the Lumber River Indians. They appeared on the scene at a particularly difficult period in the history of the Indians. At this time the armed resistance of the plains Indians was being smashed, their numbers decimated, while the Indians of the eastern seaboard had known little but defeat and increasing humiliation for a hundred years. With the triumph of a frankly racist party during Reconstruction, it appeared that nothing could stop the winners from putting the Lumber River Indians into the same half-free "place" in which they generally succeeded in putting the blacks. But this effort failed. It appears to have failed, furthermore, to a great extent because of the bold deeds of the Lowrys, which filled the Lumber River Indians with a new pride of race, and a new confidence that, despite generations of defeat, revitalized their will to survive as a people.

Yet despite its local success this Indian counterattack could only be limited in scope, as a result, not of the quality of the Lowrys' efforts, but of the larger historical circumstances within which it arose. In the nonwhite world a very few nations, such as Japan, have been able to resist white conquest and to save most of their own basic way of life. Many others, however, including the American Indians, have seen much of their culture destroyed and have found themselves enclosed within the white world's ghettos. It appears that the last good opportunity the American Indians had to escape conquest and cultural devastation was during the period between 1763 and 1815, the time of the American Revolution and the War of 1812, when the white conquerors were quarreling or fighting among themselves. Some Indians, especially Tecumseh, grasped the importance of these events and attempted to unite all the Indian peoples from Florida to the Great Lakes into a federation that sought political recognition and military support from Great Britain, the more remote of the two rivals.

But Tecumseh's movement of course failed and this defeat rendered infinitely more difficult every subsequent effort at resistance, as the victorious Anglo-Saxons overran the valley of the Mississippi and penned up the conquered peoples in a series of widely separated enclaves, the direct forerunners of the reservations and Indian ghettos of later years. Indian history at this point tended to become local history, each enclosure appearing to its inhabitants as an isolated world to itself, rendered land-poor by the ever-tightening encirclement of the white world, humiliated by defeat, poverty, and racism.

No longer was it possible, as it had been in the days of Tecumseh, for an Indian victory to send a thrill of excitement rippling across the heartland of America from one brown-skinned people to another. Thus the victories of the Seminoles in Florida in the 1830's could not serve to revitalize resistance in the region of the Great Lakes. Nor could the revolt of the Lowrys thirty years later. No Indian resistance, however heroic, could produce more than local results at best. Perhaps the impact of the Lowrys will be fully felt only when the level of Indian historical consciousness has reached the point at which Indians will come to regard every defiant act in every rural enclave and in every urban ghetto as constituting a part of the common history of all.

In addition to its meaning in relation to Indian history

the Lowry conflict may also furnish us with some insights into the nature of American institutions. To what extent does the American system of government provide a group such as the Lumber River Indians with legal and peaceful solutions to grievances which are all too familiar in our society? Clearly the Conservative, or, as it later came to be called, Democratic, Party offered them few solutions. The chairman of the state executive committee of that party, who was likewise editor of a newspaper widely regarded as its official voice, was Colonel William L. Saunders, who was also head of the state organization of the Ku Klux Klan.[2] Both the parliamentary and the pillowcase branches of the party were working to put back together as many as possible of the broken pieces of the old slave society, which had reduced the Indian to a half-free status. The Conservatives furthermore had scarcely ever surrendered a single feature of the old way of life except as the direct result of armed force.

But an American election ordinarily offers more than a single list of candidates on a one-party slate. The two-party system, then as now, offered a measure of choice. If the Lumber River Indians were unhappy about the murders that had occurred under the Conservative regime or if they did not approve of flogging people with a cowhide whip or branding them with hot iron—features of the old society's legal code that the Conservatives for a time revived—they could in that instance vote for Republican candidates, men whose Radical rhetoric was often as empty as their railroad frauds were substantial. The Indians would discover—though it was a finding that has been made independently in a number of different places—that people who lack the wealth and far-reaching connections needed for influencing the policies of a very large political party, are rendered virtually

[2] *Ibid.*, 461.

powerless by the two-party system and at election time are often confronted with a meaningless choice.

Yet, for all that, the two-party system offered more clear alternatives during the period of the Civil War and Reconstruction than it has during most of its history. The Republicans had carried out a kind of revolution against antebellum society. In a mighty sweep they had abolished slavery and wiped out the Black Codes on all the statute books from the Canadian border to the Gulf. But having made men equal —at least on paper—they turned their attention to other matters, particularly those occurring at the stock exchange in New York and at another exchange around Capitol Square in Washington, where there was a lively commerce in congressmen as well as in the nation's resources. They thus became completely absorbed in what Mark Twain called "the great barbecue." The problem of the kind of society that was to be reconstructed in the South was a bothersome distraction that could claim little of their attention and even less of their intelligence.

For one thing, if we judge the administration of President Ulysses S. Grant by its deeds rather than its rhetoric, Republican leaders appear to have been blind to the nature of their opposition in the South. The southern Conservatives had revived almost completely the antebellum military establishment—men who functioned as county militias wherever the Democrats were in control and as extralegal terrorists, such as the Ku Klux Klan or Red Shirts, wherever legal violence belonged to the Republicans. The psychological makeup of these men was shaped by the habits of a lifetime and sometimes by family tradition extending over many life spans. It was almost instinctive with them, and required little reflection, to commit bloody deeds in defense of property, privilege, and status. However much the Republicans might stress the difference between violent acts committed by legal, Conservative county patrols and those acts committed by the Klan, the Conservatives realistically recognized that their harsh actions in either costume served essentially the same purpose: that of preventing any further reconstruction of society along Radical lines or, better still, making things more like they used to be. The constituency whom they served, when confronted by a bloody deed, was often far more impressed by the magnitude of the perpetrator than by the magnitude of the violence.

Even though the homicide rate in the South was at least two and one-half times the rate prevailing in the North[3] and despite the numerous indications that the same political ground rules which applied east of the Hudson were not always appropriate south of the Potomac, the Republican Party repudiated the defensive or retaliatory violence practiced by the Lowrys and generally insisted that southern Republicans behave as if they were in New England. Yet, although the Conservative press did not disapprove of this legalistic absurdity quite so vehemently as they did the eye-for-an-eye feud law of the Lowrys, at the same time the Conservatives were not sufficiently impressed with the more commendable policy of the Republicans to adopt it for themselves. In fact, during the thirty-six months following the Republican repudiation of the Lowrys, the Klan in North Carolina murdered some 26 people and flogged 213.[4] Thus the nonviolent Republican policy of teaching respect for law and for democratic processes by the force of good example, produced an appalling list of martyrs, mostly black, and left much to be desired as a means of instructing wolves in the ethics of sheep.

[3] Sheldon Hackney, "Southern Violence," *American Historical Review*, LXXIV (1969), 906–25; H. C. Bearley, "The Pattern of Violence," in W. T. Couch (ed.), *Culture in the South* (Chapel Hill: University of North Carolina Press, 1934), 681.
[4] Hamilton, *Reconstruction in North Carolina*, 477.

With this turn of events, anyone who believed the official rhetoric of the Republicans about law and order must have expected to see the federal government fall upon the Klan with the same ferocity with which it was currently moving against the plains Indians, who in most cases were upheld by the most respectable legal documents. But when forced by events to translate political bluster into action, the language of sincerity, the government roar of indignation faded into a feeble squeak: Congress organized an investigation to determine whether the wave of murders that had just swept the South had in fact taken place. Not only would an investigation without fail produce documentary material for more "bloody shirt" demagoguery, which would be currently useful to cover the stench of fraud that hung over the Grant administration. It had an additional advantage: an investigation would never break the bones of the pillowcase defenders of property and the status quo, men who would prove to be quite as tractable to control by money and by patronage as had the southern Republican rivals.

But such an investigation was not without its disadvantages for the Republicans. In the first place, it could not last forever. In fact, it did not even last long enough to convert a political dilemma into an academic controversy. Even worse, an investigation implied a commitment to some sort of substantive action. So again interrupting "the great barbecue," Congress passed the Ku Klux Klan acts of 1870–71, under which the Ku Klux trials were conducted.

The trials were a sad indication that, though the Republicans had abolished the Black Codes, they had nevertheless now come to accept the same double standard of justice that the southern Conservatives had long held: that a deed of violence committed by a person of low status was one type of crime, whereas one committed by a person of high status or powerful connections was an offense of an entirely different order. Although the Republican regime in North Carolina was fighting for its life against the Klan, President Grant wired Governor Holden to release his Ku Klux prisoners.[5] Throughout the South only about 10 percent of the persons arrested for Ku Klux offenses were ever indicted; and of these only about half were convicted.[6] Of the thirty-seven convicted in North Carolina, probably none served longer than Randolph Abbott Shotwell, sentenced to six years, but released after two.[7] During the previous two years the Klan in North Carolina had averaged a murder a month.

The Republicans, of course, were not responsible for the outbreak of the Lowry conflict, which was based on antagonisms that long antedated the appearance of the party in the South. Yet had they been able to make good their claim of the oneness of mankind before the law they could have ended it. But the Republicans, despite all they had done to legislate human equality, in the end could not free themselves from that double standard of justice that has characterized so much law enforcement. Yet along the Lumber River there had been justice of sorts long before there had ever been an Anglo-Saxon court—justice based on a simple principle of retribution and compensation. So after a brief respite, during which the Lowrys listened to the claims of the

[5] Lefler and Newsome, *North Carolina*, 467–68.

[6] Rembert W. Patrick, *The Reconstruction of the Nation* (New York: Oxford University Press, 1967), 157. It is perhaps indicative of the degree to which historians share our society's double standard toward acts of violence that no one has investigated the extent that those convicted were actually punished and the extent that they were quietly pardoned. In view of the preference that scholarly foundations have shown for "quantitative studies" which keep historians busy with counting instead of more free-ranging speculation, it is surprising that there are some quantities that would seem to tell us something about American society that have not yet been counted: just how much punishment did Klansmen, who were supported by high-status people, get for crimes against low-status people?

[7] J. G. de Roulhac Hamilton and Rebecca Cameron (eds.), *The Papers of Randolph Abbott Shotwell* (3 vols.; Raleigh: North Carolina Historical Commission, 1936), III, 174–429 *passim*.

new regime and observed its performance, they turned back to their ancient feud law, a system which, though primitive, at least did not make distinctions as to the status of a killer or his victim. To these men there had to be retribution for the willful killing of a man, whether he was a poor white like Zachariah McLauchlin, a black like Benjamin Bethea, or one of the numerous Indians that had been slain. They were willing for that retribution to be exacted under written law if the courts were structured to serve such a purpose. But if the courts were set up to serve some other end, then the responsibility for retribution fell to the kinsmen and friends of the slain man.

There is not room here to account very fully for the failure of the Republicans in Reconstruction. But important among the reasons, besides their inability to provide equal justice in the courts, was the failure of their political tactics. They read lectures to pillowcase Conservatives about law and order, about democratic processes, while acquiescing to their bloody deeds. The history of Reconstruction is the history of the failure of this tactic from the Potomac to the Rio Grande. Henry Berry Lowry's followers, on the other hand, left the lectures to others, and repaid bloody deed with bloody deed. Like the Republicans, they also were defeated and suppressed. But in the country of the Lumber River Indians they have left a mark that the years have not erased.

Essay on Sources

The beginning point for anyone studying the Lowry conflict is likely to be the local traditions of the Lumber River region because documentary sources are scarce and scattered in this region where primitive conditions lingered, where illiteracy was especially high, and where no newspaper was published before 1870. Yet the people of the Lumber River area have definite ideas about their own history, and the accounts that they relate are exciting and rich in detail.

Perhaps one episode will serve to illustrate the strength of this popular tradition. In 1967, I was driving with the local historian Lewis Randolph Barton, who was helping me locate the site of a cabin where Henry Berry Lowry and Rhoda had lived in 1867. We stopped to ask directions from two young men whom we saw loading a truck. Barton did not know them, but from their speech, he immediately recognized that they, like himself, were Lumbee Indians. He asked them simply if they knew where "the cabin" had been located. I expected the reply to be "what cabin?" But to my surprise, they launched into an animated discussion about two theories as to the exact site. Generations had passed since the encroaching undergrowth had wiped out the last visible remains of that cabin. But these young Indians had not forgotten that near where they stood Henry Berry and Rhoda had once lived.

The problem is not so much to discover the popular tradition, which is all-pervasive, but rather to evaluate it critically. There are a number of books which provide some information about the historical circumstances in which the Lowry conflict arose and about the Lumber River region in general. Especially useful is Hugh Talmadge Lefler and Albert Ray Newsome, *North Carolina: The History of a Southern State* (Chapel Hill: University of North Carolina Press, 1963). For a sharper focus on

Reconstruction the standard statewide study is still the "Dunning school" work of Joseph Grégoire de Roulhac Hamilton, *Reconstruction in North Carolina* (New York: Columbia University Press, 1914); W. McKee Evans, *Ballots and Fence Rails: Reconstruction on the Lower Cape Fear* (Chapel Hill: University of North Carolina Press, 1967) is an interpretation of eight counties in southeastern North Carolina from a revisionist point of view.

Especially useful among works dealing directly with Robeson County is a spritely county history, Robert C. Lawrence, *The State of Robeson* (Lumberton, N.C.: Robert C. Lawrence, 1939). There are also several valuable histories dealing directly with the Indians: Clifton Oxendine, "A Social and Economic History of the Indians of Robeson County, North Carolina" (M.A. thesis, George Peabody College, 1934); Clarence E. Lowrey, *The Lumbee Indians of North Carolina* (Lumberton, N.C.: Clarence E. Lowrey, 1960); and Lew[is Randolph] Barton, *The Most Ironic Story in American History: An Authoritative, Documented History of the Lumbee Indians of North Carolina* (Charlotte: Associated Printing Corp., 1967).

The defiant attitude taken by the Lowry band often has been assumed to have some connection with the Indian past of Henry Berry and many of his supporters. Yet we know entirely too little about that past. Our knowledge of the Lumber River region in the eighteenth century is sketchy, and the seventeenth century and before is virtually a closed book.

Perhaps scientific archaeology in the immediate area could shed some light on the various interesting theories concerning the origin of the Lumber River Indians. Also a more thorough study of William L. Saunders (ed.), *The Colonial Records of North Carolina* (10 vols.; Raleigh: State of North Carolina, 1886–90) might yield some clues. The more voluminous unpublished Colonial Records at the North Carolina Department of Archives and History in Raleigh would probably provide even more.

Some works on the seventeenth and eighteenth centuries, though not particularly concerned with the Lumber River region, are nevertheless helpful. William P. Cumming, *The Southeast in Early Maps* (Chapel Hill: University of North Carolina Press, 1958) helps make some sense out of otherwise confusing travel accounts. Chapman J. Milling, *Red Carolinians* (Chapel Hill: University of North Carolina Press, 1940) is a good overall survey of Indian society in the larger region. A leading authority on southeastern Indians, John Reed Swanton, suggests in *Probable Identity of the "Croatans"* (Washington: U.S. Office of Indian Affairs, 1933) that the tribal group most closely related to the Lumber River Indians were the Cheraws, a Siouan-speaking people. This theory would seem to give added significance to Alexander Gregg, *The History of the Old Cheraws* (Columbia, S.C.: State Co., 1925), a reprint of a book that first appeared in 1867.

Hamilton McMillan, *Sir Walter Raleigh's Lost Colony* (Wilson, N.C.: Advance Press, 1888) is a classic statement of the "Lost Colony" theory of the origin of the Lumber River Indians. This view is further elaborated in Stephen B. Weeks, "The Lost Colony of Roanoke: Its Fate and Survival," *Papers of the American Historical Association*, V (1891), 441–80; and also by Barton, mentioned above. Other studies of Indians having some relationship to the Lumber River community are E. Lawrence Lee, *Indian Wars in North Carolina, 1663–1763* (Raleigh: Carolina Charter Tercentenary Commission, 1963); and the articles of Charles R. Holloman, "Fort Nohoroco: Last Stand of the Tuscaroras," *We the People*, December, 1965, pp. 15–18, 30–32, "Palatines and Tuscaroras," *We the People*, January, 1966, pp. 21–22, 28–29, and "Expeditionary Forces in the Tuscarora War," *We the People*, March, 1966, pp. 15–17, 30. An important recent book is Charles M. Hudson, *The Catawba Nation* (Athens: University of Georgia Press, 1970).

A thoroughgoing scholarly treatment of the first large-scale white settlement of the Lumber River area and the surrounding territory is Duane Gilbert Meyer, *The Highland Scots of North Carolina, 1732–1776* (Chapel Hill: University of North Carolina Press, 1961). His failure to deal with the smaller group of non-Scottish whites coming into the area about the same time has been offset by Mrs. Furman Biggs's "Colonial Robeson and Its Contribution to the Revolutionary War," a typescript deposited in the North Carolina Department of Archives and History in Raleigh.

Indispensable to an understanding of the economic power relationships in the Lumber River region on the eve of the Lowry conflict are U.S., Bureau of Census, Eighth Census of the United States (1860), Free Population, North Carolina, XIII, Robeson County, and Slaves, North Carolina, IV, Robeson County. These are the unpublished reports that the census taker made as a result of his visit with each family, which are deposited in the National Archives.

For the Civil War years the documentary source material is by no means plentiful. In the North Carolina Department of Archives and History in Raleigh are the Minutes of the Robeson County Court and a group of criminal action papers called the Henry Berry Lowry Papers. Both of these are the barest kind of records. So are the captured Confederate records in the National Archives. The latter, however, verify the local tradition that Indians were conscripted for the construction of the Cape Fear forts, though the plodding clerks in the Confederate Department of Engineers seem to have missed all the wrath and poetry that the victims passed down to their descendants. See U.S., War Department, Captured Confederate Records, Payrolls (Record Group 109, National Archives).

For the closing months of the war, the sources become slightly more abundant. In part this is due to the passage of Sherman's army through the Lumber River country. Thus one can begin to use *The War of the Rebellion: A Compilation of the Official Records of the Union and Confederate Armies* (128 vols.; Washington: Government Printing Office, 1880–1901). Also valuable for this phase are the excellent studies of John G. Barrett, *Sherman's March Through the Carolinas* (Chapel Hill: University of North Carolina Press, 1956), and *The Civil War in North Carolina* (Chapel Hill: University of North Carolina Press, 1963).

The most important source directly concerning the Lowrys in the early part of 1865 was a result of the killing by the Home Guard of some Indians. Two years later, the circumstances surrounding these deaths were thoroughly investigated by William Birnie, an agent of the Freedmen's Bureau. Birnie conducted hearings, recorded sworn testimony, and collected depositions and letters. See U.S., War Department, Records of the Army Commands (Record Group 393, National Archives).

The leanest period for source material on the Lowrys is from the second half of 1865 until 1869, as the federal army moved on and the Indians waited expectantly for better things to come because of the Union victory. Fortunately, during this period, as indeed during the entire span 1862–74, the official Governors' Papers in the North Carolina Department of Archives and History in Raleigh, including the papers of Governors Zebulon Vance, William Woods Holden, Jonathan Worth, and Tod R. Caldwell, consistently yield a small flow of information about the Lumber River region, as does the collection of Governor Holden's private papers which is located at Duke University. These documents include letters, usually from local politicians and other prominent persons, advising the various governors about political currents and economic conditions in the area.

Probably the best single source for the first four years after the war are unpublished reports from the Lumberton office of the Freedmen's Bureau. See U.S., War Department, Bureau of Refugees, Freedmen, and Abandoned Lands (Record Group 105, National Archives). A surprisingly good source, however, for this period has proved to be the records of the Presbyterian Church, located in the Synod of North Carolina Building in Raleigh. Another valuable source for the same years is the journal of the Reverend Washington Sandford Chaffin (MS in Duke University Library).

An investigation the United States Senate conducted in 1871 into activities of the Ku Klux Klan yields some information on the Lowrys during the years just after the war. See *Report of the Joint Select Committee to Inquire into the Condition of Affairs in the Late Insurrectionary States (Ku Klux Conspiracy)* (13 vols.; Washington: Government Printing Office, 1872). The investigators took considerable testimony from Giles Leitch, a Conservative lawyer and old resident of Robeson County, concerning the activities of the Lowrys.

Newspapers became the most important source after the Lowrys began offensive actions late in 1868. Coverage by the state papers, however, remained spotty and confused for a time because of a failure of their writers to understand the unusual racial and political situation in Robeson County. This coverage changed dramatically in 1870 with the appearance of the first issues of the *Robesonian*, edited by the Reverend W. S. McDiarmid. It is extremely unfortunate that the only known file of the early *Robesonian* was destroyed some years later by a fire, for this paper appears to have been the ultimate source of some of the most reliable information about the Lowry conflict when it was at its height. It is not surprising that the Reverend Mr. McDiarmid, assisted by his brother W. Wallace McDiarmid and the able local historian Hamilton McMillan, could speak with real authority on the local situation. It is surprising, however, that, though sympathetic to the Conservatives and publishing in the storm center of the conflict, they are comparatively objective —more judicious than the *Daily Journal*, for example, written from the safety of Wilmington, or the Fayetteville *Eagle*.

But, fortunately for the historian of the Lumber River region, in addition to a few surviving issues of the *Robesonian* there are reprints of its articles and even reprints of reprints appearing in other newspapers for which more complete files have been collected. The historian also benefits from a wider, and unacknowledged, influence of the *Robesonian*: after the appearance of this paper in 1870, other press reports about the Lowry conflict became more precise and sophisticated.

An important group of journalistic writings that appear to be largely, though not entirely, independent of the *Robesonian* are those that appeared in the New York *Herald*. At various times the Lowry conflict was covered for the *Herald* by George Alfred Townsend (who was also a popular fiction writer), by E. Cuthbert, but most extensively by A. Boyd Henderson. Their writings were later combined into a book: George Alfred Townsend (comp.), *The Swamp Outlaws: Or, the North Carolina Bandits, Being a Complete History of the Modern Rob Roys and Robin Hoods* (New York: M. De Witt, 1872). These writers made some effort at fairness to both sides in their coverage of the conflict, but unfortunately their accounts are somewhat marred by attempts at sensationalism.

Second to the newspapers the most important source for 1870–72 is the Wishart Papers, in the possession of Clifton Wishart, White Plains, N.Y. Colonel Francis Marion Wishart (1837–72), with his extensive espionage system and his personal connections in both the Republican and Conservative parties, was probably the most knowledgeable person in the anti-Lowry camp. His papers include letters (or copies of letters) that he wrote, letters that he received, a twenty-eight-page manuscript by an anonymous but well-informed author on the origins of the Lowry band, maps, military orders, and especially his pocket-sized notebooks in which he made brief dated notations. Since an entry in this diary may consist only of a single word or a name, intended to call something from his own memory, the meaning of some of these was forever lost once the Lowrys succeeded in assassinating the writer. Later Mrs. Lydia Wishart married W. B. Harker of Shoe Heel (Maxton), and the Wishart Papers were lost. More than a half-century later they were rediscovered by her son, William Clifton Wishart (1872–1965), who carefully edited them. They now belong to the great-grandson of the officer who fought the Lowrys.

Voluminous but sterile are the records of the federal army units sent to suppress the Lowrys. These documents are found in two groups, both located in the National Archives: U.S., War Department, Records of the Adjutant General's Office (Record Group 94), which was the information Washington was getting about the Lowrys; and U.S., War Department, Records of the Army Commands, Post of Lumberton (Record Group 393), which included the reports of officers in Robeson County to their immediate supervisors. Judging from these letters and reports, it appears that few people in the Lumber River area knew as little about the Lowrys as the federal army officers. According to one newspaper account, Henry Berry made one of his seemingly miraculous appearances and disappearances in the midst of a federal camp. If this report was true, it does not seem to have disturbed the federal officers in their preoccupation with routine military housekeeping.

North Carolina Adjutant General John C. Gorman did better. He spent weeks interviewing people of all races and opinions and became an advocate of redressing Indian grievances as opposed to military suppression. Mary Bridgers Norment claimed that he was related to the Strong brothers and to Rhoda Strong Lowry, whose father had been white. His interviews with the press are good sources. Disappointing, however, is his twenty-six-page "Henry Berry Lowry Paper," a manuscript in the North Carolina Department of Archives and History in Raleigh. Though it bears no date, it appears to have been written some twenty years after the end of the conflict. It lacks the sharpness that characterizes his press interviews.

Mary C. Norment, *The Lowrie History, as Acted in Part by*

Henry Berry Lowrie, the Great North Carolina Bandit, with Biographical Sketches of His Associates, Being a Complete History of the Modern Robber Band in the County of Robeson and the State of North Carolina (Wilmington, N.C.: Daily Journal Printer, 1875) was intended as a Robeson County Conservative's reply to Townsend (comp.), *The Swamp Outlaws*, which she thought was too partial toward the Lowrys. A member of the prominent Bridgers family, she married a militia officer, who was killed by the Lowrys. Though she refers modestly to her husband as a "mechanic by trade," he was nevertheless from a family that put him very near the top of the county establishment both before and after the Civil War. Although Mary Norment borrows considerably from *The Swamp Outlaws*, the book that she is answering, at the same time her effort must be regarded as a separate and valuable source. She uses testimony of individuals on aspects of the conflict about which they claimed personal knowledge, and she had access to issues of the *Robesonian* that have since been lost. She is strongly partisan, but seems to make few factual mistakes.

One scholar has asserted that Mary Norment did not actually write the book that bears her name as author. The real author, he says, was Joseph B. McCallum, presumably her brother-in-law. See Weeks, "The Lost Colony of Roanoke: Its Fate and Survival," 474. I have found no substantiation of this statement. In any event the second edition again bears her name as author (Weldon, N.C.: Harrell's Printing House, 1895), as does a serial version published March 19–June 11, 1905, in the Charlotte *Daily Observer*. The third edition (Lumberton, N.C.: Lumbee Publishing Co., 1909) does not carry her name as author, though the editors say that "the facts of this book have been written" by Mary C. Norment, from whom the copyright had been purchased. The third edition is considerably enlarged and includes additional background material about the Indians.

Mary Norment's *Lowrie History* thus came to be regarded after 1875 as the standard work on the subject. She had begun with Townsend (comp.), *The Swamp Outlaws* and had constructed solid new information on it. But after 1875 writing about the Lowry conflict came to consist of repeating Mary Norment.

Even worse, when a later writer did on occasion venture out on his own, far from adding anything important to what Mary Norment had written, he introduced new mistakes. An example may be seen in James J. Farris, "The Lowrie Gang: An Episode in the History of Robeson County, N.C., 1865–1874," *Historical Papers Published by the Trinity College Historical Society*, Series XV (Durham: Duke University Press), 55–93. Farris was a trained scholar and made use of at least one source, the *Ku Klux Conspiracy*, which she apparently did not use. But she had access to more valuable evidence that had since been lost: the Wishart Papers, the early issues of the *Robesonian*, and oral testimony about recent events. The result was, in this case, that the trained scholar is less accurate in factual detail than the amateur local historian. Furthermore, Farris made a mistake that a scholar should not have made and Mary Norment would not have made: he thought that Radical Reconstruction in Robeson County began in 1865. This mistake creates an important distortion because it was in fact the Conservative regime of Governor Jonathan Worth (1865–68) that outlawed Henry Berry Lowry and drove him and his followers back into the swamps. When the Radicals took power in 1868 they confronted the accomplished fact of a fugitive outlawed by a legal government.

For most of the twentieth century almost all of the new material added to the writings on the Lowry conflict has been drawn from the maturing popular tradition, often appearing in the form of a newspaper interview of an elderly Indian. Thus one is likely to end a study of the Lowrys by returning to the point of beginning, to the glowing tales of the people: "My grandmother said that when she was small, a strange child used to come to her door and ask her mother, my great-grandmother, if it was 'all right.' If assured that it was, the child would go away and then a band of armed men would come. The child was a Lowry scout." How does our study of the documentary evidence help us to evaluate these stories? It seems clear that the stories we listen to today concerning Reconstruction are not as reliable as historical evidence as those that A. Boyd Henderson and Mary Norment listened to a century ago. Yet one comes to recognize that the folk tradition, even in its maturity, has a certain integrity: most of the occurrences that these tales purport to describe appear really to have happened. In the very few cases that I have been able to compare I have noted a striking correspondence in detail between newspaper accounts written a few days after an event and the oral tradition of the same episode related a century later.

Nevertheless, things happen to an account as it is retold over the passing years. The historian is struck by the almost complete absence in the popular tradition of any concept of time. The narrator is likely not to give even approximate dates. It is as though it all happened the day before yesterday. Closely related to the loss of time perspective is the tendency to simplify the story, to omit distracting crosscurrents. Accuracy thus suffers as the artistic quality of the tale is enhanced.

Also, in the mature popular versions of the Lowry conflict, the chief actors do not seem to be the matter-of-fact kind of people one meets every day, but heroes that loom larger than life. Lesser figures have been forgotten and their deeds attributed to the central characters. The inept federal army officers have become men without names, without faces, as the conflict has developed into an epic struggle between Wishart and Henry Berry. In studying the Lowry conflict and the tradition it created, one can easily understand the belief of the ancients that giants once walked the earth.

Index

THE Iroquois AND THEIR NEIGHBORS

Laurence M. Hauptman, *Series Editor*

This series presents a wide range of scholarship—archaeology, anthropology, history, public policy, sociology, women's studies—that focuses on the indigenous peoples of Northeastern North America. The series encourges more awareness and a broader understanding of the Iroquois Indians—the Mohawk, Oneida, Onondaga, Cayuga, Seneca, and Tuscarora—and their Native American neighbors and provides a forum for scholars to elucidate the important contributions of the first Americans from prehistory to the present day.

Selected titles in the series include: